IMAGES
of America

ASHEVILLE

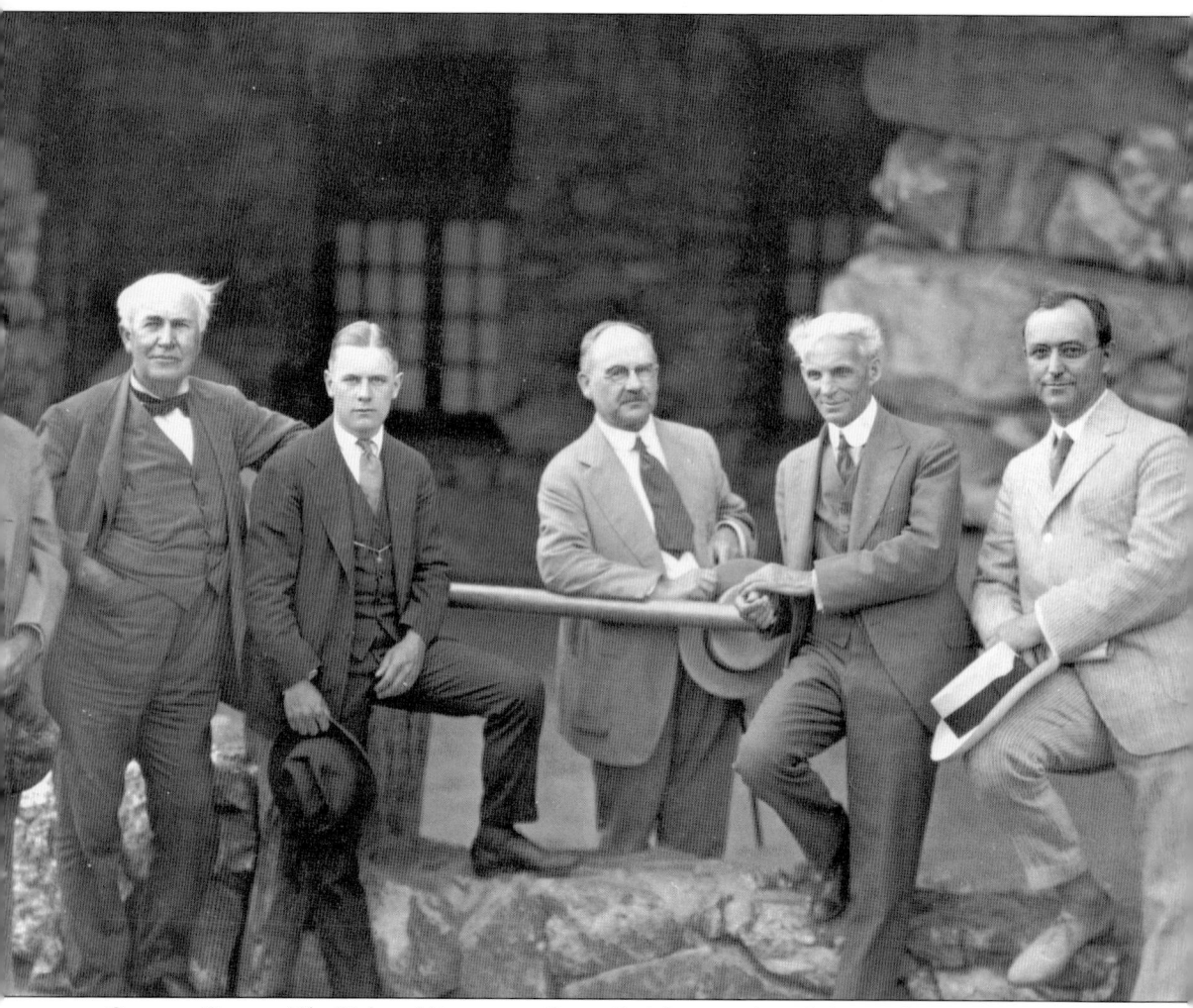

ON THE COVER. *The Rich and Famous at Grove Park Inn* are, from left to right, Harvey Firestone Sr., Thomas Edison, Harvey Firestone Jr., Edwin Wiley Grove, Henry Ford, and Fred Seely. The photograph is dated 1917.

IMAGES
of America

ASHEVILLE

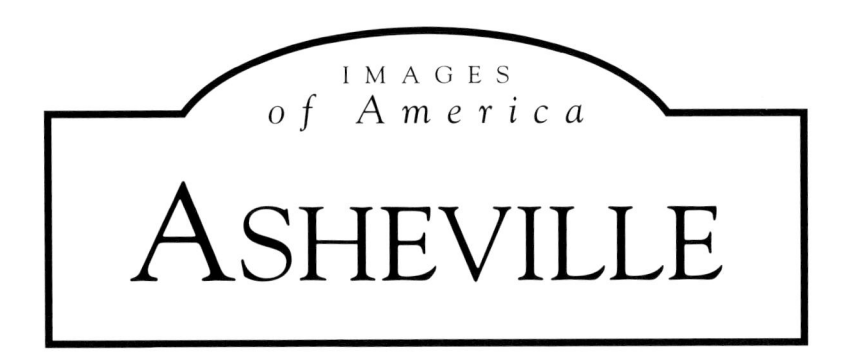

Douglas Stuart McDaniel

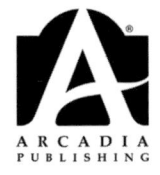

ARCADIA
PUBLISHING

Copyright ©2004 by Douglas Stuart McDaniel
ISBN 978-0-7385-1619-6

Published by Arcadia Publishing
Charleston, South Carolina

Printed in the United States of America

Library of Congress Catalog Card Number: 2003116596

For all general information contact Arcadia Publishing at:
Telephone 843-853-2070
Fax 843-853-0044
E-mail sales@arcadiapublishing.com
For customer service and orders:
Toll-Free 1-888-313-2665

Visit us on the Internet at www.arcadiapublishing.com

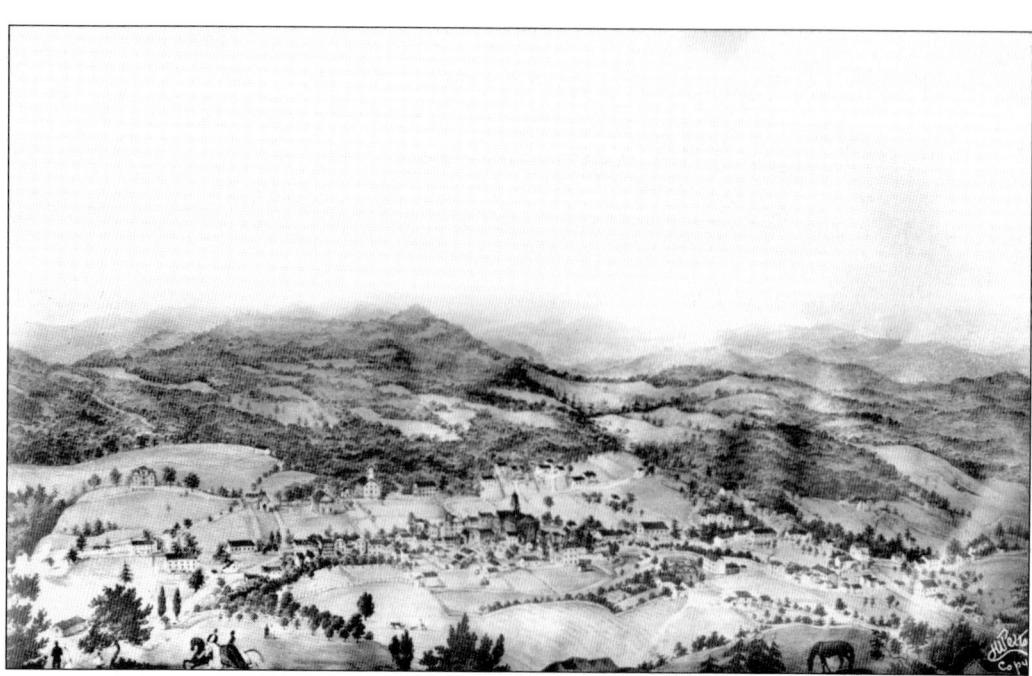

VIEW OF ASHEVILLE, NORTH CAROLINA, AND THE MOUNTAINS FROM THE SUMMER HOUSE, FROM THE EAST. Pictured here is a lithograph by Sarony and Major, published by James M. Edney in 1851. "Summer House" may refer to James W. Patton's summerhouse, built on Beaucatcher Mountain in 1850.

Contents

Introduction		6
1.	Native Travelers and Warriors	9
2.	The Early Europeans and Africans	13
3.	Early Images of the Asheville Area	15
4.	A City is Born	37
5.	Planning and Development	63
6.	A City Emerges	75
7.	The Artisans	99
8.	An Architectural Time Capsule	115
Acknowledgements		127
Bibliography		128

INTRODUCTION

There were no natives of Asheville or of Western North Carolina; they were all travelers. For more than a thousand years, American Indian tribes including Cherokee, Creek, and Shawano passed through these lands and built towns and villages, complete with defensive palisades and plazas for ball play, along the banks of the Swannanoa and the French Broad; humans have actually traveled through these mountains for much longer.

Spanish conquistadors rested in the area when they traveled through the mountains in the 16th century. As slaves of the Spanish, Africans may have in fact preceded the first Europeans settlers, who established the first settlement in the Swannanoa Valley in October of 1784. From Asheville's early development and rich history as a commercial center for livestock drovers until after the Civil War, Asheville became a haven for the wealthy elite of Charleston and Philadelphia. As the resort era blossomed, so too did the city of Asheville.

Put aside what you thought you knew about the history of Asheville and the surrounding area. Second only to Miami in its treasure trove of Art Deco landmarks, Asheville is an architectural and historical time capsule of national significance. It is also a community with a rich heritage and history in the arts, including textiles, pottery, modernist art, and residential and commercial architecture.

Today Asheville is at a crossroads. Travelers have embraced this area throughout its history and prehistory; visitors and residents still do today. Readers can take away a cautionary tale for the future of Asheville's history from the lessons of its past and its history of fast-paced growth. Balancing the environmental and natural attractions of the area with commercial development is and will be one of Asheville's greatest challenges.

All photos in this book, unless otherwise noted, are from the North Carolina Collection and the William Barnhill Collection, Pack Memorial Library, Asheville, North Carolina.

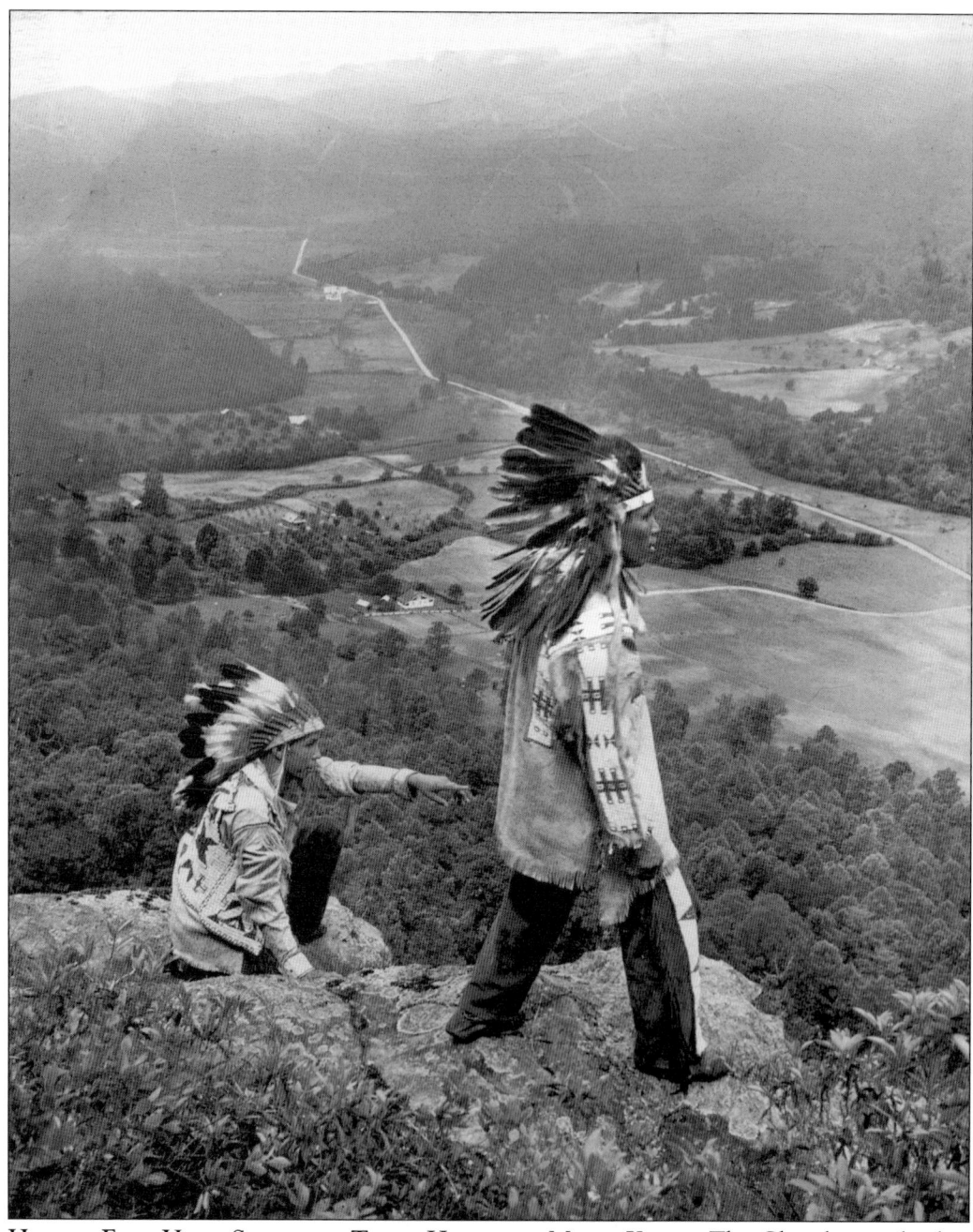

HUMAN EYES HAVE SURVEYED THESE HILLS FOR MANY YEARS. The Cherokee and other Native American tribes have traveled the mountains of Western North Carolina for thousands of years.

One

NATIVE TRAVELERS AND WARRIORS

In Henderson County, up Connelly Road, near the Buncombe County line just below Avery's Creek, there is a cornfield with a prominent mound in the middle that no one has ever bothered to investigate.

For decades, local residents have collected arrowheads from this fertile soil in the small valley that adjoins the Pisgah National Forest, under the watchful eye of the mountain named Doublehead, the name of a Cherokee chieftan. Others call it Double Knob.

For many, arrowheads are very disconnected from a basic understanding of Native Americans in western North Carolina. Year after year, many make the journey to Cherokee, browse the leather shops for Indian headdresses and feathers while children beg their parents for a leather belt with inlaid turquoise-colored plastic beads. But they learn little of the heritage of the people who populated our region for over 6,000 years. Only in the last few years are we more clearly understanding the ancient legends of native travelers and warriors who previously inhabited these lands, how they lived, with what tribes they married, and with which tribes they fought.

Many native travelers and warriors have journeyed across these mountains of Western North Carolina and stopped to call it home. In the Western tongue, they were Creek, Cherokee, Shawano or Shawnee, Catawba, Wateree, Tuscarora, and Saxapahaw, just to name a few, although they did not call themselves these names. The Cherokee likely came from the North, pushed south after the Iroquois wars, just as they themselves pushed the Creek Indians further to the south to Alabama and Mississippi.

Who was here first? Who were the "first" natives? It is anyone's guess.

Others came from the South. The Shawano were perhaps from the banks of the Savannah River. Savannah. Shawano. Swannanoa. Sewanee. Swanee. Suwanee. These place names will tell you much about where these people traveled, lived, fought and died, from the Savannah River in the east to the Overhill Country of Tennessee in the west, where these place names still linger. In this time, Hernando DeSoto had not yet brought the plagues and misery of conquest. British colonial powers from coastal South Carolina were not yet seeking western frontiers.

For thousands of years Native American travelers have camped along the banks of the French Broad and Swannanoa Rivers. Plentiful food and game abounded. They began growing corn around 200 B.C. After 500 A.D., their small campsites had grown to villages, and over the next 1,000 years, larger and more established villages emerged.

James Mooney (1861–1921) worked for the Bureau of American Ethnology in Washington, D.C. He stayed there the rest of his life, studying the mythology of the Cherokee, Kiowa, and the Sioux Tribes. One of his most famous writings is about the American Indian Ghost Dance, a ritual common among American Indian tribes. Mooney's explanations illuminate much about the native Cherokee, and even speculates about earlier peoples.

"Some say that the mounds were built by another, earlier people. Others say they were built by the ancestors of the old Ani'-Kĭtu'hwagĭ for townhouse foundations, so that the townhouses would be safe when freshets (rains) came. The townhouse was always built on the level bottom lands by the river in order that the people might have smooth ground for their dances and ballplays and might be able to go down to the water during the dance."

Still other legends make reference to earlier peoples. Were they "giants of the west," as Mooney proposed in his Myths of the Cherokee, his interpretations and transcriptions of Cherokee legend? One story Mooney relates tells of Cherokee man, born in 1806, whose grandmother told a folk legend of giants visiting the Cherokee from very far away in the direction the sun goes down.

Whoever was here first, they were not the last. These indigenous, aboriginal peoples were not pastoral or peaceful. They fought, they made treaties, and they built towns with open plazas encircled by a palisade or stockade. Their homes were constructed with upright wooden posts, generally square or rectangular in shape and usually about 20 feet on a side. Wall coverings included bark and possibly daub or mud. These were many of the characteristics of Pisgah village sites of the southern Appalachian region, especially those along the French Broad and Pigeon Rivers and their tributaries.

Long before Samuel Davidson would ever embark his family on a journey to become some of the first white settlers west of Old Fort in the Swannanoa Valley, the area that is now Asheville and Buncombe County was inhabited by peoples as complex, as creative, as insular, as contradictory, and as war-like, as any Spanish conquistador or colonial settler that would follow.

Mooney's explanations of the French Broad and the Swannanoa illuminate much about the native Cherokee. He critiques a magazine writer for claiming that the Cherokee called the French Broad "the racing river." He clarifies this, explaining that the Cherokee have no name for the river as a whole, but the district through which it flows about Asheville is called by them Un-ta'kiyasti'yĭ, "Where they race." The name of the city they translate as Kâsdu'yĭ, "Ashes place."

His explanation of the term "Swannanoa" is equally interesting. Again, he challenges a magazine writer, who has translated this name "the beautiful." The word, according to Mooney, is a corruption of Suwa'li-nûññâ'(-hĭ) "Suwali trail," the Cherokee name, not of the stream, but of the trail crossing the gap toward the country of the Ani'-Suwa'lĭ or the lands of the Cheraw.

As in contemporary society, where we refer to northern, southern, western and other regional nuances, the Cherokee called the Delaware Indians Anakwan'`kĭ, or in the singular Akwan'`kĭ. This word in turn is derived from Wapanaq'kĭ—"Easterners," a generic name the Delaware and other eastern bands called themselves.

The Delawares also referred to the Cherokee as Talega, Tallige, and Tallige-wi. Later on, they call the Cherokee Kĭtu'hwa.

The majority of the Tuscarora fled from eastern North Carolina to Iroquois lands around 1713, after an unsuccessful war with American colonists. Both the Cherokee and the Catawba aided the colonists in defeating the Tuscarora.

The Catawba knew the Cherokee as Ani'ta'gwa, singular Ata'gwa, or Ta'gwa. They were the immediate neighbors of the Cherokee on the east and southeast. Lasting Catawba place names further to the west, indicating their further travels, include Toccoa Creek, in northeastern Georgia, and Toccoa River, in north-central Georgia, both names being derived from the Cherokee Tagwâ'hĭ, "Catawba place." An old Cherokee personal name is Ta'gwädihĭ', "Catawba-killer."

The two tribes were bitter enemies. and Mooney indicates that the only case on record of their acting together was in the war of 1711–1713, when they cooperated with the colonists against the Tuscarora.

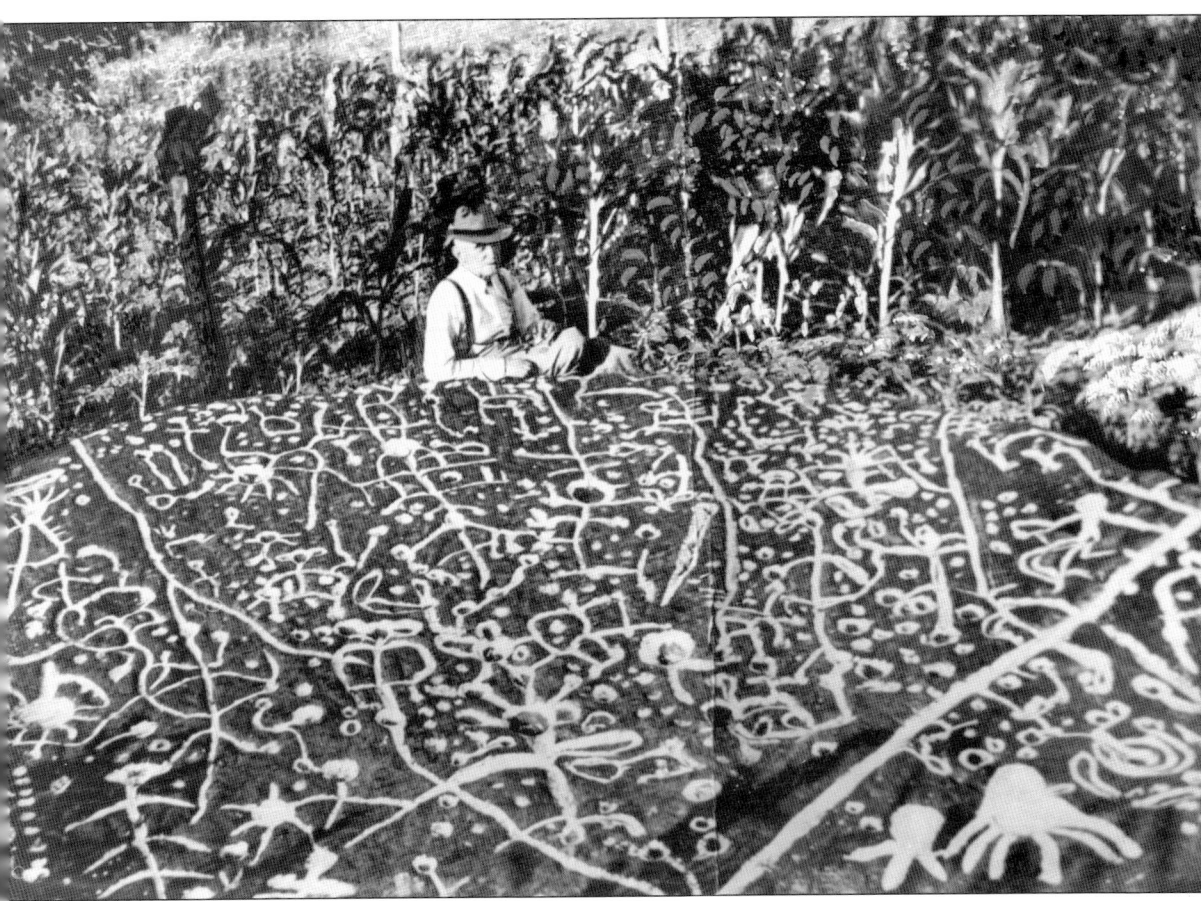

HERE THERE BE GIANTS. According to 19th-century ethnologist James Mooney, a being named Judaculla (called Tsul-ka-lu, or the Great Slant-eyed Giant, by the Cherokee) was a giant hunter who lived atop a mountain at the head of the Tuckaseegee River in Jackson County. Judaculla was very powerful and could control the wind, rain, thunder, and lightning. The carvings on the boulder represent scratches made by Judaculla's feet as he jumped from the top of the mountain to the creek below. The seven-toed foot at the lower right hand side of the boulder is said to depict Judaculla's footprint. The actual meanings of the Judaculla Rock symbols are a mystery. It is possible these figures may represent humans, animals, or figures of religious importance. As late as the 1880s and 1890s, Cherokee groups would assemble at Judaculla Rock to hold ceremonies. Today the land around the Judaculla Rock has been turned into a small park, where visitors can view the boulder and ponder its meaning.

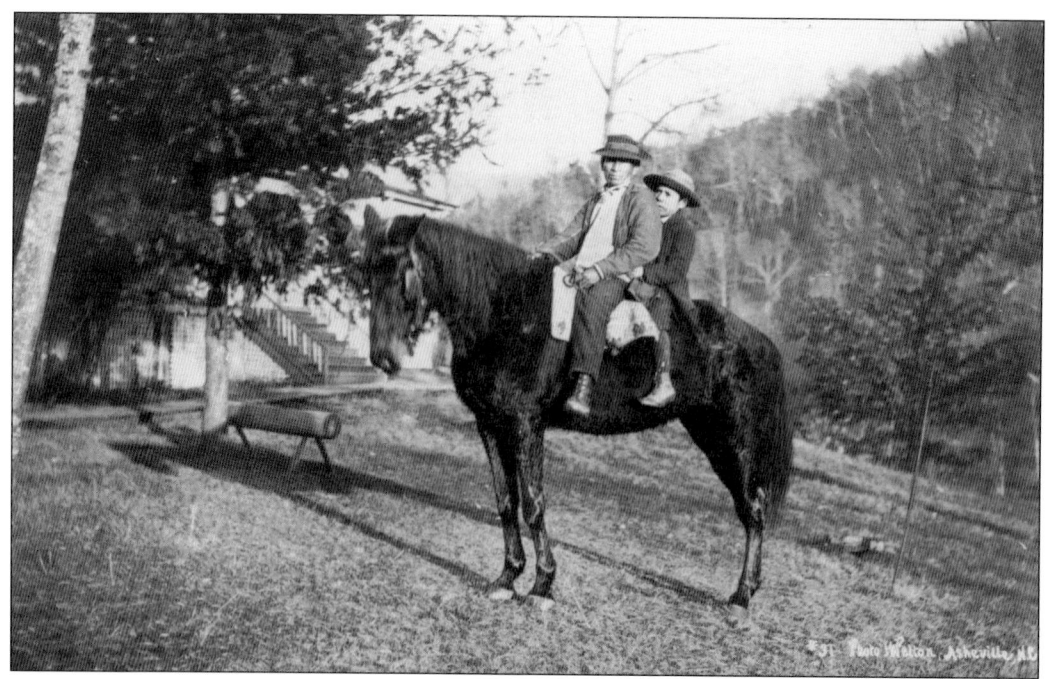

A RARE GLIMPSE. Two Native American men sit on horseback with a partial view of a home behind tree, mountainside to the right. It is assumed that these people are Cherokee, c. 1910–1930. This photograph was purchased on eBay on June 20, 2000, by the Pack Memorial Library. Two other similar photos were for auction but not purchased by Pack Library.

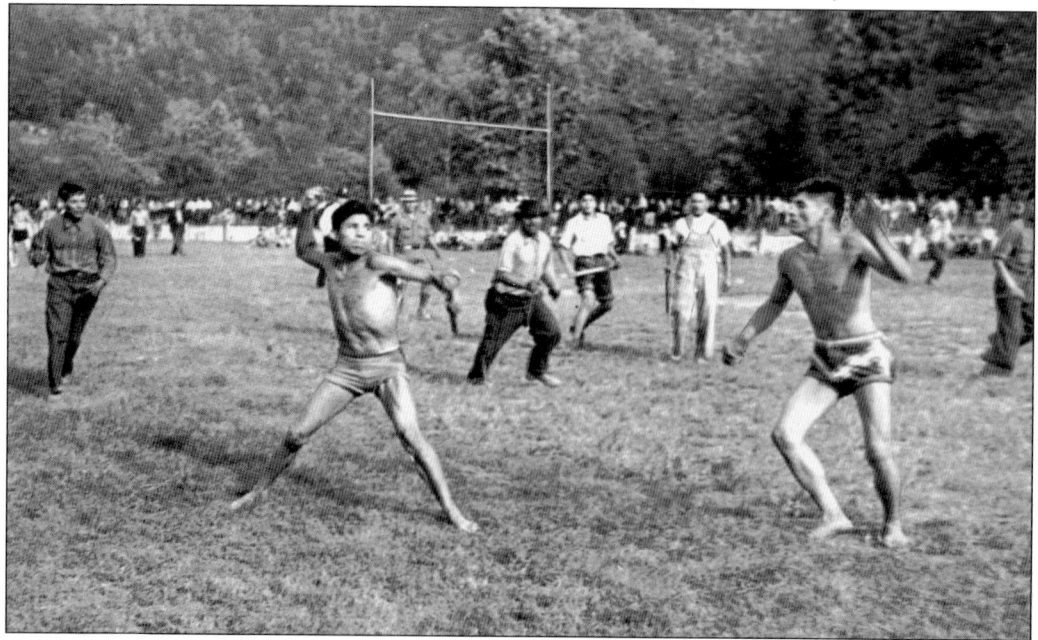

AN ADVANCED CULTURE. The Cherokee and other Mississippian tribes of the Southeastern United States had developed villages with defensive palisades, plazas, and ball courts long before Europeans and Africans arrived on the continent. This photo of Cherokee ball-play is undated.

Two

The Early Europeans and Africans

After conquests of the Aztecs in Mexico and the Incas in South America, Spanish conquistadors turned northward in search of more land and riches. Hernando de Soto and his army traveled from Florida through North Carolina in 1540, decimating and plundering native villages and cultures. In 1566, Juan Pardo departed the Spanish town of Santa Elena in coastal South Carolina in search of an overland route to Mexico.

Since 1939, when the U.S. de Soto Expedition Commission presented its final report to Congress, historians have debated the routes of the Spanish through Western North Carolina. Recent archaeological discoveries of 16th-century Spanish ceramics and hardware at the Berry site in the upper Catawba River Valley, as well as more recent translations of 16th-century texts, tend to validate the understood routes of the Spanish through the Carolina Piedmont. The Berry site, north of Morganton in Burke County, is a large archaeological site of almost 12 acres that dates to the 15th and 16th centuries and is believed to represent the ancestral Catawba town of Joara. Archaeological work began there in 1986. The routes across the Appalachian Mountains have been more in dispute. The name of the mountains themselves are attributed to de Soto himself from the word "Apalachee"—the first village he encountered in Florida after leaving Havana, Cuba.

In a 1997 article that appeared in the professional journal Southeastern Archaeology, *Robin A. Beck Jr. describes the journeys of the conquistadors:*

> The Hernando de Soto expedition arrived at Xuala (Pardo's Joara) on May 21, 1540. They departed four days later, and according to Ranjel, "crossed that day a very high mountain range." After traveling through the mountains for about five days, the army arrived at Guasili, located on the upper Nolichucky River near present Erwin, Tennessee. Two days later, the expedition passed through Canasoga, also on the Nolichucky, though camped in the open. After four more days of travel, they entered the town of Chiaha, probably located on Zimmerman's Island, now submerged by Douglas Lake near the present town of Dandridge, Tennessee.

And of the Pardo expedition, he relates:

> In January, 1567, Juan Pardo arrived at the aboriginal town of Joara (north of present-day Morganton). Due to heavy snow in the mountains, he and his company were unable to continue their westward trek. After building a small fort, San Juan, where he stationed twenty men, Pardo returned to Santa Elena.

A later expedition by one of Pardo's sergeants places the Spanish directly on the French Broad and Swannanoa Rivers, near present-day Asheville.

> In the Spring of 1567, Hernando Moyano, Pardo's sergeant at Fort San Juan, departed from Joara with a small force of Spaniards and Indians. He burned the "Chisca" village of Maniateque, near present-day Saltville, Virginia, then returned to Joara. Shortly thereafter, he attacked and burned Guapere, the town of a "mountain cacique," which may have been located on the upper Watauga River. Six days after departing from Guapere, he arrived at the town of

Chiaha, where he built a small fort and waited for Pardo. Upon his return to Joara in September, 1567, Pardo learned that Moyano was "undersiege" at Chiaha; Pardo left several men at the fort and hurried with the others to his sergeant's defense. Crossing the mountains in three or four days, the company arrived at Tocae, which was probably located near present Asheville, then continued on to Cauchi, near present Canton. Five days later, having briefly passed through Tanasqui, Pardo and his men arrived at Chiaha, where they found Moyano and company "hard pressed," but safe.

A commonly held belief in the history of America is that the arrival of African-Americans in Southern Appalachia coincided with British colonial expansion. In many histories of Asheville, it is claimed that the first African in this area was a female slave of Samuel Davidson, who arrived in the Swannanoa Valley between 1781 and 1782. Davidson was killed by natives, and his wife, daughter, and female slave fled back to the safety of Old Fort.

While this event did occur, it is more of a convenient, poetic story than accurate history. It is more likely that the expeditions of the Spanish conquistadors placed Africans in Western North Carolina as early as the 1500s. Lucas Vasquez de Ayllon brought with him 100 slaves from Virginia when he established a short-lived settlement on the Pee Dee River in South Carolina around 1526. It is thought that at some point, these slaves revolted and fled to the Cherokee nation, the original occupants of Southern Appalachia. Expeditions of de Soto in 1540 and Pardo in 1566 also included slaves.

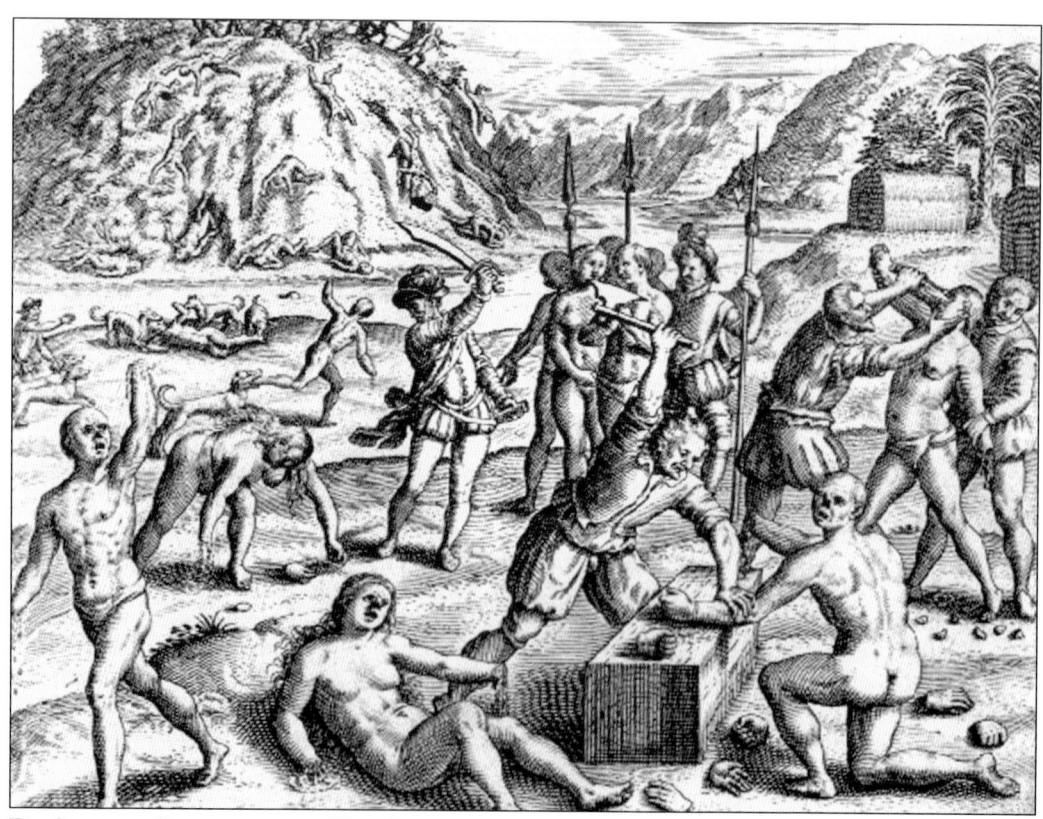

DE SOTO AS PORTRAYED BY HIS CONTEMPORARIES. This illustration is by Theodore de Bry for a German edition of *Brevisima relacion de la destruycion de las Indias*, which translates as *A Brief Relation of the Destruction of the Indies*, by Bartolome de las Casas, written in 1552. The illustration documents the savage abuse of Native Americans by the Spanish, including the cutting off of hands and noses, dogs hunting natives, and mass slaughter. (From *Knights of Spain, Warriors of the Sun: Hernando de Soto and the South's Ancient Chiefdoms* by Charles Hudson.)

Three

EARLY IMAGES OF THE ASHEVILLE AREA

Until the early 1700s, there was little contact between native tribes in Western North Carolina and English settlements in the East. The relationship between fur traders and the Indians deteriorated by the 1740s as the number of traders increased and became more hostile; the Cherokee retreated further into the mountains until their final defeat and removal to Oklahoma in the late 1830s.

Col. David Vance and William Davidson introduced the bill in the North Carolina legislature that created Buncombe County in 1791. Buncombe County was formed in 1792, with William Davidson hosting the first meeting of the Buncombe County courts; the first courthouse was built the following year. Davidson had received a land grant from the State of North Carolina of 640 acres in 1787; John Burton, who received 200 acres next to Davidson, laid out a street plan along old Indian paths. First known as North and South Main Street, these later became Biltmore Avenue and Broadway.

The area located on the French Broad and Swannanoa Rivers that became Asheville was a natural trading center; it was incorporated as Morristown in 1797. It was quickly designated as the county seat for Buncombe County. A post office was established in 1801, and the public square that would later become Pack Square was built in 1815. The town was renamed Asheville several years later in honor of the popular North Carolina governor Samuel Ashe. While the Pattons staked out land in Chunns Cove, David Vance settled in the Reems Creek community. James Alexander's family originally settled in the Bee Tree area of Swannanoa. The first census of Buncombe County in 1800 recorded a total population of 5,185 including 347 slaves. The 1860 population in Buncombe County climbed to 12,654 and the population of Asheville was 1,100.

The area remained inaccessible for much of its early history. Drovers walked on foot, herding their livestock to market. Farmers often drove teams of oxen pulling wagons, hauling supplies over Saluda Mountain to Asheville and to points beyond. Asheville proved to be a convenient rest stop, offering drovers' stands and hotels. Alexander's Inn was first a drovers' stand. Other inns and stands included Vance Inn and Barnard's Inn to the north, and Forster's Inn, Fletcher Tavern, McDowell Hotel, Farmers Hotel, and Tabor's Place to the south. Even by this time, travel was increasing. The Eagle Hotel, the town's first luxury hotel, second to Alexander's Inn, was built by James Patton in 1814. Frequent visitors came up the mountain from South Carolina and Georgia, even then realizing the healthful climate and escape from Southern summer heat.

Asheville's first "boom" occurred after the completion of the Buncombe Turnpike in 1828. This linked Asheville with South Carolina and Tennessee and provided a way for farmers and lumber producers to move goods around and out of the mountains. This inter- and intra-mountain commerce was greatly enhanced with the establishment of stagecoach service around the same time.

In 1800, William Mills owned 20 slaves. The more familiar families of the region and their slaveholdings for 1800 were as follows: Pattons, 26; Samuel Chunn, 5; Thomas Alexander, 3; Bedant Baird, 2; John Davidson, 7; William Davidson, 8; George Swain, 3; and David Vance, 10.

While Buncombe County's geographical size decreased over the next several decades, the number of slaves it owned actually increased. These slaves, often overlooked in the history of Asheville, proved to be instrumental in building the city of Asheville and profoundly influenced its culture. According to the slave schedules enumerated on August 16, 1860, Asheville held 750 slaves. The 1860 census yielded approximately 1,932 slaves for all of Buncombe County. Even in 1860, slaves represented nearly 15 percent of the population of Buncombe County and 68 percent of the population of Asheville. Frederick Law Olmstead traveled through the region in 1853, and he took note of who these slaveholders were: mainly professionals, doctors, lawyers, merchants and holders of public office, as well as "land owners with some ties, loosely or extensively, to agriculture."

Asheville struggled after the Civil War. Physically, no battles had been fought in the area, but the area was financially bereft. By the 1870s, after rail connections between Tennessee, Georgia, and Alabama were established, west Tennessee no longer sought goods via the Buncombe Turnpike. An ambitious plan to build a railroad through Asheville and across the mountains had emerged in the 1850s. It had gotten as far as Morganton when the Civil War began. Construction continued in 1877, finally reaching Asheville in 1880. The railroad, as in many cities, proved to be a watershed event.

By 1886, the year Frank Coxe built the first Battery Park Hotel, it is estimated that the population of Asheville was boosted by approximately 30,000 summer visitors, many from Philadelphia, South Carolina, and further south. Coxe's landmark hotel, along with many other hotels and boarding houses, marked turning point for Asheville, as its economy diversified into the tourism industry. It is said that from the terrace of the original Battery Park Hotel, George Vanderbilt decided to build his massive estate. And while Vanderbilt was perhaps the most prominent visitor, the sheer number of visitors indicated Asheville's growing importance as a summer resort town. Of particular interest in this book is a photo of the interior of one of the many boarding houses of the time, illustrating how perhaps the lesser of the summer visitors spent their time.

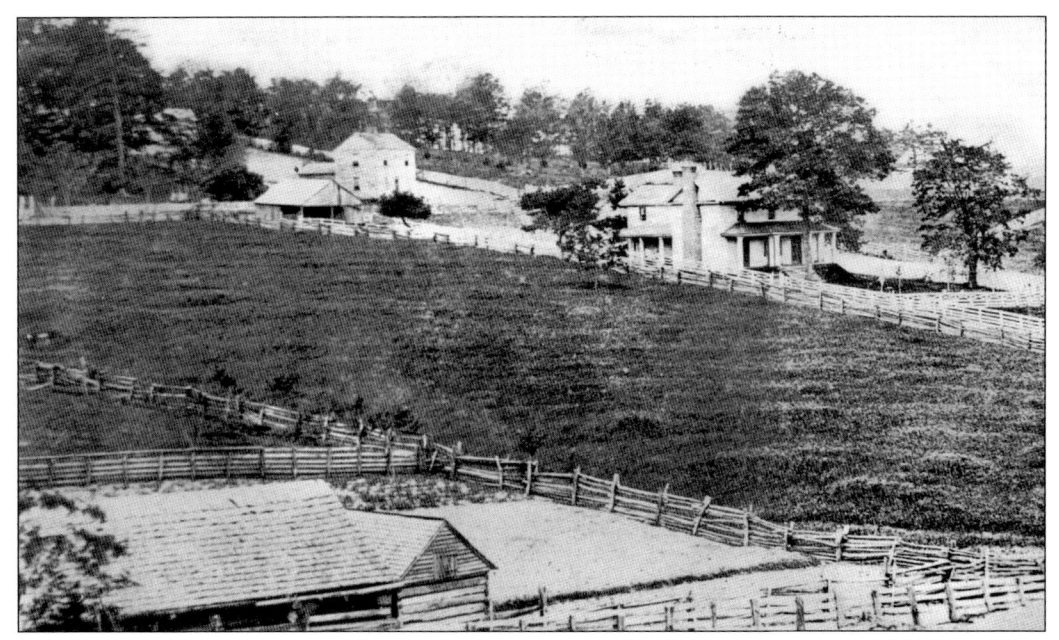

BEFORE THE CITY. This c. 1866 photo of present-day Lexington Avenue and Walnut Street looks towards Haywood Street and shows the Roberts House and its stable. What is now Walnut Street runs between them. The stable, in the lower left corner, would be near Lexington Avenue.

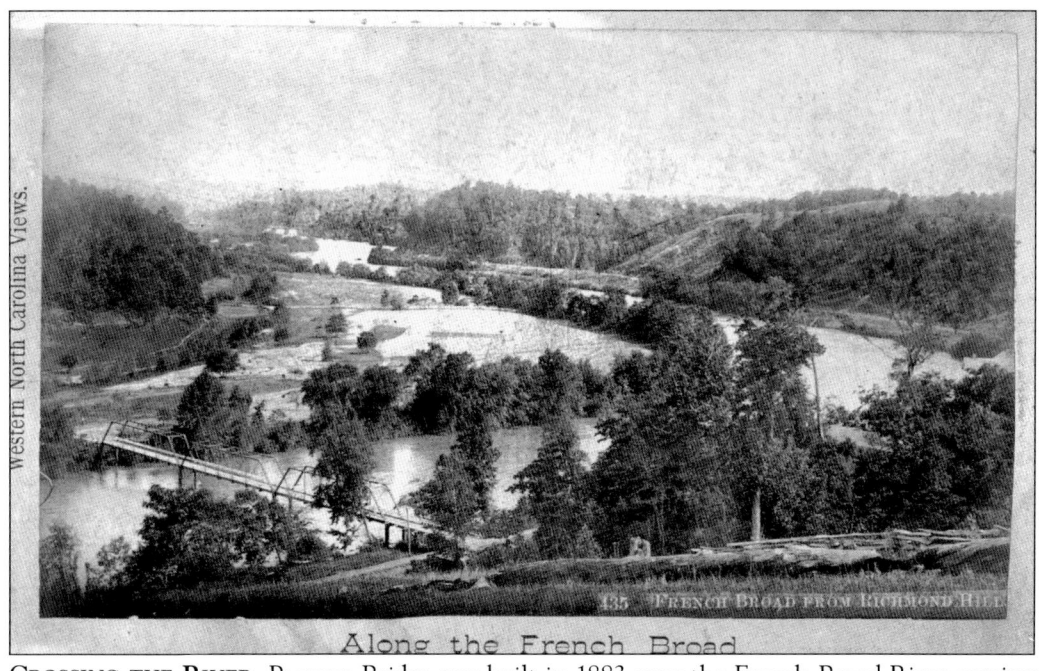

CROSSING THE RIVER. Pearson Bridge was built in 1883 over the French Broad River coming from Richmond Hill. The photograph was taken c. 1885.

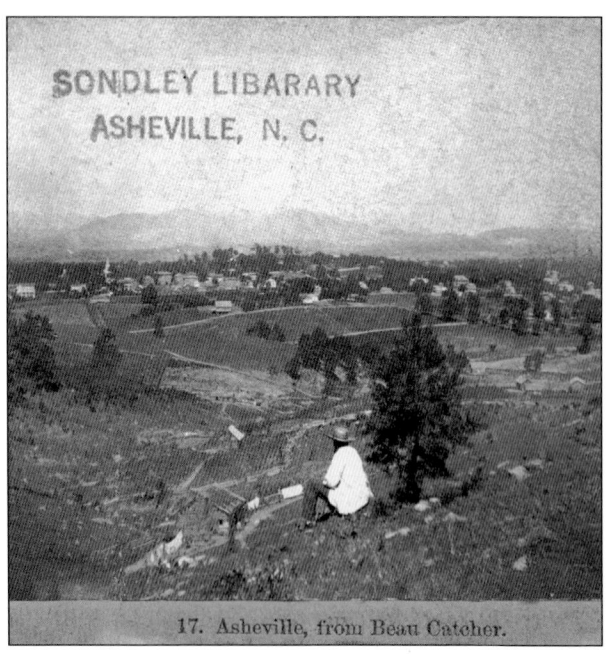

ASHEVILLE FROM BEAUCATCHER. This photograph was taken by W.T. Robertson before 1886, as the Battery Park Hotel had not yet been built. Robertson was active in Asheville from 1872 to 1884.

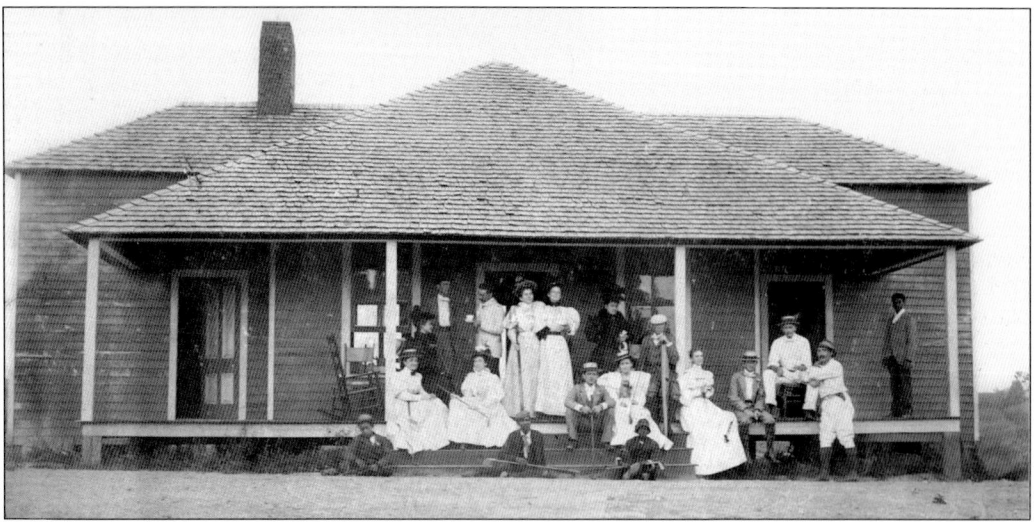

EARLY CULTURE. Members of the Swannanoa Country Club pose with golf equipment in front of the clubhouse on Charlotte Street in Grove Park. Originally organized in West Asheville as the Swannanoa Hunt Club, the club changed its name to the Swannanoa Country Club and moved in 1899 after George Pack donated a building and land for a golf course at the end of Charlotte Street. The name changed to the Asheville Country Club in 1909. Identified members are James Edwin Rumbough (in white cap to the left of post), Miss Sarah Keyes Rumbough (his sister), Miss Elizabeth Fitzgerald Forbes, Miss Laura Carter, Miss Minnie Tucker, Miss Raidee Tucker, Miss Chism, Miss Sarah Mills (of Savannah, Georgia), Dr. Charles S. Jordan, William R. Porter (of Key West, Florida), John Charles, "Jack" Rumbough (John Rumbough's brother), Dr. and Mrs. Thomas Cheeseborough, Mr. Williams, and Joseph J. McCloskey. Three small African-American boys, who served as caddies, are sitting at the foot of the steps, and a young African-American man, who was a servant, is on the far right side of the porch. The photograph is dated August 1896.

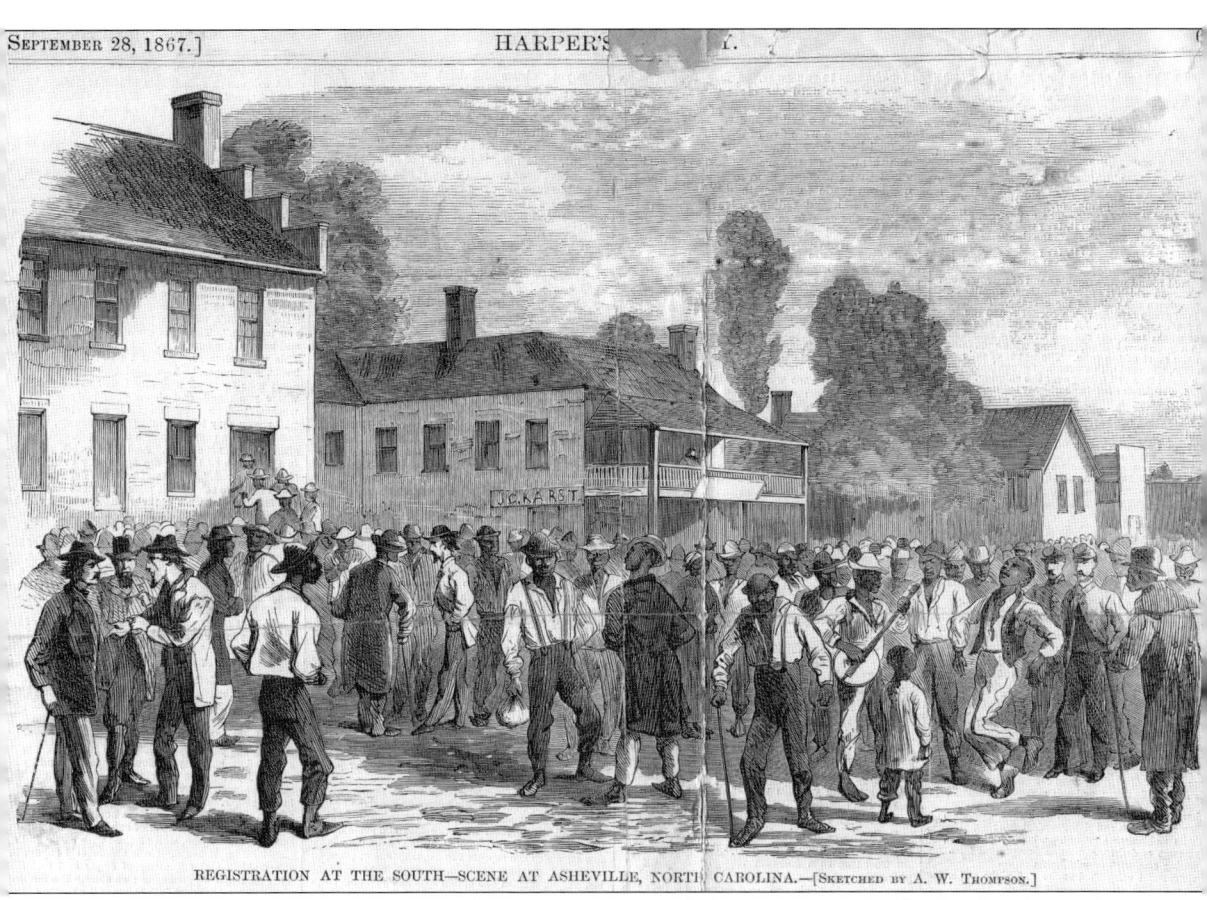

VOTER REGISTRATION IN 1867. The engraving, entitled *Registration At the South—Scene At Asheville, North Carolina*, by A.W. Thompson, was printed in the September 28, 1867 edition of *Harper's Weekly*; it shows African Americans registering to vote.

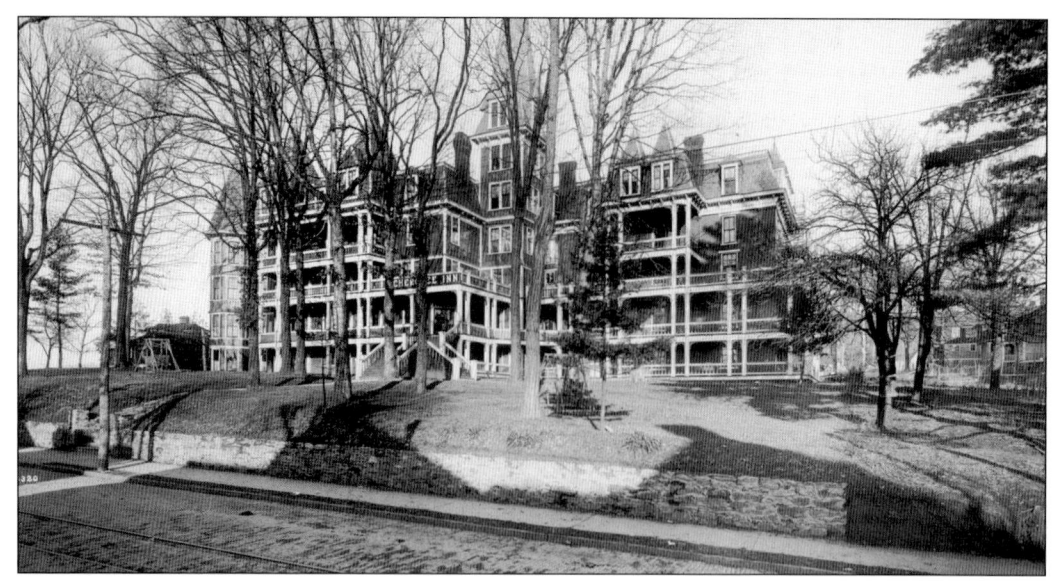

EARLY HOSPITALITY. Cherokee Inn was at the corner of Oak and Woodfin Streets. Built c. 1856, the inn was used as a dormitory for Asheville Female College until about 1887. It was sold in 1889 to H.G. Greenwell from Kentucky, who enlarged and remodeled it and opened the Oaks Hotel. It sold again in 1908 to R.R. Robinson, who changed the name to Cherokee Inn. The inn was sold in 1920 to the YWCA and again in 1924 to the First Baptist Church. It was demolished in 1925. It had four floors with wrap-around porches on each level and at least three conical towers. On the back, it reads "Oakes Hotel where Baptist Church is, floor fell once during a ball after that it became a third rate hotel."

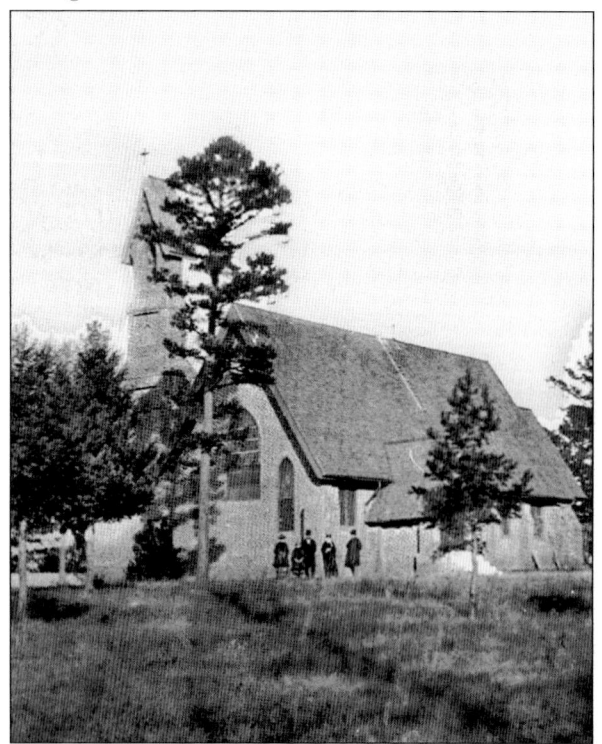

THEY WERE FAITHFUL. This quarter-view of Calvary Episcopal Church was taken by Thomas A. Weston, who visited the Asheville area in 1878 before he bought Rock Hall, also known as the Blake House, in Arden. The caption includes "Shufordsville Church—Episcopal, Rev. E.A. Osborne, Valley of the French Broad River, 12 miles south of Asheville on stage road to Hendersonville and Flat Rock."

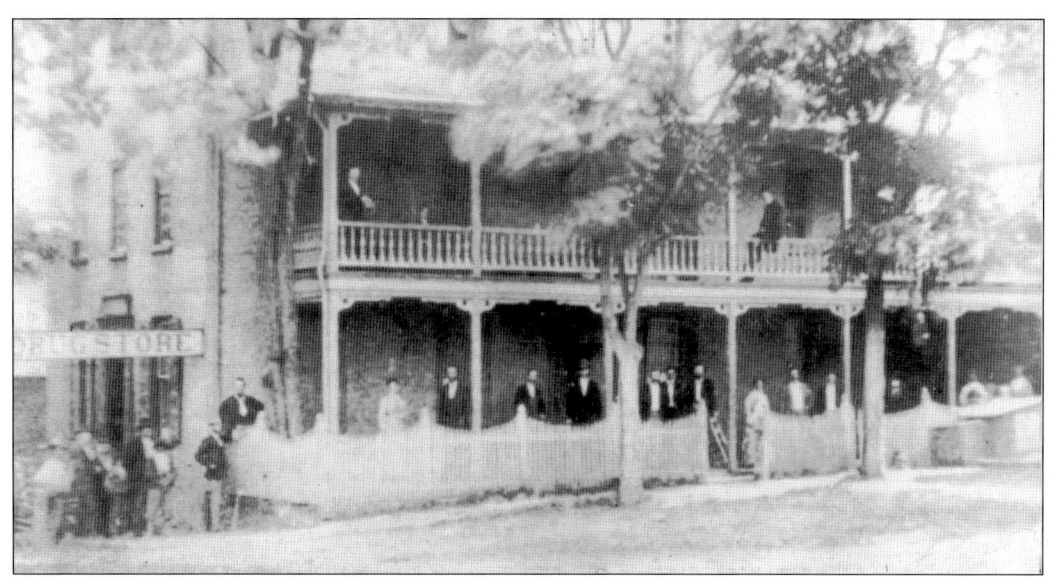

THE DROVERS. This *c.* 1880–1900 stereoscopic view, from the northeast, shows Alexander's Inn on the east bank of the French Broad River, along the Buncombe Turnpike. The inn was built and operated by James Mitchell Alexander in 1827–1828. A general store, shoe shop, wagon factory, gristmill, sawmill, and river ferry operated at the inn. The two-and-one-half–story weather-boarded structure with roof dormers, exterior end chimneys, shed rooms, and semi-engaged double-tier porch faces the river. The Turnpike is visible between the building and the river. The inn was sold to Robert Brank Vance, who, with his son James Vance, operated the inn as Alexander Hotel and as Vance Hall. It was sold again to Dr. Frank P. Meriwether before it burned in 1924. One Flemish bond brick chimney remained in 1981.

EARLY PACK SQUARE. This stereoscopic view of the Bank Hotel is from the south on the Public Square, now Pack Square, *c.* 1860. The hotel, also known as Hilliard Hall or Hilliard House, was built by James Mitchell Alexander in 1815 and torn down in 1889. Alexander operated the hotel and a harness shop until 1828. In 1827, the Buncombe Turnpike opened and Alexander built Alexander's Hotel and moved there. Dr. P.C. Lester, M.D., operated a drug store here after 1850.

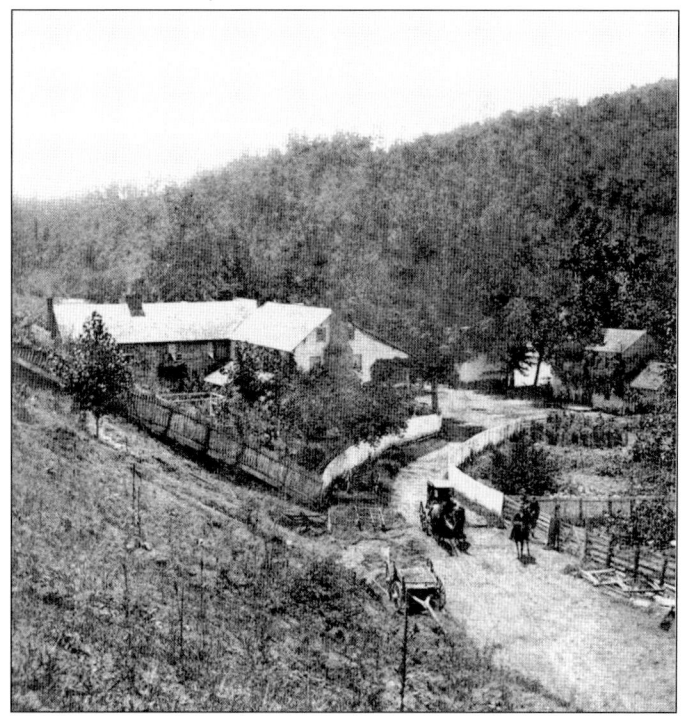

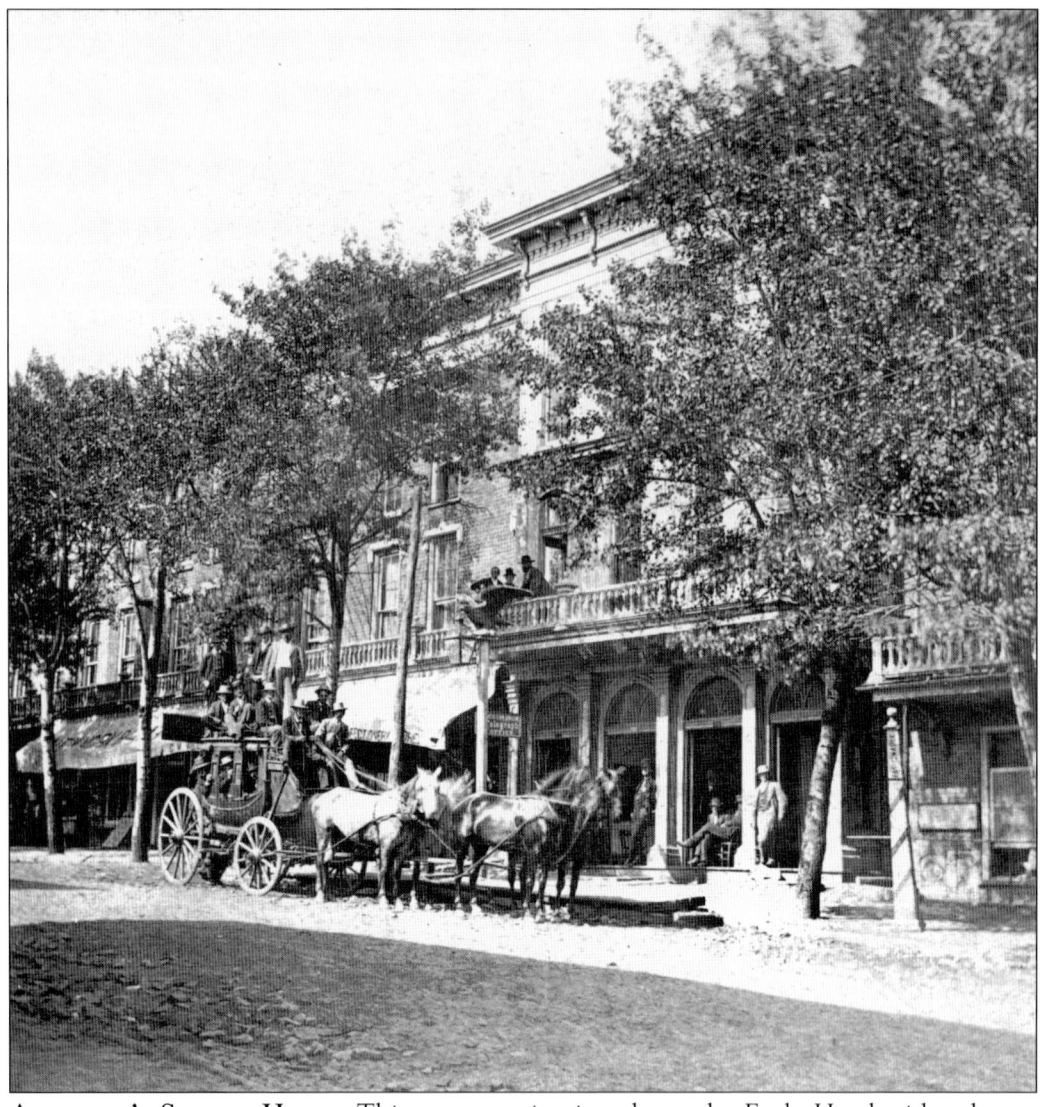

ASHEVILLE'S SECOND HOTEL. This stereoscopic view shows the Eagle Hotel with a horse-drawn stagecoach in front. Asheville's second hotel, it was established c. 1814 by James Patton; the hotel was probably named for the gold eagle over the entrance. Originally a frame building, it was enlarged to a three-story brick and covered a block between Eagle and Sycamore Streets on the east side of South Main. William P. Blair operated the hotel in the 1870s. The hotel was demolished 1934 when Main Street was widened.

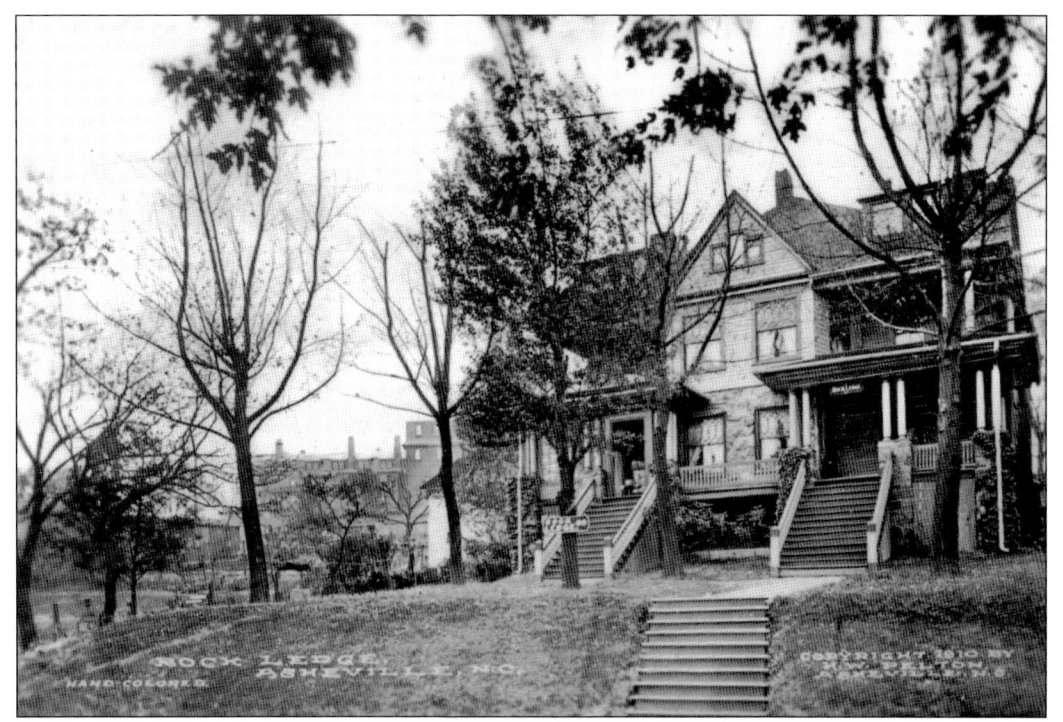

ASHEVILLE FROM SUNSET DRIVE. This view, c. 1886–1895, shows Battery Park Hotel, operated from 1886 to 1921, in the center background; the courthouse, built in 1876, is at the extreme left. Notice the rural appearance, with open fenced areas.

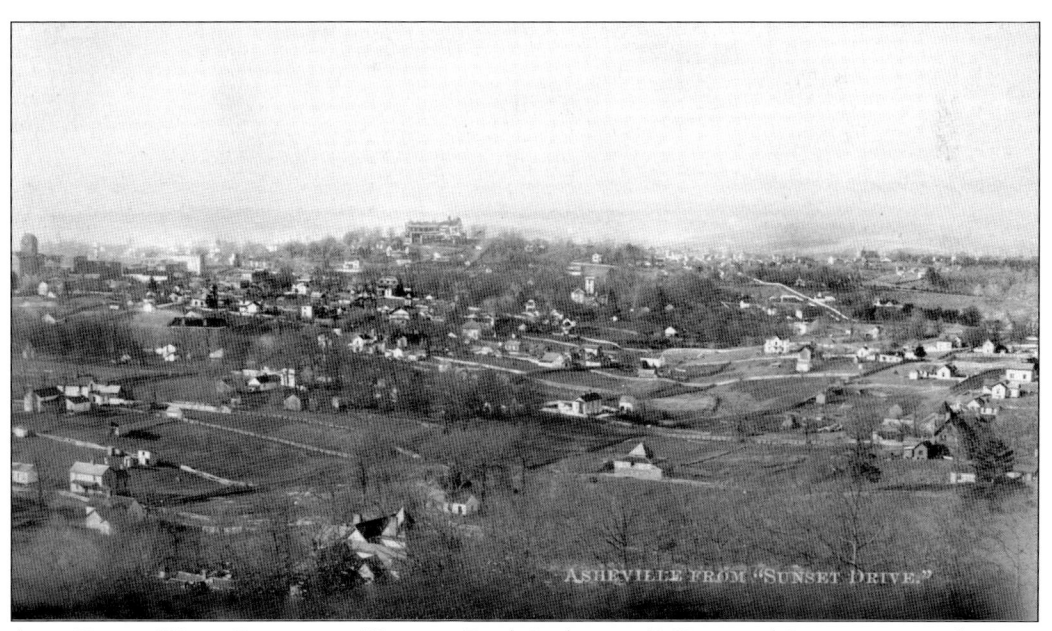

AND THERE WERE BOARDING HOUSES. Rock Ledge, at 68 Haywood Street, was run by Mrs. M.J. Corcoran. Battery Park Hotel is in the left background.

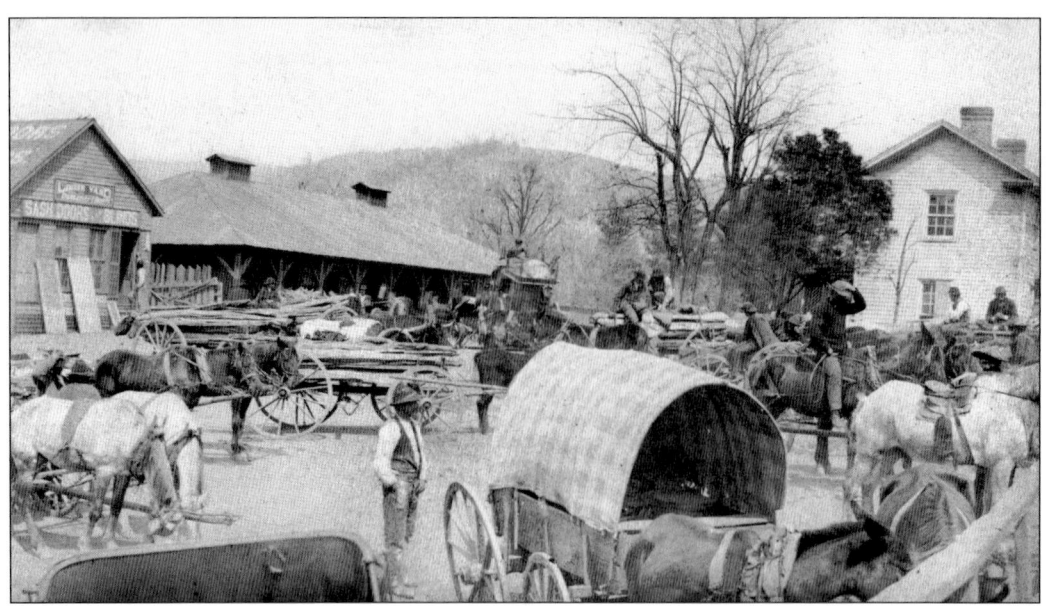

EARLY COMMERCE. This is an 1890 image of the Asheville Wood Yard near Depot Street. The businesses carried building materials of all kinds—lumber, sash, doors, and blinds.

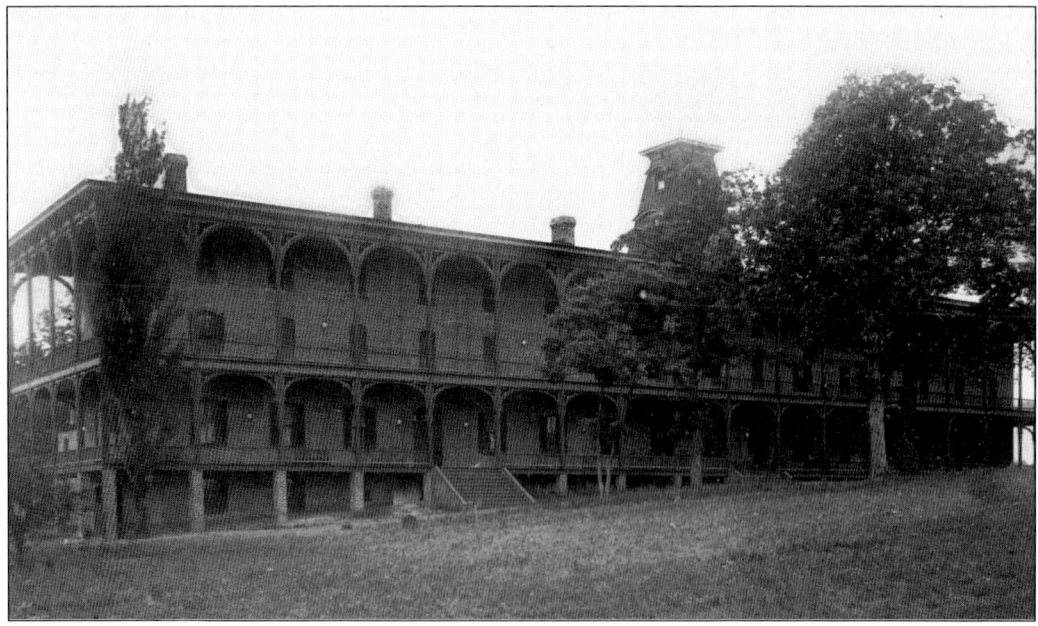

THE RESORT ERA BEGINS. Sulfur Springs Hotel was located five miles west of Asheville near School Road in Malvern Hills. The springs were discovered in January 1827 by Robert Henry, a veteran of the Revolutionary War battle of King's Mountain and the first schoolteacher in Western North Carolina. The original wooden hotel was built c. 1831 by Henry and his son-in-law, Col. Reuben Deaver. It was L-shaped with double piazzas in front. By 1848 the hotel could accommodate 200 guests. It burned in December 1862, and was rebuilt by E.G. Carrier as the brick building pictured here in 1887, but burned again in 1892; concrete ruins of the structure still remain. A railway ran between Asheville and the springs from 1889 to 1894.

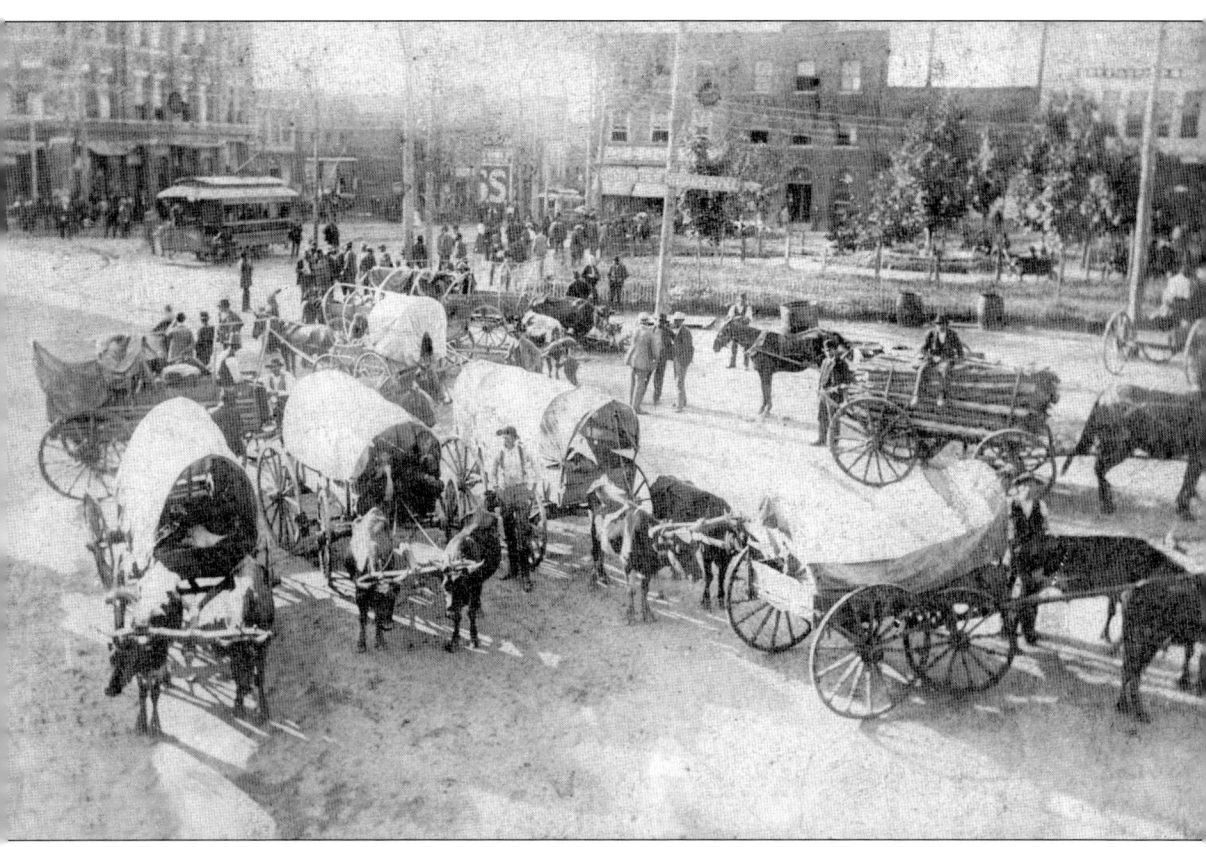

A Very Busy Pack Square as Drovers Await Their Orders. This view of Pack Square, then Court Square, from the south to the northwest, dates from 1890. Ten ox-drawn wagons stand in the foreground. The sign on the utility pole promotes the Western Union telegraph office. Buildings include Barnard (also known as Revell) Building; C.D. Blanton & Co. clothing; A.D. Cooper, grocer; several newspapers, including *Asheville Methodist* (weekly), *Daily Citizen*, *Democrat* (weekly), *Evening Journal* (daily), and *Farmer & Mechanic*; a restaurant; and M. Alexander, harness maker.

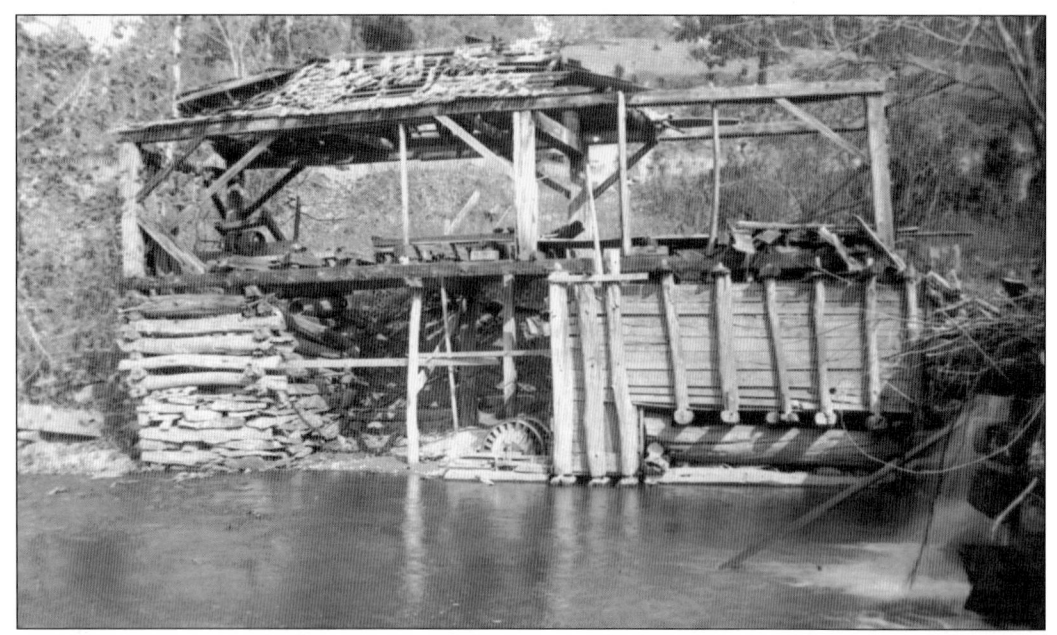

A Pioneer Mill. Pictured are ruins of an old sawmill on Reems Creek. It is a vertical mill type, which has since been replaced with a more modern, circular type.

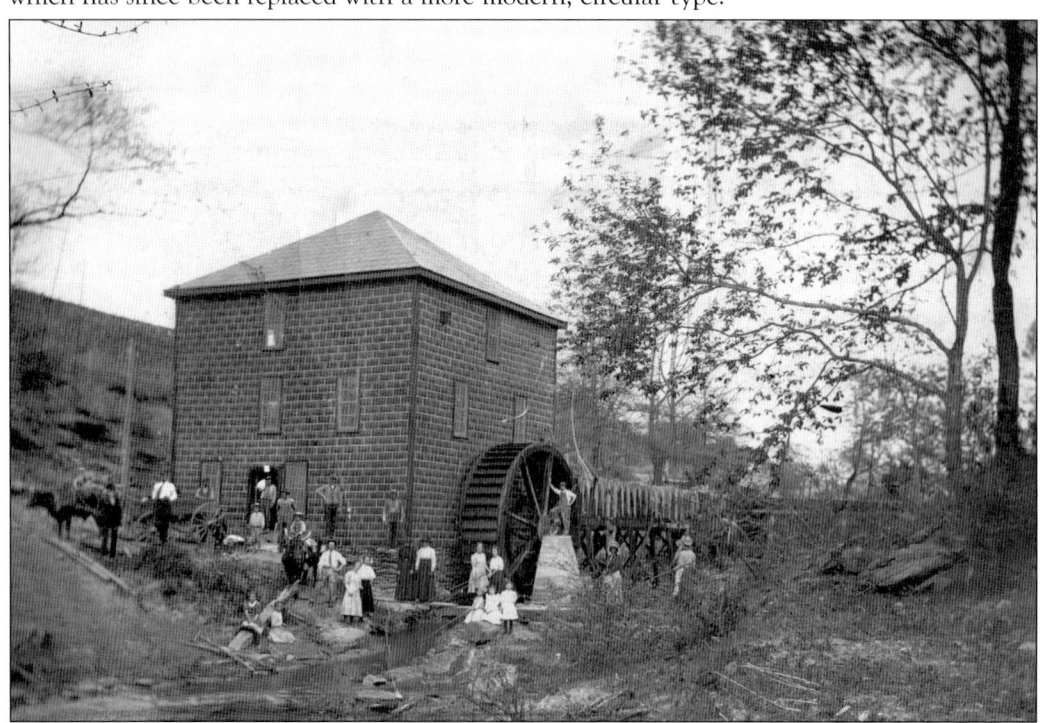

The Family Business. M.J. "Will" Jones's mill stood in Fairview, about two miles west of Court Square, c. 1880–1900. It was a cubical, three-story, brick-and-block building. Cane Creek runs from center-right under the bridge to the lower left. Several men, women, and children stand in front of the mill. An ox-drawn wagon is at the left of the building, and a steep hill is behind it.

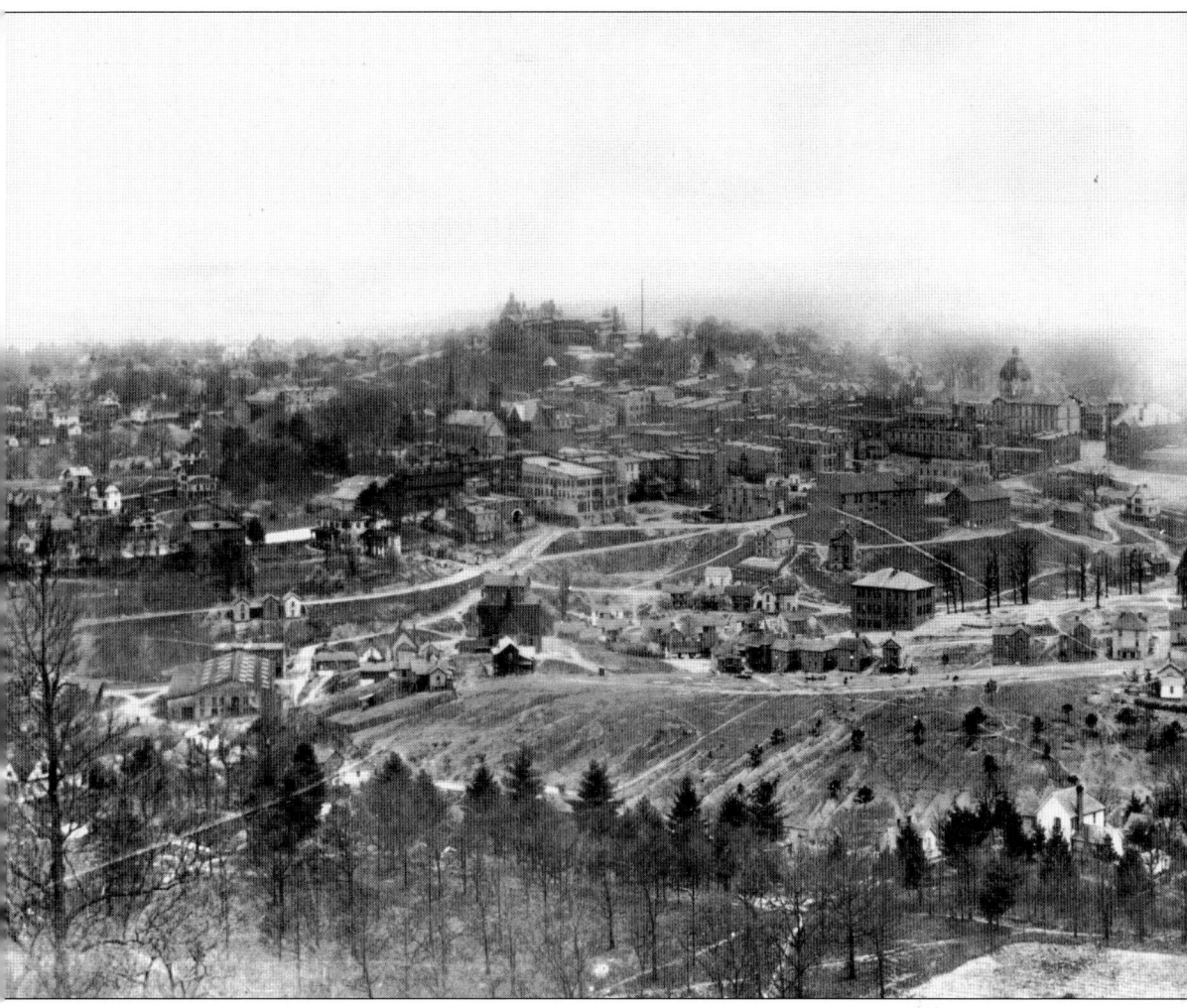

THE DAWN OF A NEW CENTURY. This view of Asheville from Beaucatcher was taken between 1898 and 1903 with a clear view of the area from South Main Street above Atkin Street over to East Pack Square. Buncombe County Courthouse, in use from 1876 to 1903, and Asheville City Hall with its inverted cone tower, built in 1892, are at right. Battery Park Hotel, built in 1886, is in the center background on the hill. The tower of the Drhumor Building, built in 1895, is to the lower right of the Battery Park Hotel. The pyramidal tower is the post office, in use from 1892 to 1930. Catholic Hill School, which burned in 1917, is the dark three-story building at lower right along Velvet Street/Dixon Street. The First Presbyterian Church, built in 1884, and the Methodist Church across from it, built in 1857, with its square steeple, are in the center. Many other buildings are clearly visible.

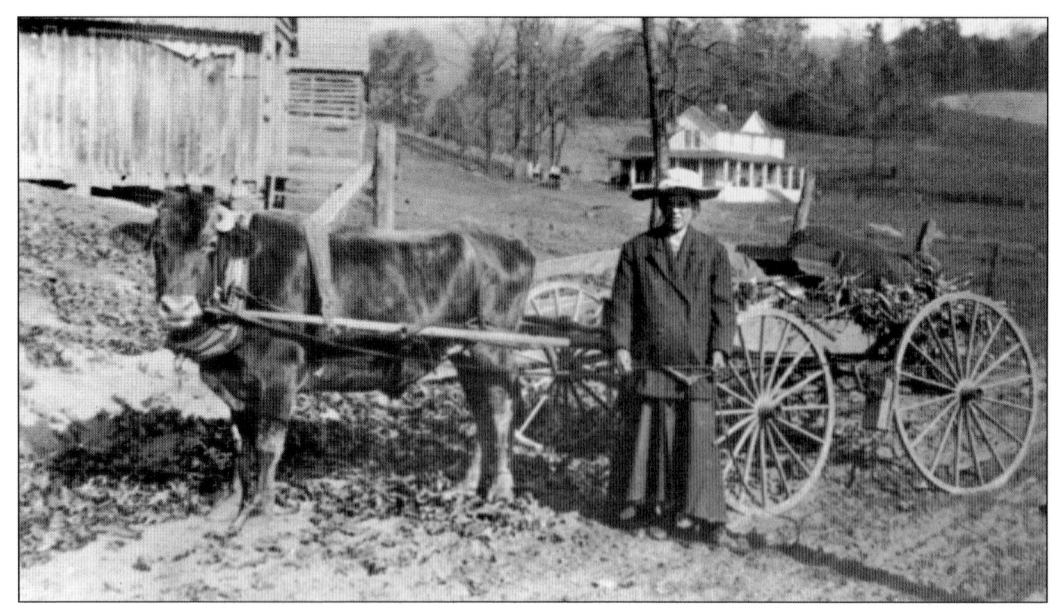

TO THE MARKET. This woman, in the Reems Creek area of Buncombe County c. 1915–1917, is leading her loaded ox-drawn wagon to market. Farm buildings are visible to the near left. The house in background belonged to George Donkel, the potter.

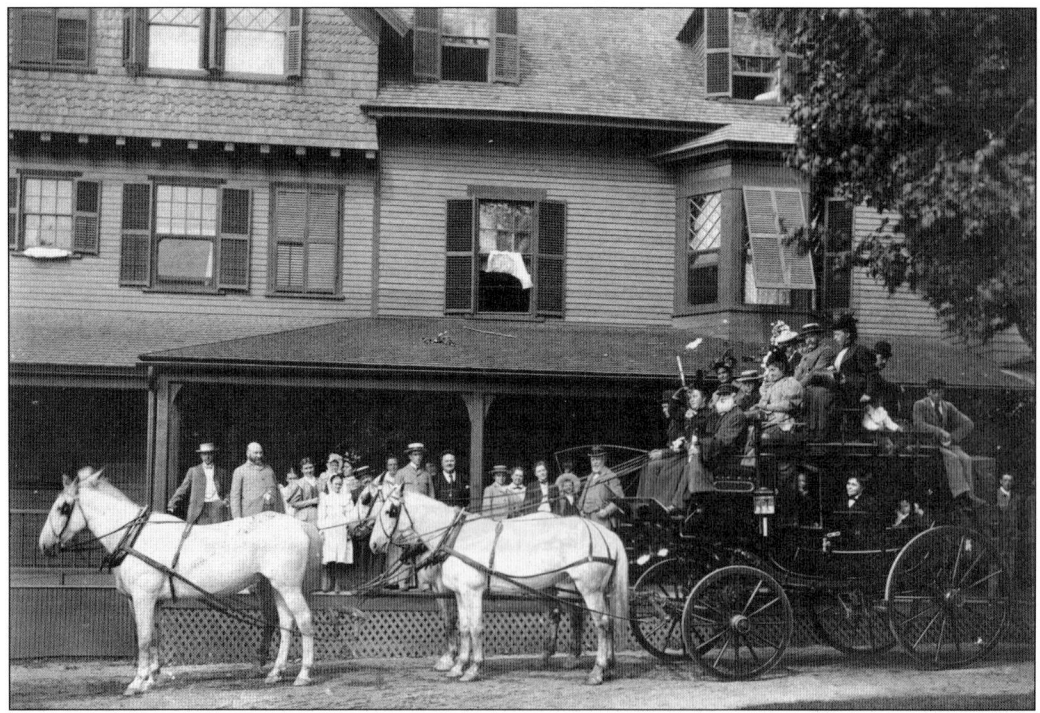

AN AFTERNOON DRIVE. This group of people by the old Battery Park Hotel is prepared for an afternoon's drive with Frank Coxe, builder and owner of the hotel. Coxe took pleasure in driving his "Tally-Ho" throughout the countryside, or in using his coach to transport guests to and from the depot. The coach drawn by four white horses is named "Wentworth." His other coach was "Maude."

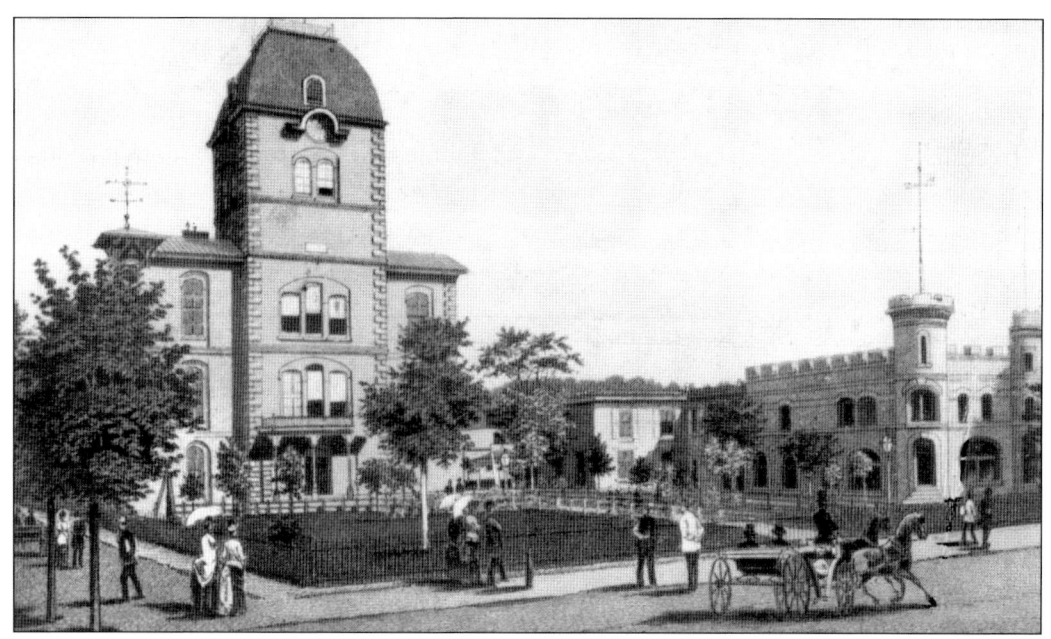

PUBLIC SQUARE IN 1887. This view of Public Square, copyrighted 1887 by Adolph Wittemann, is titled *City Hall and First National Bank*. "City Hall" is actually Buncombe County's sixth courthouse, built in 1876.

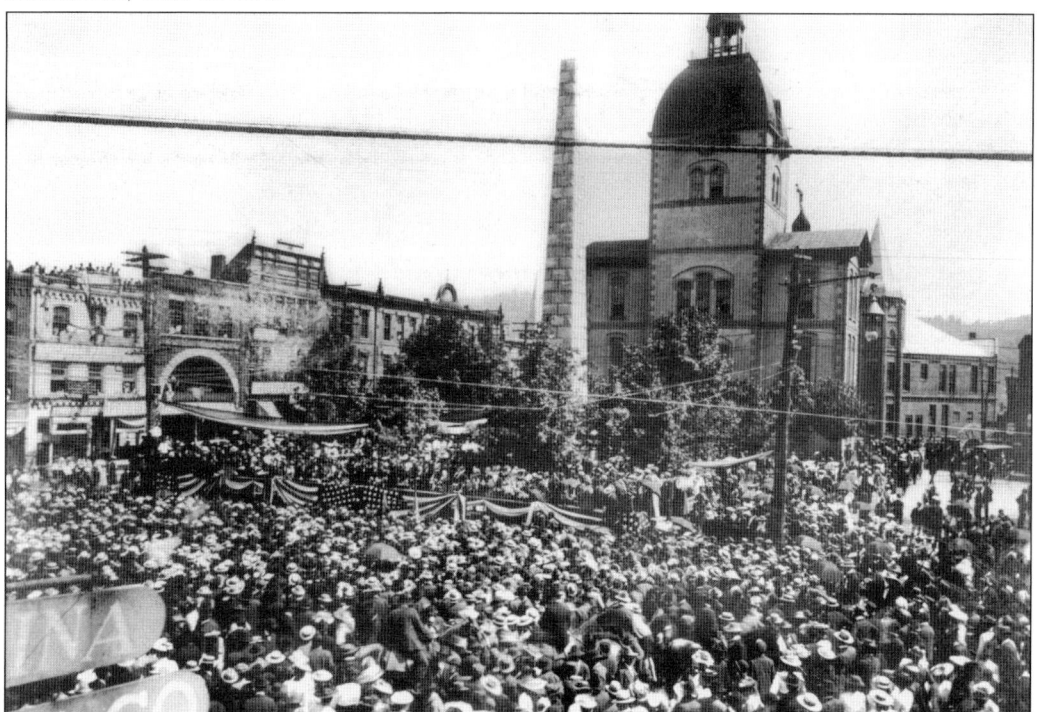

BULLY FOR ASHEVILLE. An overflow crowd jammed into Pack Square on September 9, 1902, to hear Teddy Roosevelt (on the speaker's platform) speak while campaigning for president. The 1876 Buncombe County Courthouse is in the center background, the last courthouse located at Pack Square.

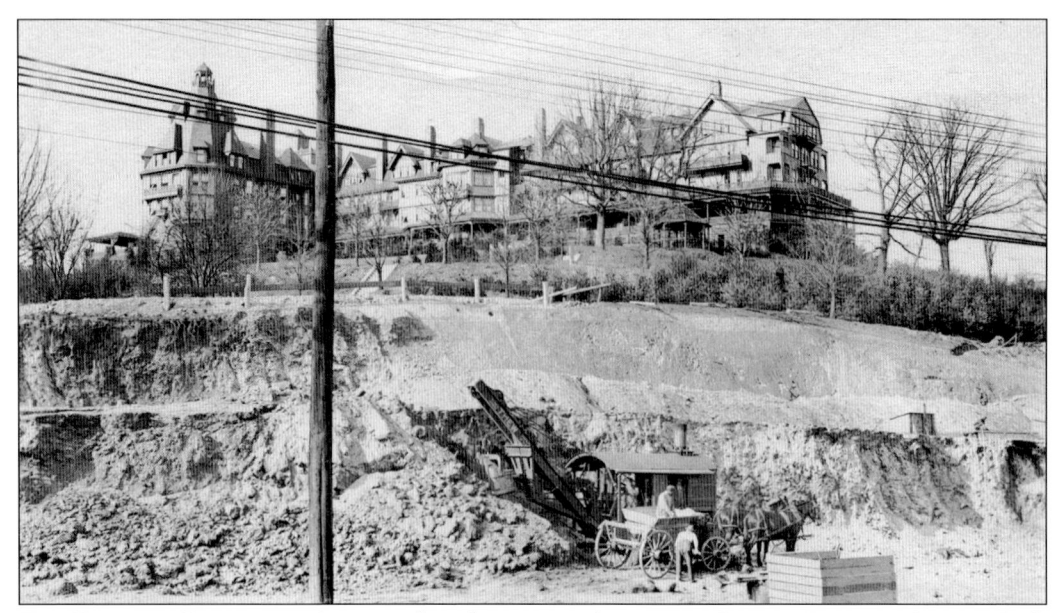

THE PRICE OF PROGRESS. A steam shovel is pictured removing Battery Porter or Battery Park Hill, c. 1922. Already obsolete for a burgeoning town, the Battery Park Hotel, shown in the background, awaits demolition.

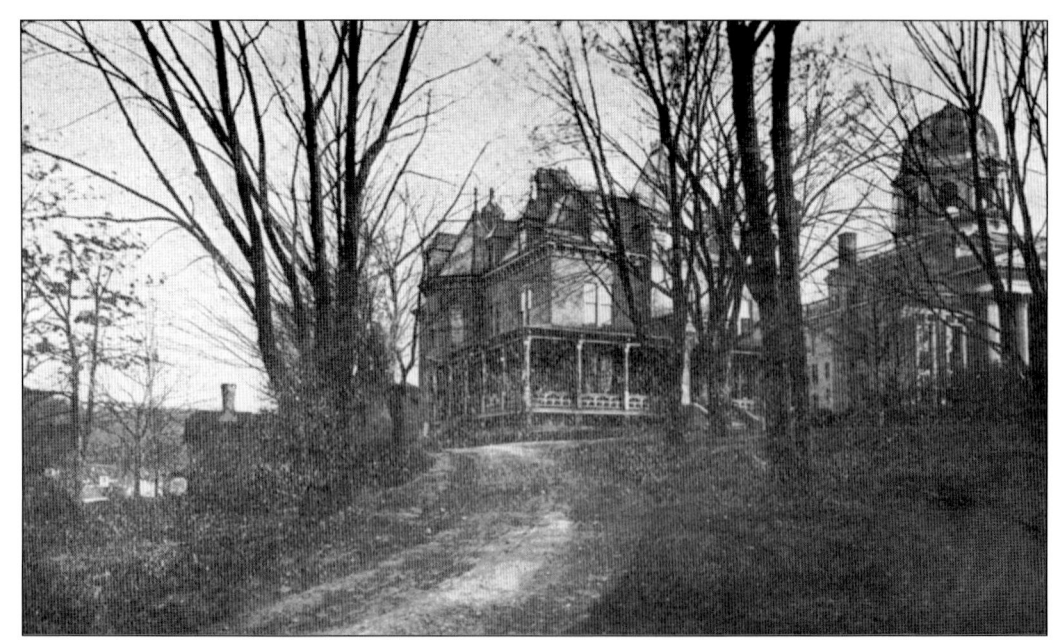

THE CHANGING FACE OF DOWNTOWN. This c. 1910 side view leads up to the Knickerbocker Boarding House, facing College Street, near the site of the present-day Buncombe County Courthouse. It has a large, wrap-around porch and pointed dormers on the third floor. The Buncombe County Courthouse with a dome, built in 1903, is to the right.

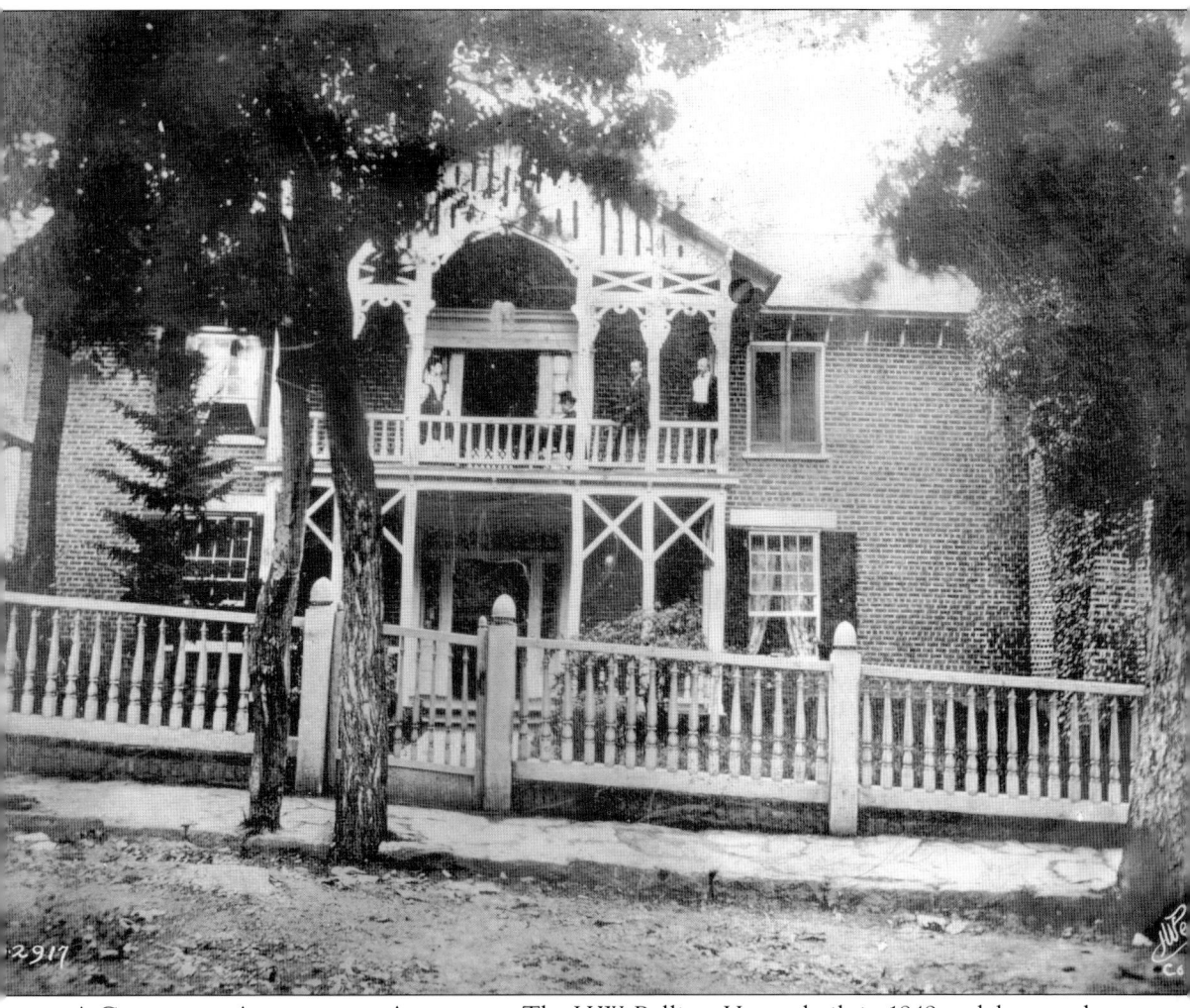

A GLIMPSE OF ANTEBELLUM ASHEVILLE. The H.W. Pulliam House, built in 1849 and destroyed in 1890, is located about midway up the first block of Main Street. The following people are on the balcony: Mrs. C.W. de Vault is standing, Col. H.W. Pulliam is seated in the chair (he was superintendent of the Asheville munitions works during the War between the States), his son Lawrence Pulliam is seated on balustrade, and Capt. C.M. McCloud (a member of the Asheville Bar and the person instrumental in bringing the first telegraph line into Asheville) is the third man on balcony. (Pelton copy of an 1878 photo.)

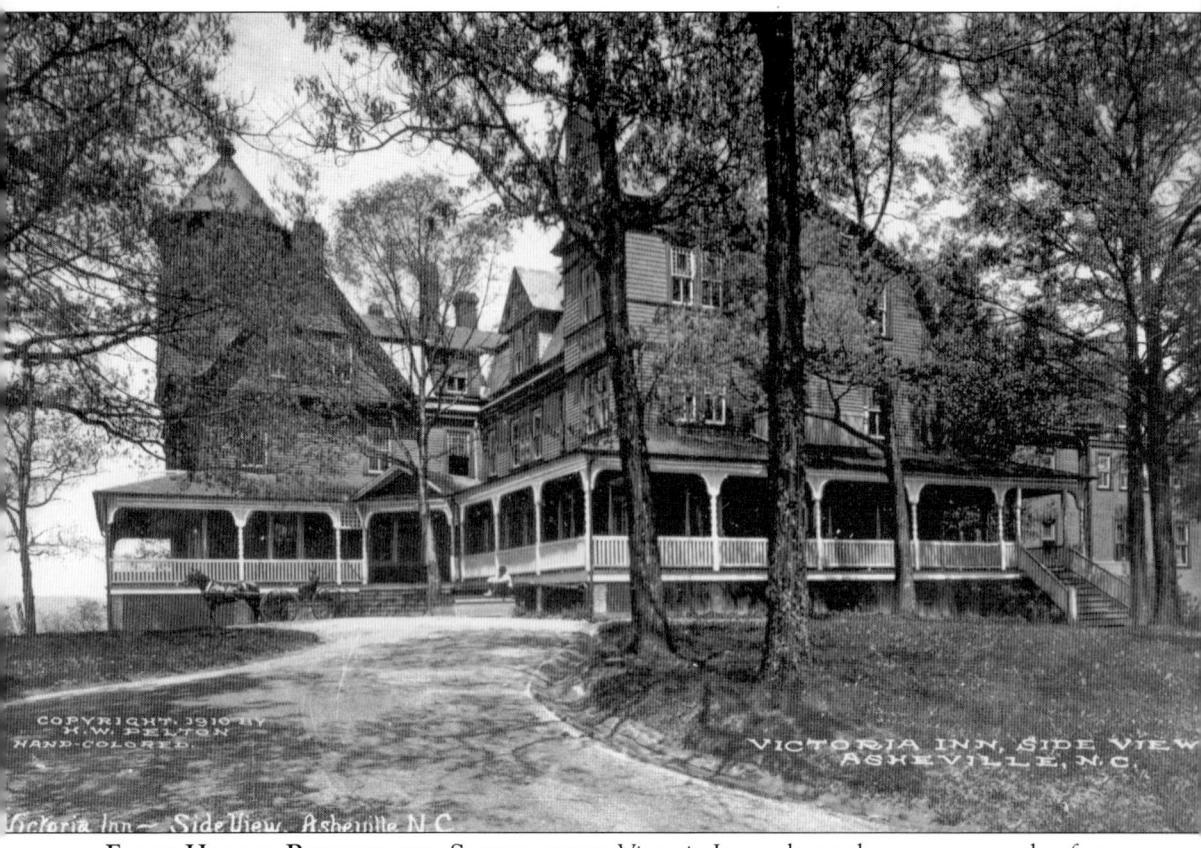

EARLY HEALTH RESORTS AND SANITARIUMS. Victoria Inn, a large three-story, wooden-frame building, sits on a hillside in Victoria Settlement above Victoria Road. It was built for $110,000 in 1889 by Alexander Garrett and deeded in 1891 to his son, Robert U. Garrett. In this photo, dated 1910, the veranda that ran around the entire front of the mansion can be seen. In 1896, the 80-room structure became Oakland Heights Health Resort, a sanitarium famous for its therapeutic baths, directed by Dr. Paul Paquin and Dr. Samuel Westray Battle. The building became the Victoria Inn c. 1909. After a fire in 1910, it was sold to the Sisters of Christian Education for St. Genevieve College, a boarding and day school for ladies that was renamed St. Genevieve of the Pines School in 1922. The tower in this photo was a landmark, advertised by the inn as holding "30,000 gallons of pure mountain water." Atop the tower was a circular room with 16 windows. Victoria Hall was used by the school for classrooms and as a convent for the sisters before it was razed in 1963. In 1923, part of the veranda was removed for construction of a new chapel.

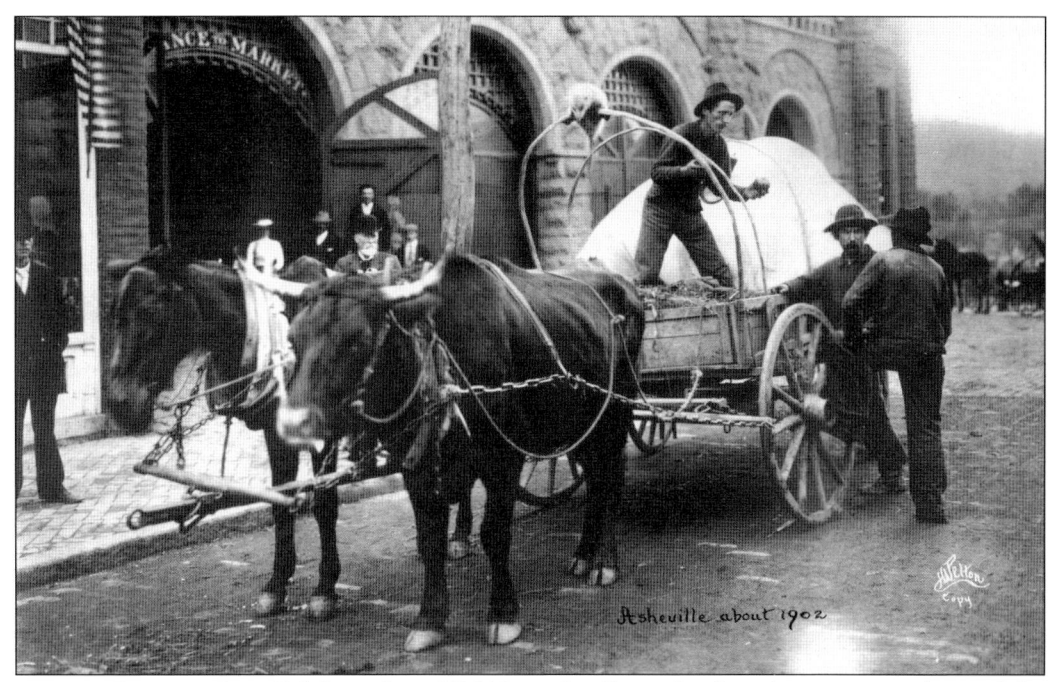

POSSUM DRIVER. Bert Calahan, from Wolf Laurel, sells apples from his wagon in front of the 1892 City Hall and Market, c. 1902. One possum is hanging onto his perch, the front rib of the covered wagon.

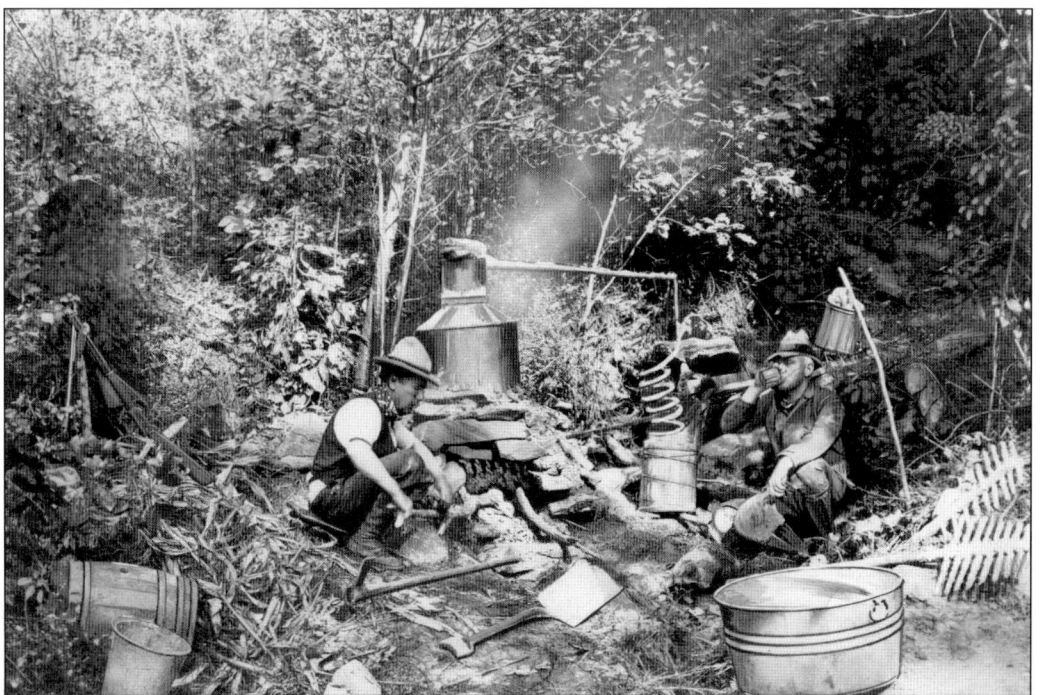

A HEALTH RESORT OF A DIFFERENT SORT. This scene of "a typical moonshine still in the heart of the mountains" is undated. The seated man at left may be Bascom Lamar Lunsford in a posed picture.

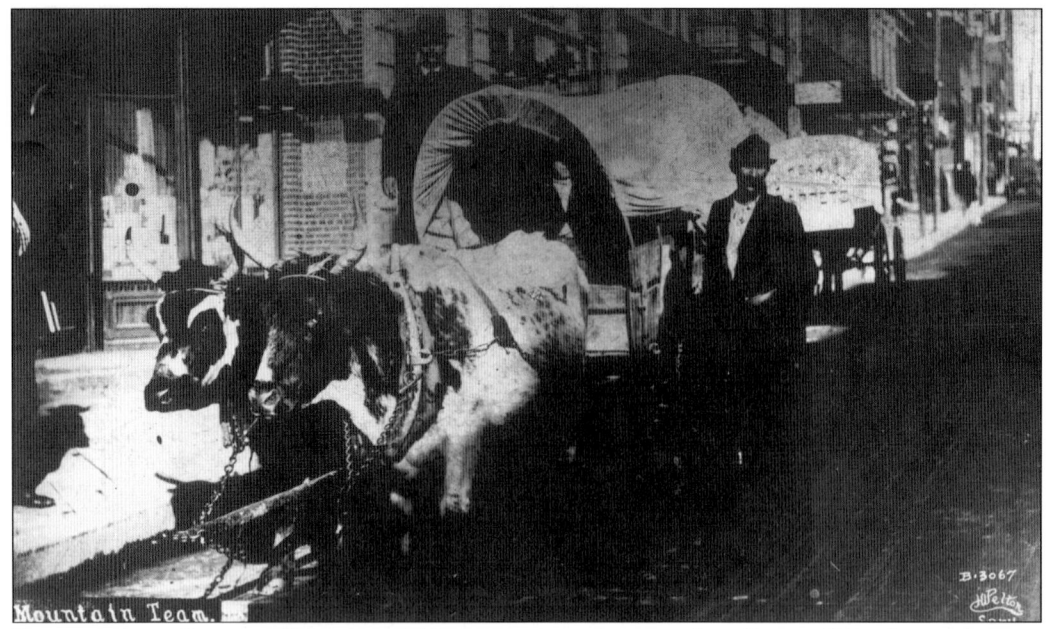

DROVERS IN A SECOND CENTURY. Old and new are contrasted in this c. 1900 photo of an ox-drawn covered wagon on Main Street. Two of the four men in this view are possibly Wiley Black "moonshiner-shooter" and his brother. The sign advertises Bonanza Wine & Liquor Co.

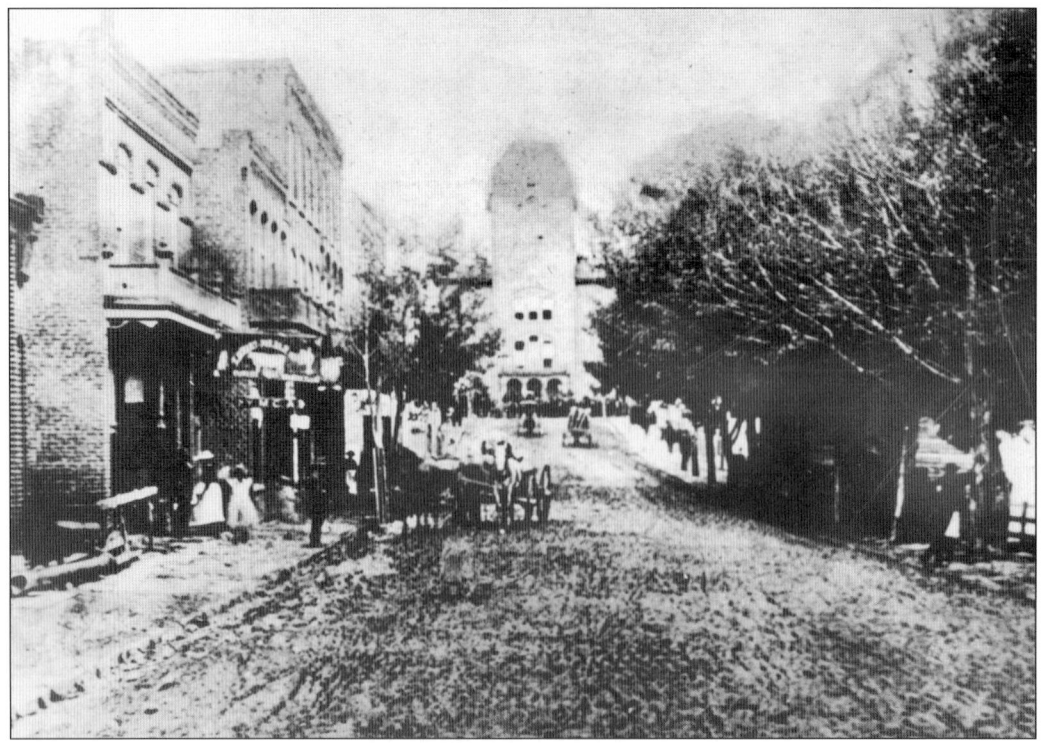

HORSE-DRAWN DOWNTOWN. This c. 1879–1884 view of Patton Avenue towards the square shows horse-drawn carriages on the dirt street. The 1876 Buncombe County Courthouse is in the center. The first YMCA, built in 1879, is on the left.

"Tree upon which Davy Crockett Said to Have Placed Targets for Shooting Matches—on Patton Farm at Swannanoa." Davy Crockett's second wife, Miss Elizabeth Patton, was the daughter of Robert Patton. Farm buildings, including a new barn under construction, are visible in the background.

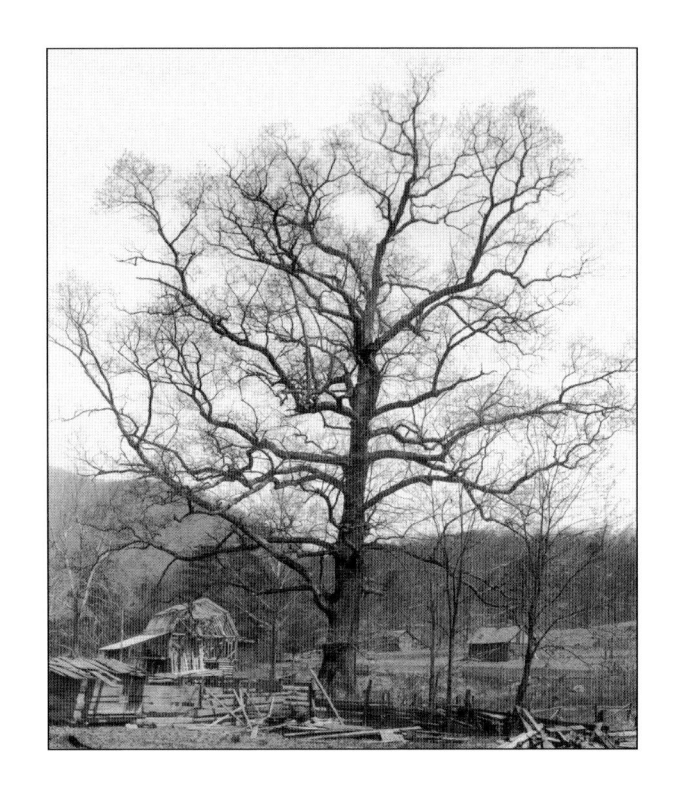

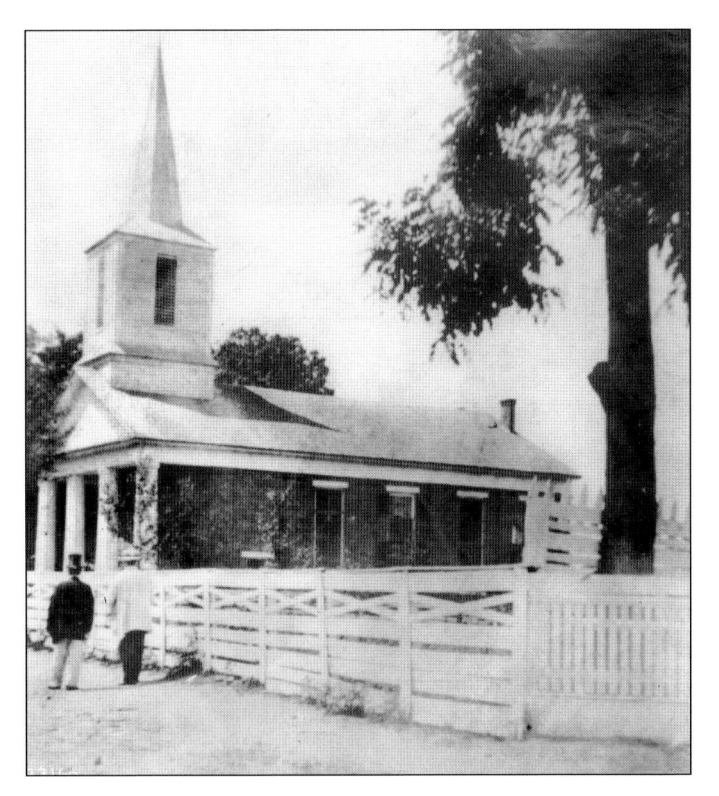

An Antebellum Snapshot. A stereoscopic view by Rufus Morgan shows Central Methodist Church, which served its congregation from 1837 to 1857. Its square steeple and columned entrance are visible in this side view. In front of church, and walking away from camera, are William Johnston, in the top hat, and Edward J. Aston, former Asheville mayor. This church building was replaced by a red brick church on the same site in 1857; the brick church was replaced in 1903, when the present Bedford limestone church was erected on the western side of Church Street.

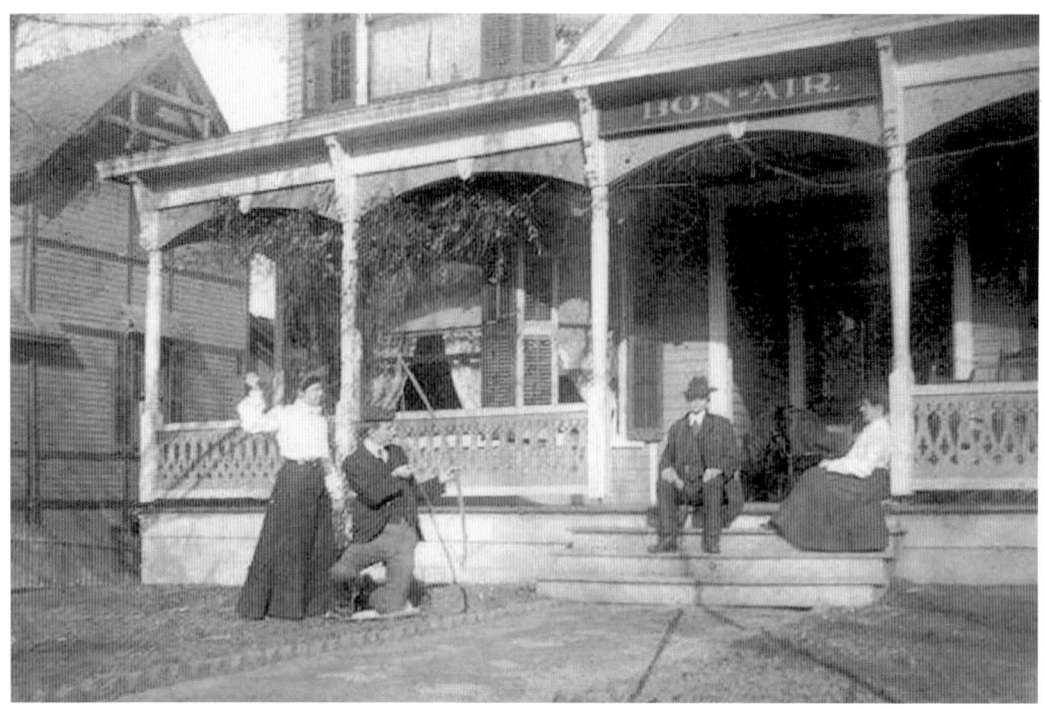

THE BON-AIR BOARDING HOUSE. Boarding houses were common around the turn of the last century. Above is a c. 1902 photo of the Bon Air Boarding House.

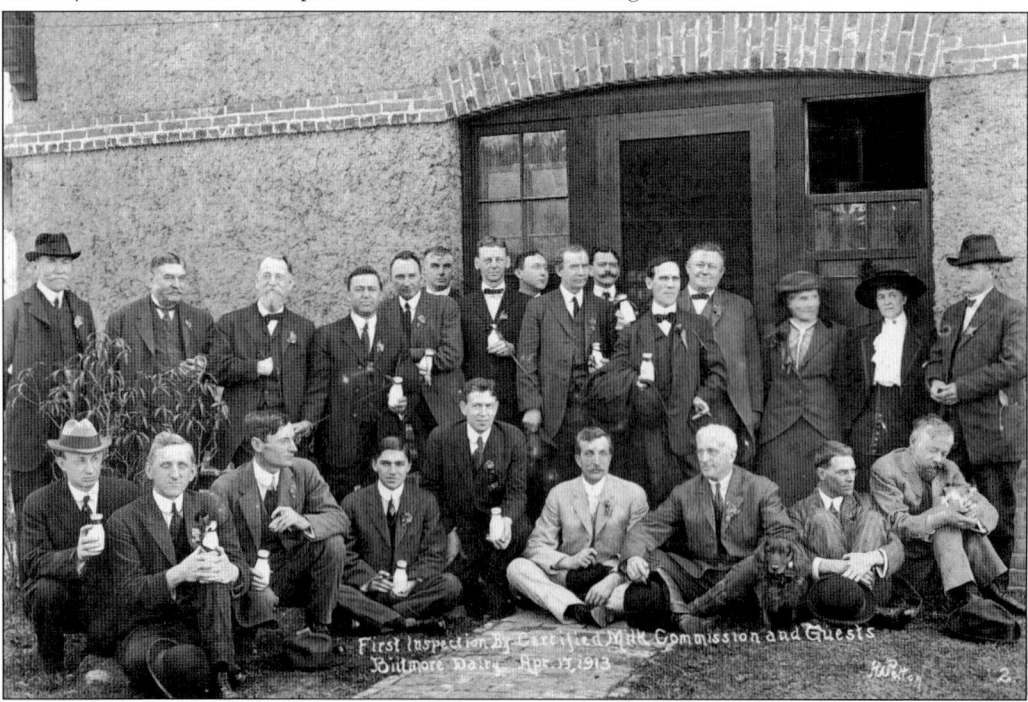

"FIRST INSPECTION BY CERTIFIED MILK COMMISSION AND GUESTS, BILTMORE DAIRY, APR 17, 1913." Twenty-two men and two women, outside the building, some holding small milk bottles, inspect the Biltmore Dairy.

Four

A CITY IS BORN

As the resort era matured, Asheville quickly boomed. Col. Frank Coxe, the man who had built the original Battery Park Hotel, was a Pennsylvania railroad tycoon, civil engineer, and bank president, who had been largely responsible for bringing the railroad to Asheville. He next turned his attention towards developing a row of commercial buildings on what is now College Street, at the foot of Battery Park Hill. He built a retaining wall in the process, which is how Wall Street got its name. In 1898, Thomas Raoul, a tuberculosis victim, built a classic English inn with the Manor and Cottages at 265 Charlotte Street. Together with his railroad developer father William Greene Raoul, he developed Albemarle Park, likely the first curvilinear neighborhood street pattern in Asheville. The architects who came to Asheville at the beckoning of the elite were also important. Rafael Guastavino, who designed the St. Lawrence Basilica, was renowned for the tile work he had done in the New York subway system, where he had also worked on the Church of St. John the Divine. Richard Sharp Smith, an English architect who came to Asheville under the direction of Richard Morris Hunt for work on the Biltmore Estate, stayed after the commission was complete and worked on commercial and residential projects, including the development of much of Biltmore Village.

George Willis Pack was originally from New York, but was successful in the lumber industry in Michigan. He and his wife came to Asheville in 1884 for health reasons. And while many came to Asheville seeking wealth, Pack was essentially retired. He therefore found time and had the resources to contribute much to what Asheville soon became. He donated land for the 1903 courthouse and gave land and a building to the Asheville Library Association that later became the city-owned Pack Memorial Library. He also donated land for Aston Park and Montford Park. Another traveler came to Asheville in 1897 and left a profound mark on the city. E.W. Grove was a wealthy pharmaceutical manufacturer from St. Louis who came to Asheville for his health. He was the owner of the Paris Medicine Company, maker of Bromo-Quinine. He suffered from bronchial difficulties but was reported also to have come to start a chemical company. He began development of another Asheville neighborhood, Grove Park, around 1905. Grove wanted the neighborhood to be both modern and artistic. In 1913, he built the Grove Park Inn, along with his son-in-law, Fred Seely. It quickly rivaled the Battery Park Hotel, which was torn down and replaced with the new Battery Park Hotel in 1920–1922.

While the slow economy of the 1890s proved difficult, Asheville continued to grow. It began to diversify from tourism into other industries. There were long-lasting benefits to Asheville with the sudden development that occurred both before and after the turn of the century. The importation of skilled craftspeople, many from overseas, added new skills to the local labor market. Stonecutters, woodworkers, experts in tile, and steel workers added new talents that were reflected in both commercial and residential buildings throughout Asheville. This new energy also led to the industrialization of many craft industries, from weaving to cabinetmaking, through such outlets as Biltmore Industries and Three Mountaineers. According to an 1899 city brochure, Asheville had "one large tobacco factory, two ice factories, three planing mills, twenty-six carriage and wagon makers, the largest cotton factory in the south, two laundries, the largest tannery in western North Carolina, two daily and four weekly newspapers, two literary clubs, four tobacco warehouses, and several golf clubs."

The rapid growth in population—from "consumptives" seeking the clean mountain as well as speculators seeking fortune—transformed Asheville from a quaint mountain village in the 1870s to a city in less than 25 years. The first public hospital opened in 1883, the first telephone lines in 1885, and a public school system began in the 1880s. The city began its streetcar system in 1889. Suburban sprawl began as early as the 1890s, spidering out from the center of the city along Main and Patton Avenue. Asheville in 1920 had a population of 28,000, but the number of annual visitors was approaching 250,000. Paul Roebling, the grandson of the builder of the Brooklyn Bridge in New York, built the Haywood Building in 1917. This spurred more development, including Solomon Lipinsky's Bon Marche in 1923, the Loughran Building in 1923, and the George Vanderbilt Hotel in 1924. By the 1920s, Asheville was seized with a fever for buying and selling land. Fifteen years after the fact, Thomas Wolfe even wrote about such exuberance in You Can't Go Home Again:

> The real estate men were everywhere. Their motors and buses roared through the streets of the town and out into the country, carrying crowds of prospective clients. . . Everyone bought real estate; and everyone was "a real estate man" either in name or practice. The barbers, the lawyers, the grocers, the butchers, the builders, the clothiers—all were engaged in this single interest and obsession.

At the height of this exuberance, men like Grove were bashing about, tearing down Battery Park Hill and remaking Asheville in their vision. In 1924, real estate broker L.B. Jackson built the Jackson Building, a beautiful skyscraper 13 stories tall on a parcel 27 feet by 60 feet in the Gothic style. But as much private development as there was, Asheville floated huge bonds to bring the city up to par. They outlined 94 objectives in a "Program of Progress" capped with the construction of the new city hall in 1928 and the new county courthouse in 1929. The completion of Beaucatcher Tunnel also occurred in the 1920s.

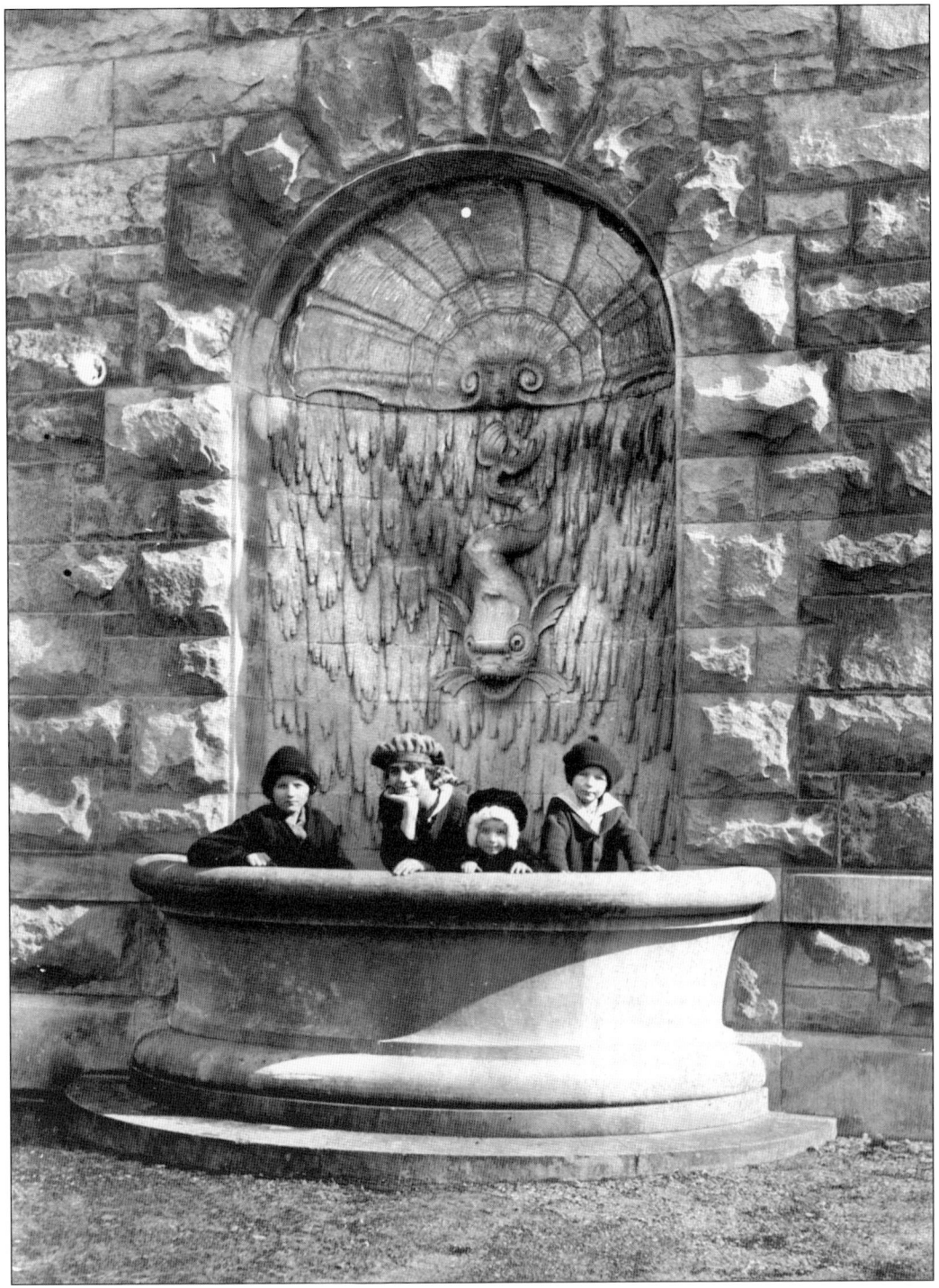

A WHIMSICAL PORTRAIT OF CHILDREN IN FOUNTAIN AT BILTMORE ESTATE. Jeanne Lance identified the children, from left to right, as Leila Pressley, Blanche Creasman, Doris Creasman, and Ruby Creasman. The Creasman family operated a photo studio that became the Plateau Studios of George Masa, who lived with the Creasmans.

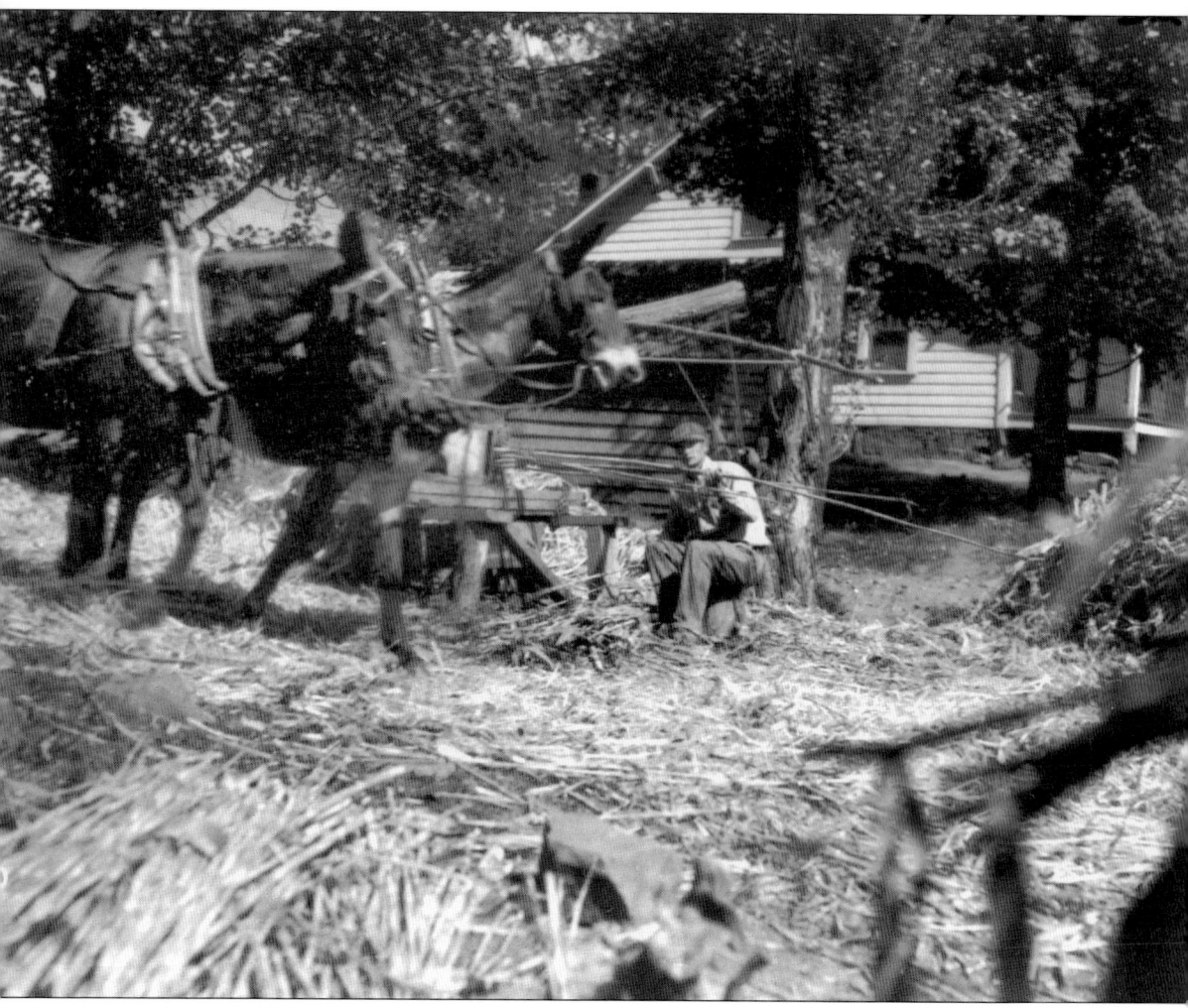

A Two-mule–powered Cane Mill for Making Molasses. This photo was taken by Jackson C. Felmet and was commissioned by Three Mountaineers in the early 1930s. It depicts a wood-frame house in the right background. Note the copyright symbol in the lower left.

TIME PASSES ON. This photo shows a man in an ox-drawn wagon in front of the Baptist parsonage at 56 E College Street and the First Baptist Church at the corner of Spruce and College Streets. The parsonage was formerly the J. Rush Oates House. Oates, who came to Asheville c. 1890, owned the Legal Building and the Oates Building; he moved to Gertrude Place in Grove Park in 1915. This is actually the third Baptist sanctuary, built in the 1890s and demolished c. 1927.

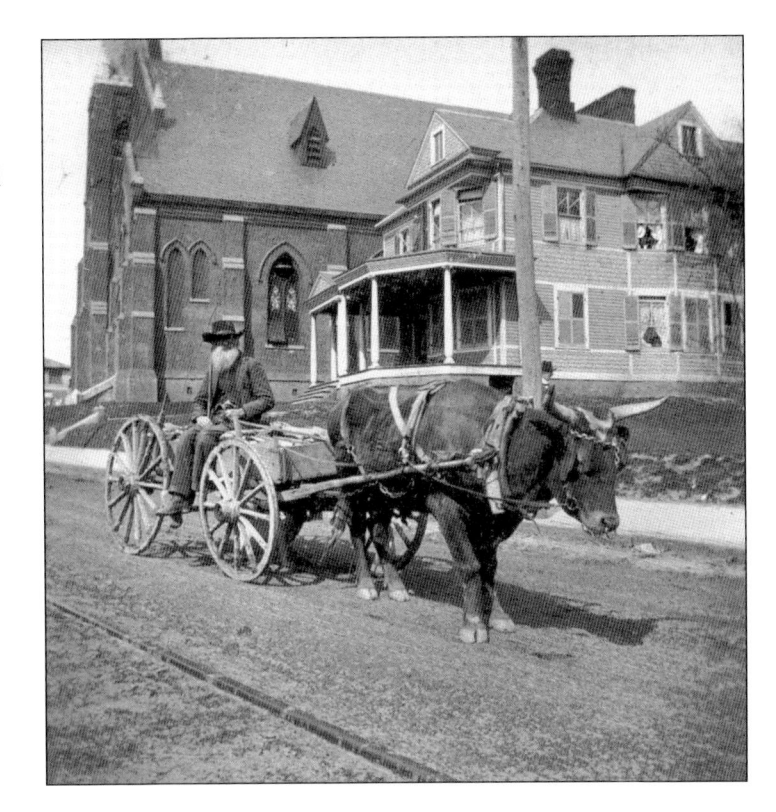

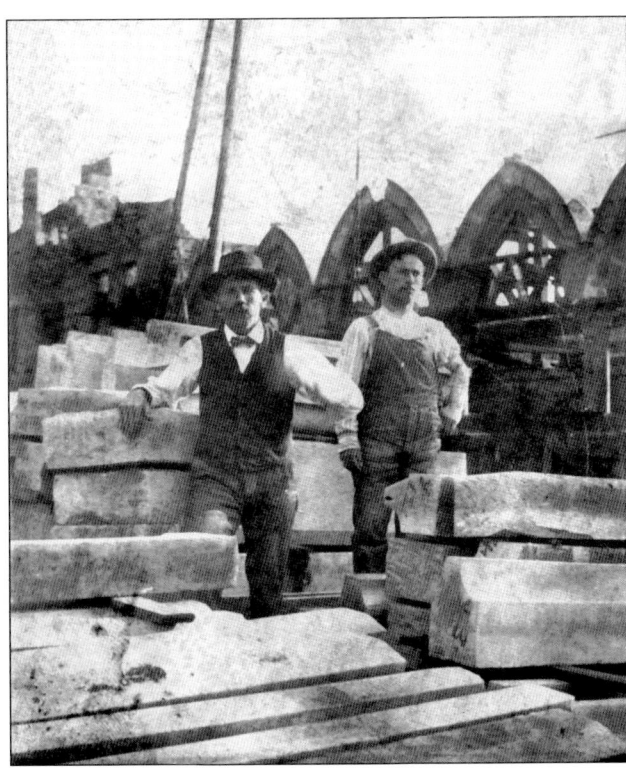

THE CRAFTSMEN. Stone mason Samuel Isaac Bean and John Corbin stand on piles of construction materials during the building of Central Methodist Church, c. 1903.

41

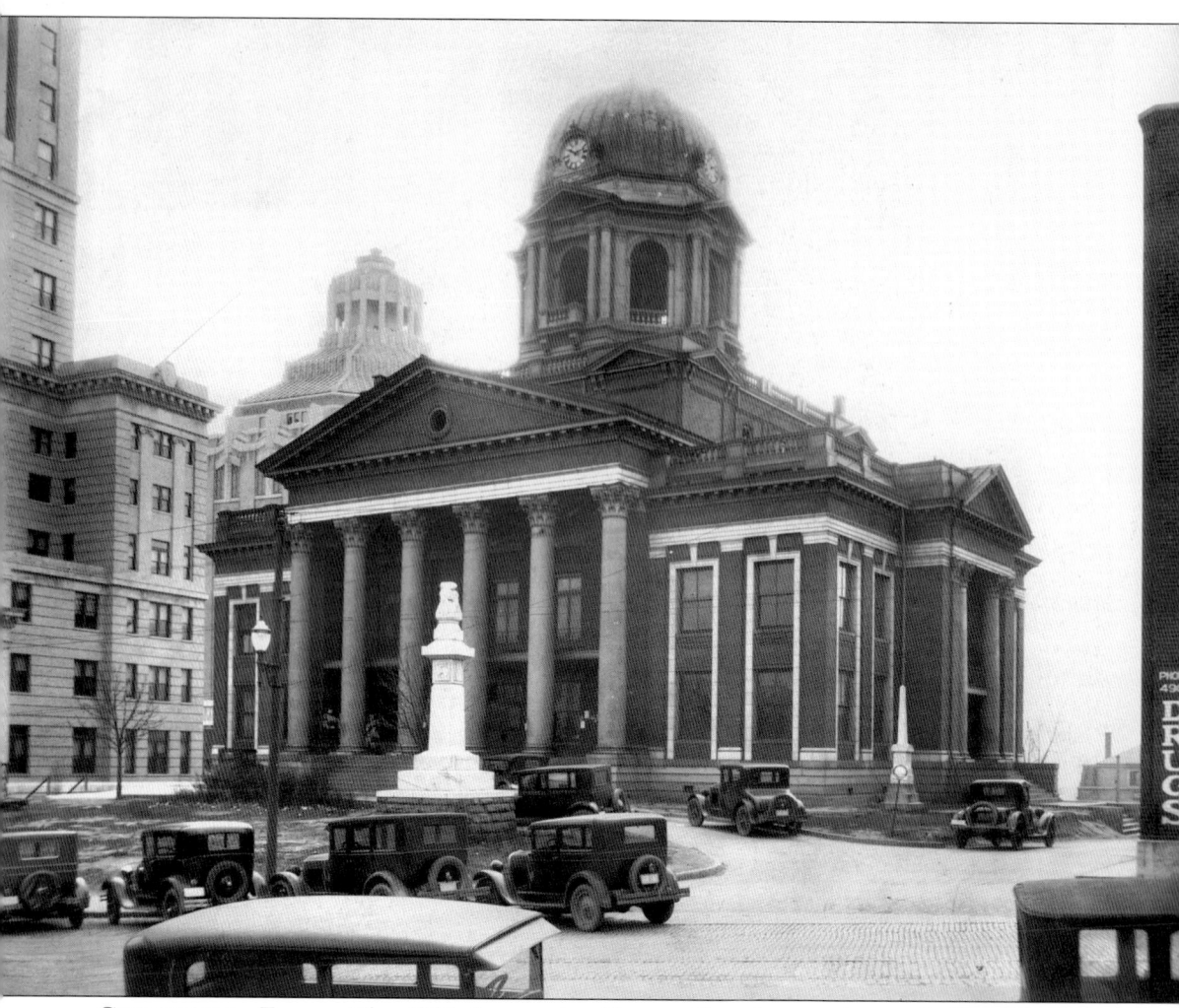

Courthouse Fever. The 1903 Buncombe County Courthouse, facing College Street, is shown here. The land for this courthouse was given to the county by George Willis Pack. This was Buncombe County's seventh courthouse; this photo was probably taken around 1927–1929, just before it was torn down. Asheville's many courthouses indicate its rapid growth. The current courthouse, which was built in 1927, is visible on the left.

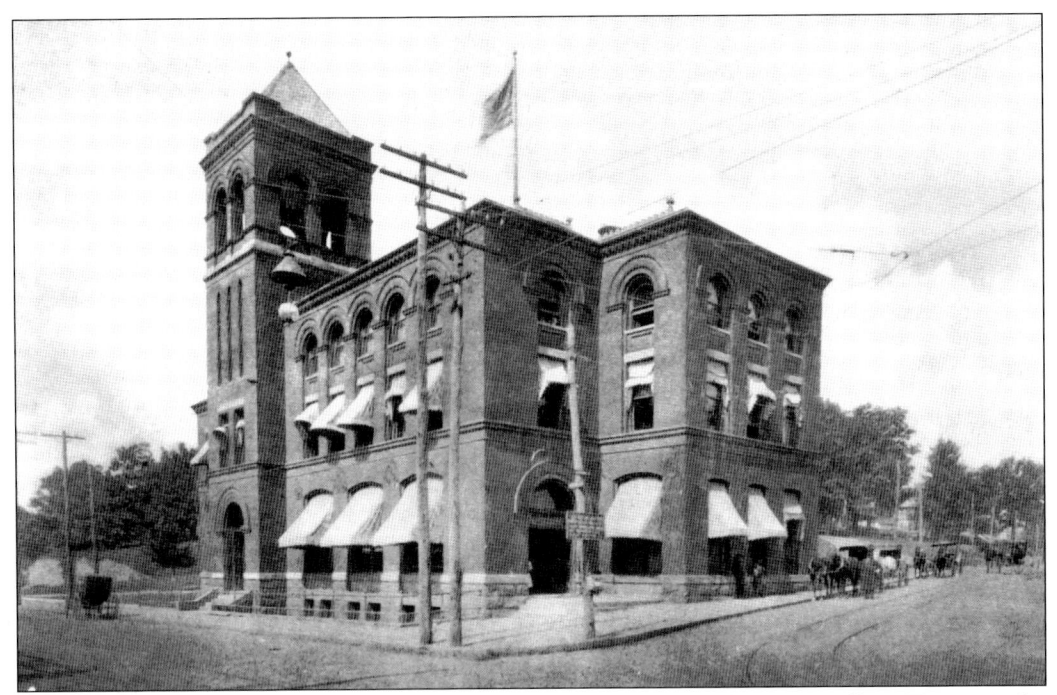

ASHEVILLE CITY HALL (1892-1926). The city hall was designed by James Albert Tennent; the Pack Square fountain is visible in front. W.O. Wolfe's monument shop at #22 Pack Square is to the right, and Stradley & Luther, grocers, and Gross Brothers Restaurant are to the right. The estimated date of the photo is 1909.

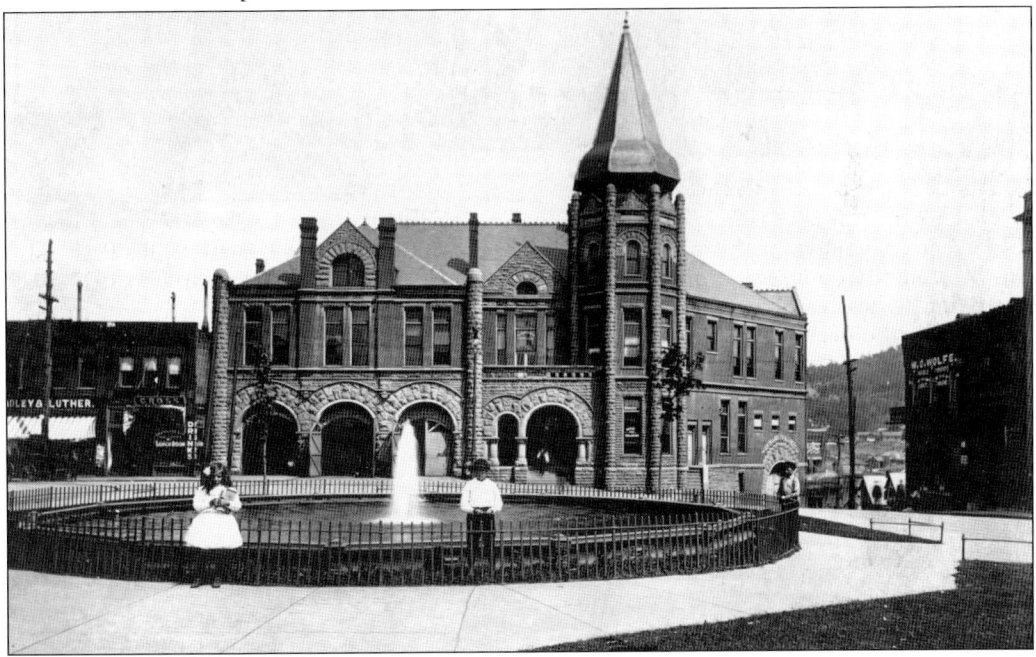

THE OLD POST OFFICE. The U.S. Post Office, built in 1892 on Patton Avenue between Haywood and College Streets, was razed in 1932; the new building on Otis Street opened in 1930.

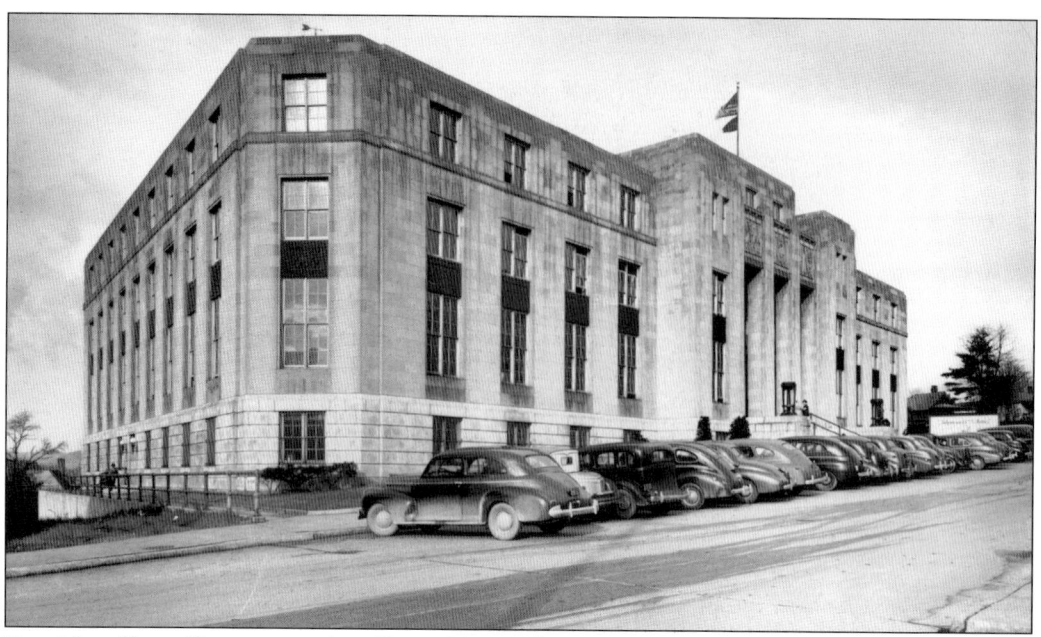

THE NEW POST OFFICE, AN ART DECO FEAT. The new post office, located at 100 Otis Street, was built in 1930. The $700,000 structure was begun in 1929 and dedicated in 1930, built on land donated by E.W. Grove and designed by the Supervising Architect's Office (Federal) under James A. Wetmore. The photograph was taken c. 1940s–1950s.

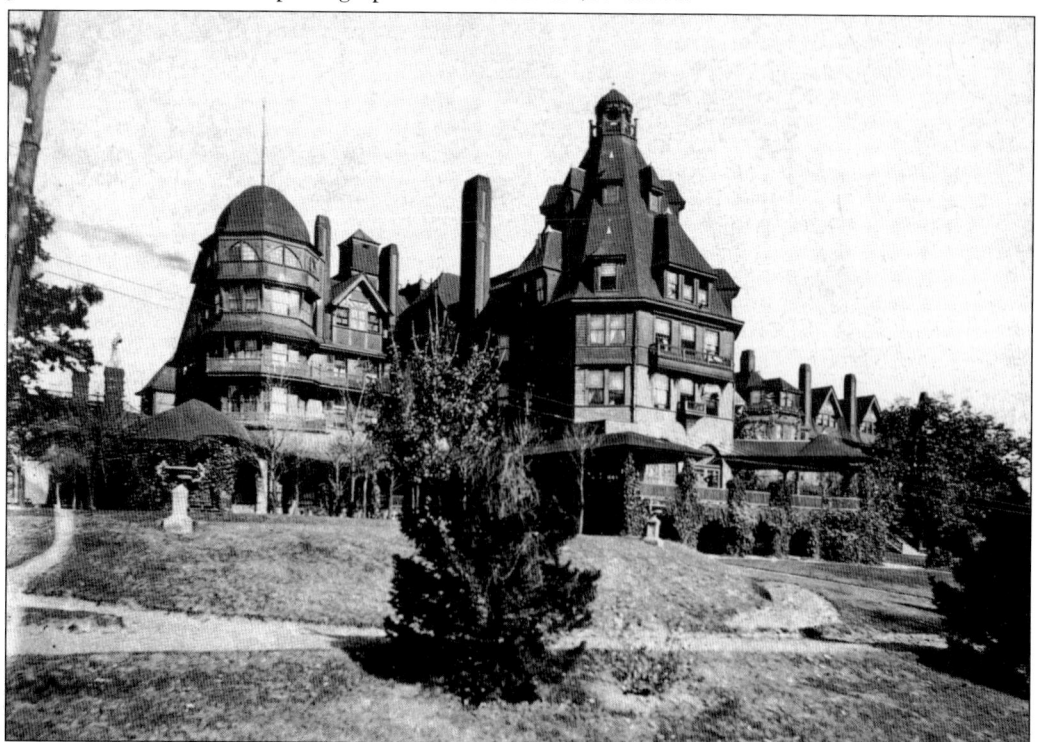

OUT WITH THE OLD. Pictured is the Battery Park Hotel, built in 1886. It is from this hotel that George Vanderbilt is said to have decided to build his grand estate in Asheville.

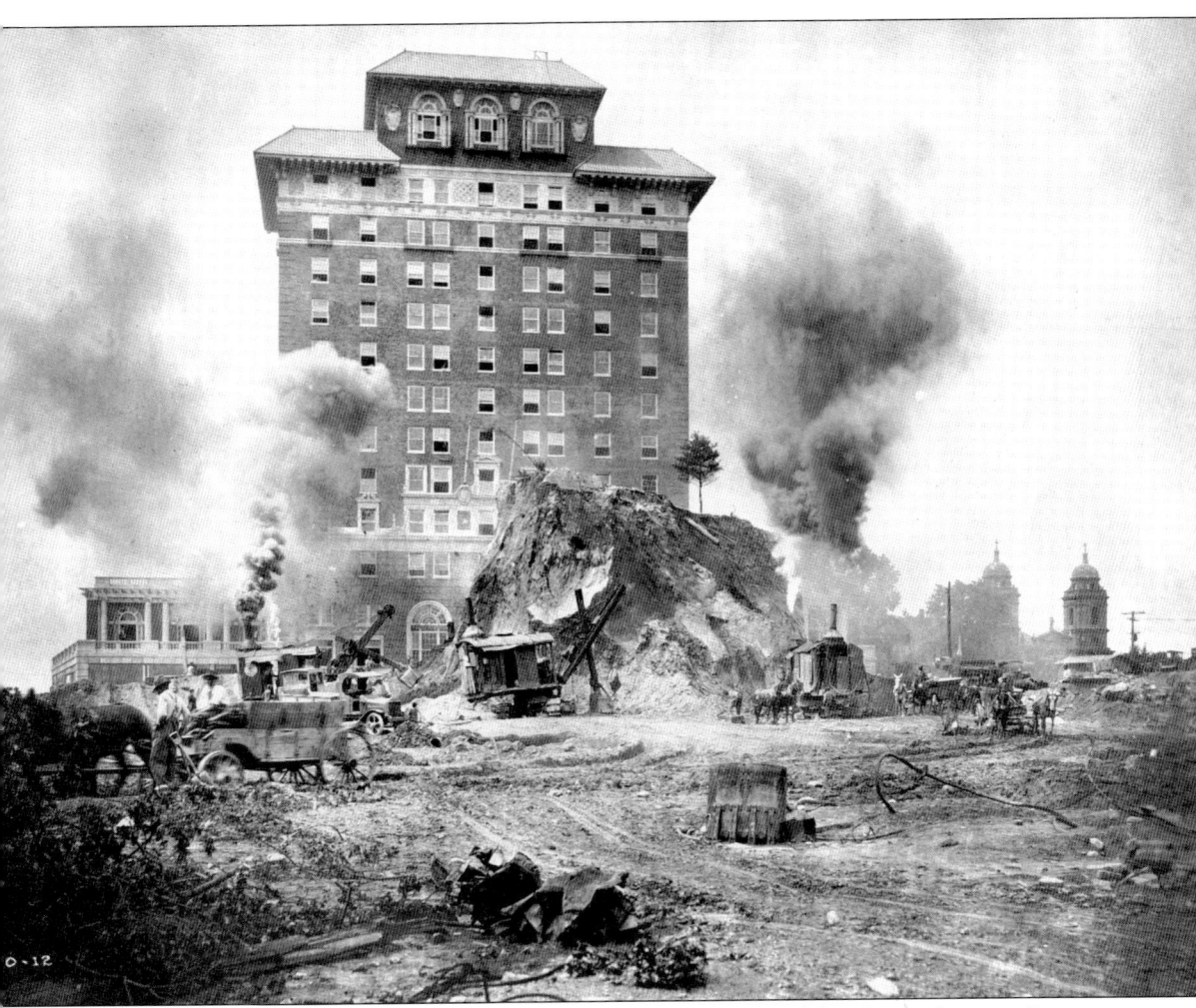

IN WITH THE NEW. In 1924 steam shovels removed the last bit of dirt from what was Battery Park Hill, also known as Battery Porter, to prepare the building site for the Grove Arcade. Battery Park Hotel is seen in the background. Earth from this site was used to fill a ravine to create Coxe Avenue.

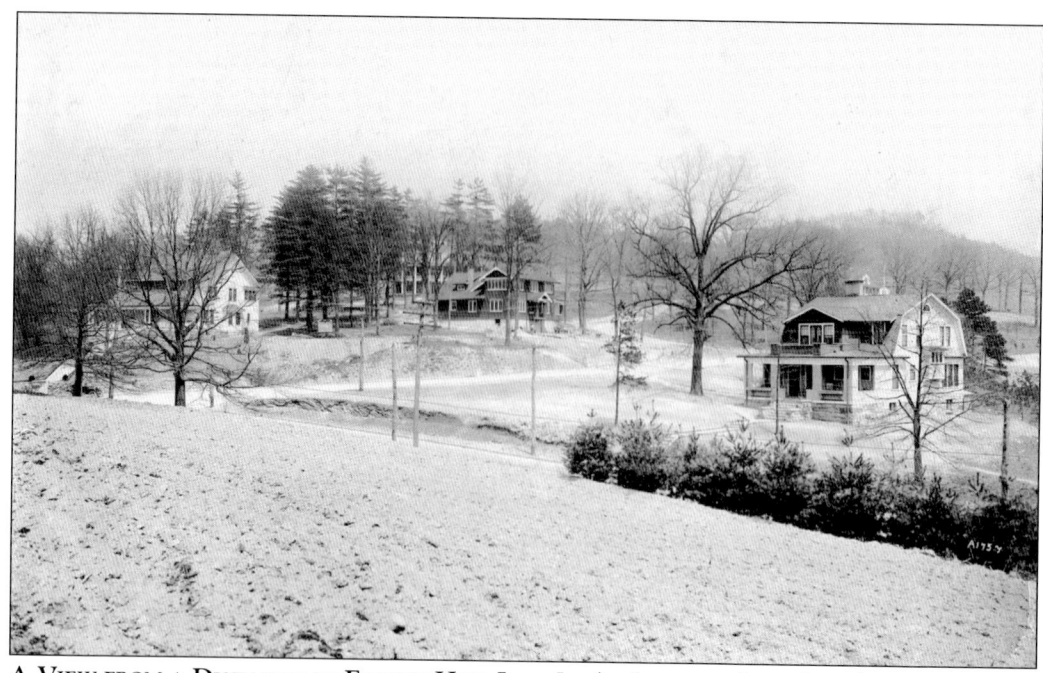

A VIEW FROM A DISTANCE OF FOREST HILL INN. In the foreground are three houses along the intersection of Biltmore Avenue and Forest Hill Drive. The columns and porches of Forest Hill Inn are visible. The photo was taken from the west side of Biltmore Avenue c. 1915–1925.

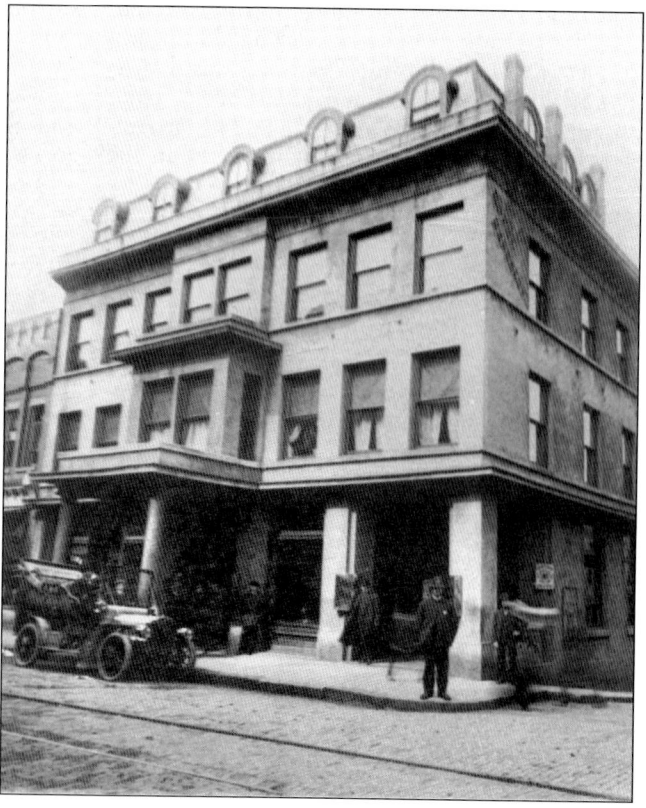

BEFORE THE KRESS BUILDING. Berkeley Hotel c. 1909, at 21–23 Patton Avenue and the northwest corner of Lexington Avenue, occupied the current site of the Kress Building. The Berkeley merged with the Swannanoa Hotel at Biltmore Avenue in 1911. Solomon Lipinsky, who had a clothing store in the Swannanoa Hotel, moved his store into the Berkley Building, where he remained until 1923 when he moved to his own building at 33 Haywood Street. The Kress Building was constructed on this site in 1926.

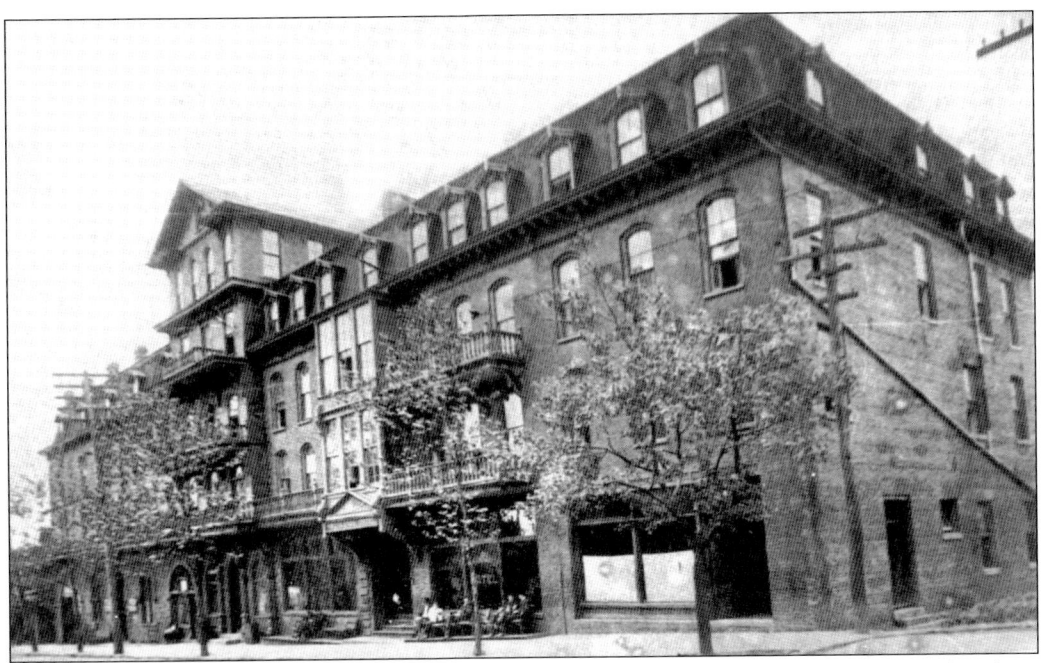

THE SWANNANOA HOTEL IN 1888. The Swannanoa was established in 1880 by brothers Charles and Reuben Rawls at the corner of South Main Street/Biltmore Avenue and Willow Street, now Aston Avenue. The hotel had Asheville's first bathroom, at the request of frequent guest George Pack. Solomon Lipinsky's clothing store, the Bon Marche, was on street level. The hotel was sold in 1905 to Frank Loughran, who added an annex and a ballroom that measured 3,400 square feet without columns. The hotel was damaged by fire in 1907 and again in 1942. In 1911 the Swannanoa merged with the Berkeley Hotel and was renamed the Swannanoa-Berkeley Hotel; in 1936 it was renamed the Milner Hotel, and in 1948 it became the Earle Hotel; it later became the Home Hotel. It was razed in 1968, and its site became a municipal parking lot.

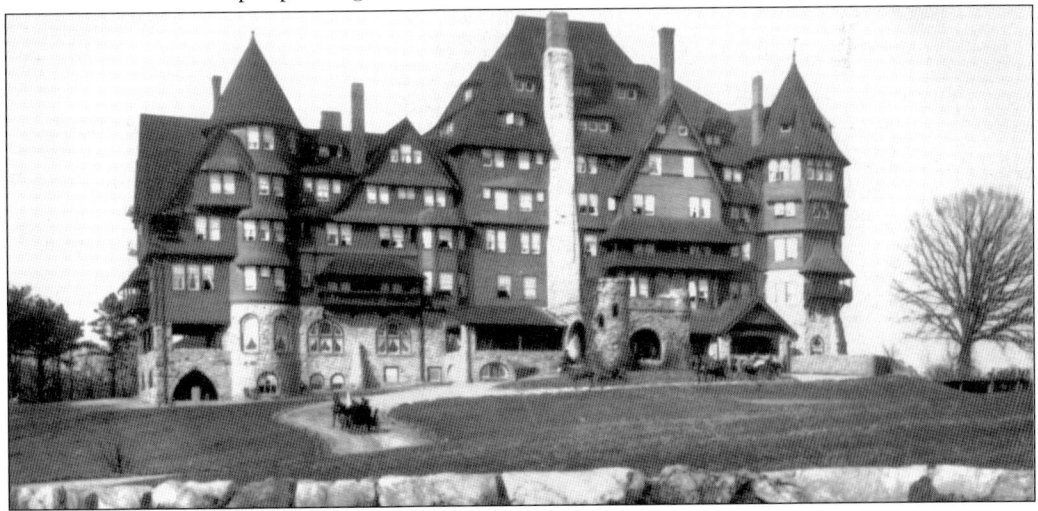

THE KENILWORTH INN. The Kenilworth was built c. 1890–1892 on 160 acres by Sen. Joseph M. Gassam & Co. of Philadelphia at a cost of $300,000. It burned in 1909 and was rebuilt c. 1913–1918.

47

NATIONAL BANK OF ASHEVILLE.

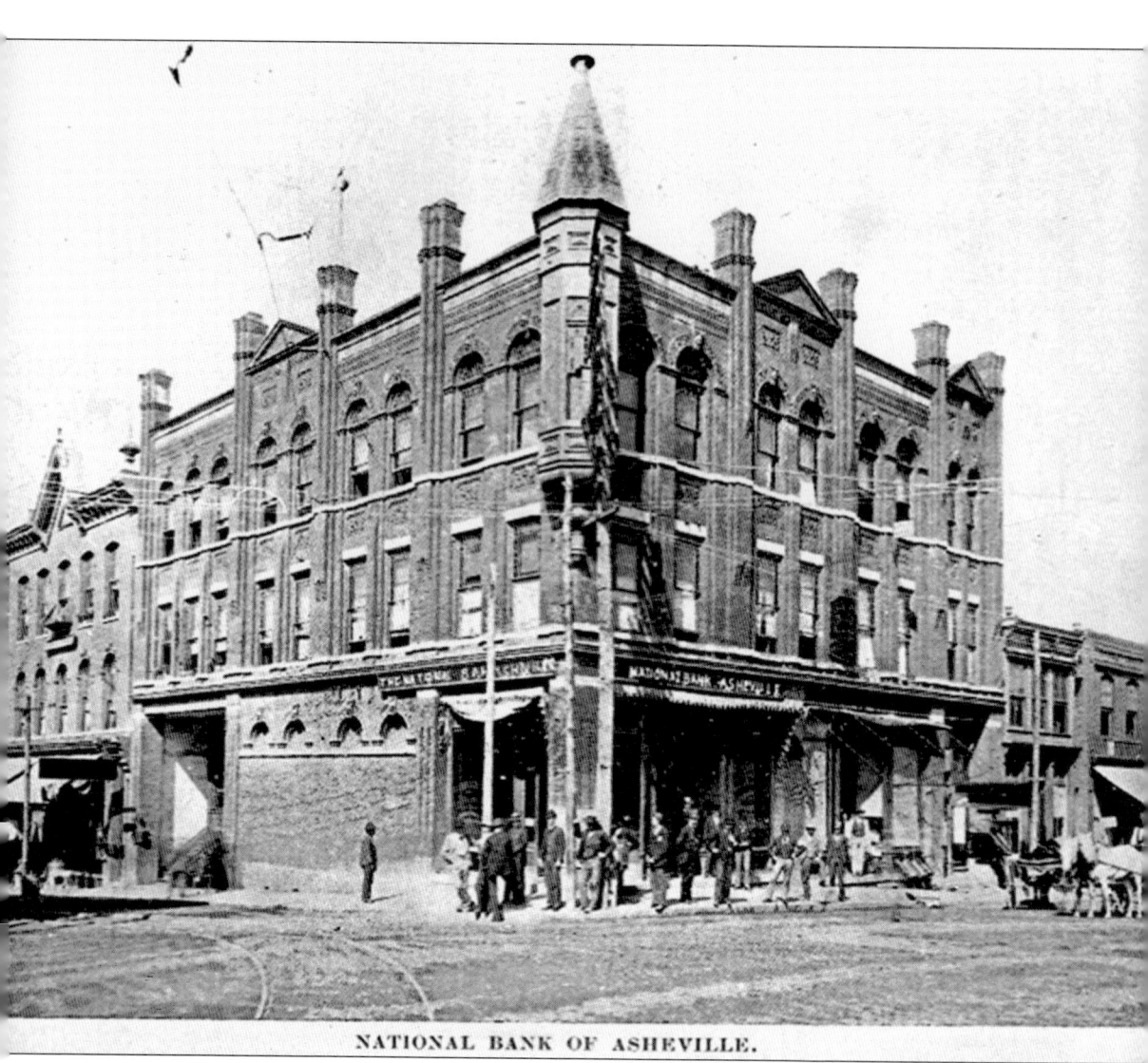

THE NATIONAL BANK OF ASHEVILLE, C. 1892. This building, on the corner of Pack Square NW and Patton Avenue, was also known as the Barnard Building and the Revell Building.

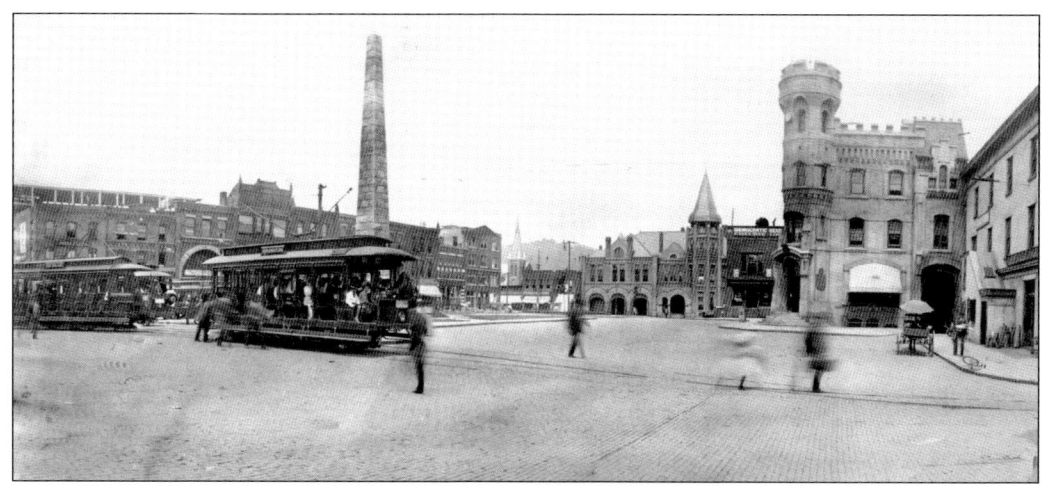

A Fascinating View of Pack Square from the Southwest Corner, 1904–1905.
Asheville Hardware, with John F. McFarland's photography studio by the stairs, and the Palmetto Building with Henry Batterham Real Estate, are on the right. In the background is the Carter Building with the Democratic headquarters, city hall, and Pack Square NE/N Spruce Street, including Owenbey (R. Lee) & Sons, grocers, and Stradly & Luther, grocers. Two streetcars are at left in front of Pack Square N and Vance Monument.

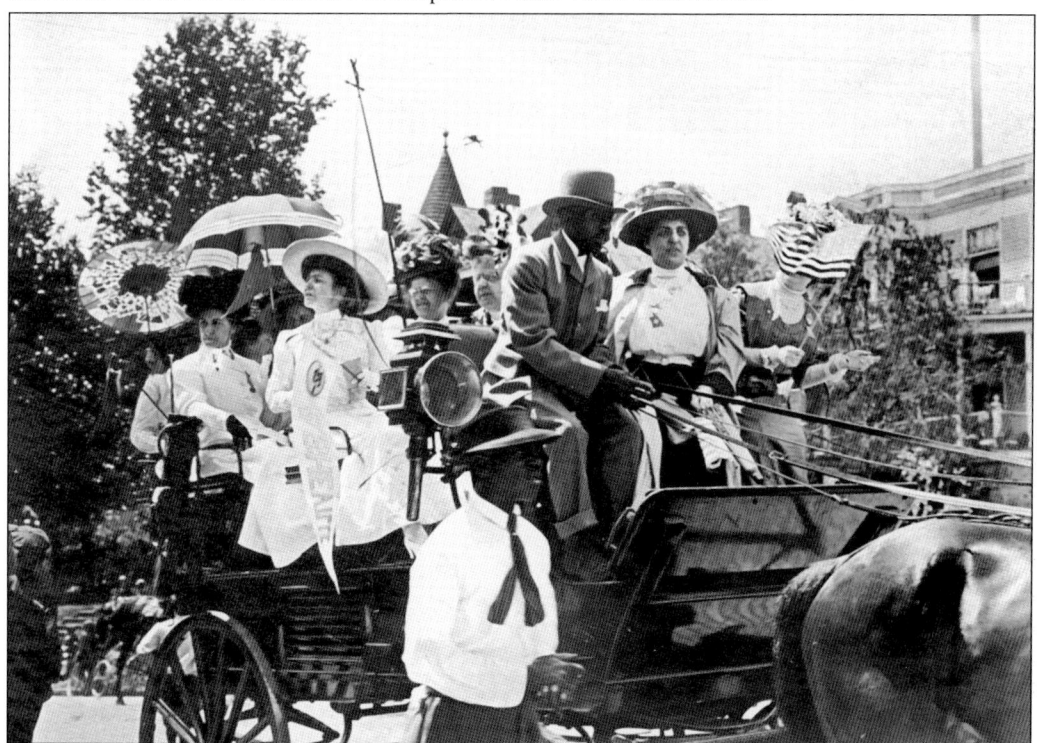

Ladies of Temperance. A carriage is driven by an African-American driver, possibly for a parade or political rally in support of prohibition. The women are carrying flags, pennants, and parasols. The banner middle front reads in reverse "Asheville." Another African-American man walks next to the carriage. There are electrical lines at top of photo, giving it a date after 1888.

49

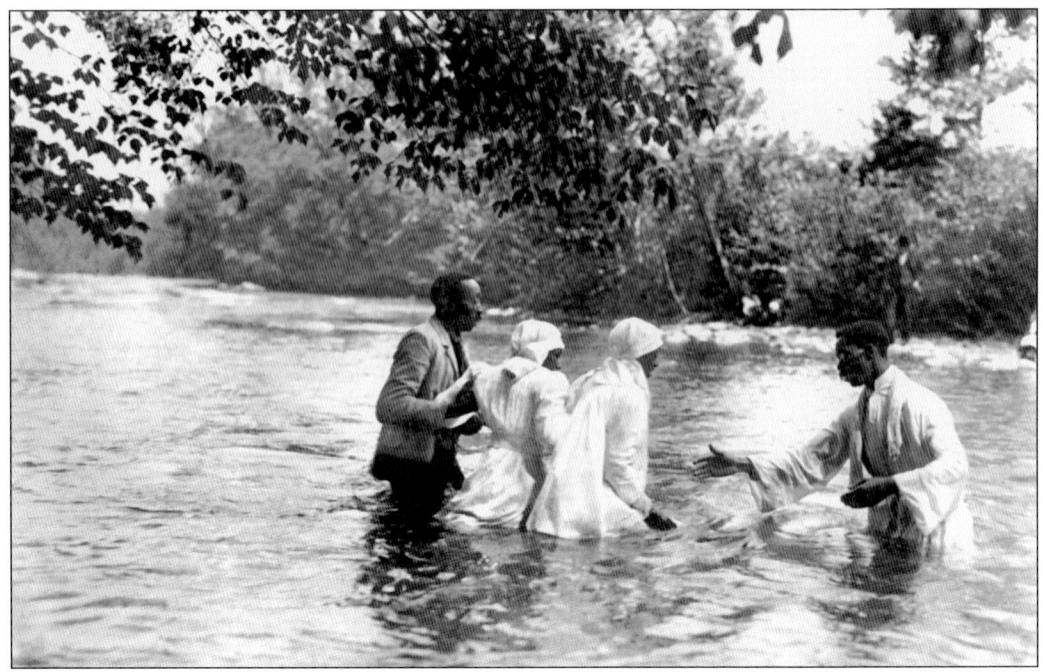

BAPTISMAL RIVER. Two men and two women take part in a baptism in the Swannanoa River c. 1900. One man at right, wearing a white robe, is reaching for one woman's hand. The women and the other man, at left, are holding hands. (North Carolina Collection, from the Vella Hendrix [Landis] family album, loaned by the Swannanoa Valley Historical Museum.)

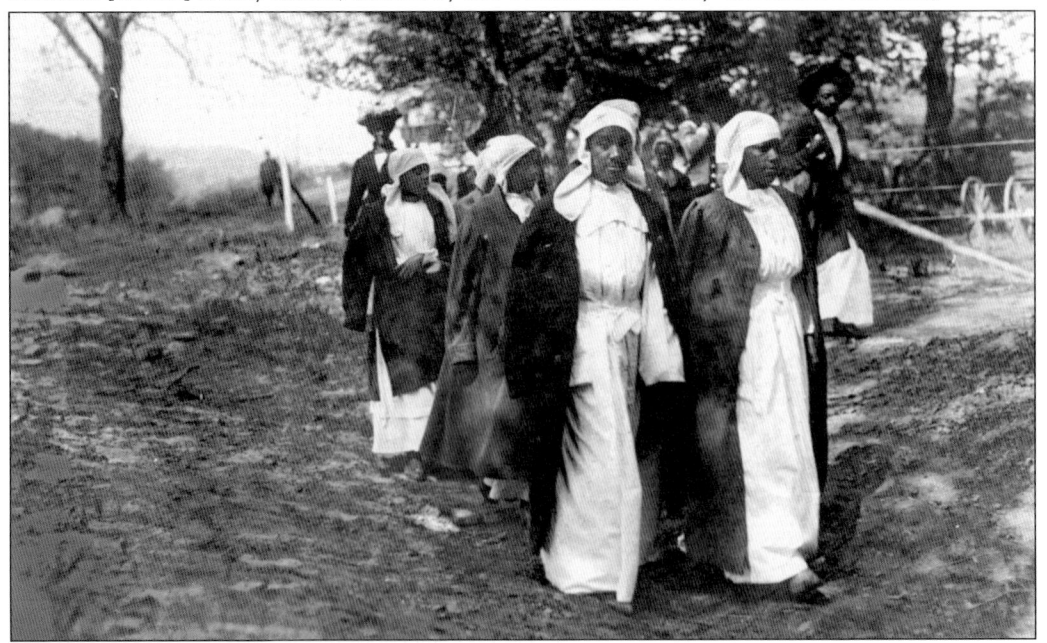

HEALING WATERS. The waters of the Swannanoa and French Broad Rivers have been a center of the community since the ancient times of Native Americans. Here, a procession of five African-American women walks to a baptism. They are wearing long robes with their coats over them. In the background are trees, a fence, and a wagon.

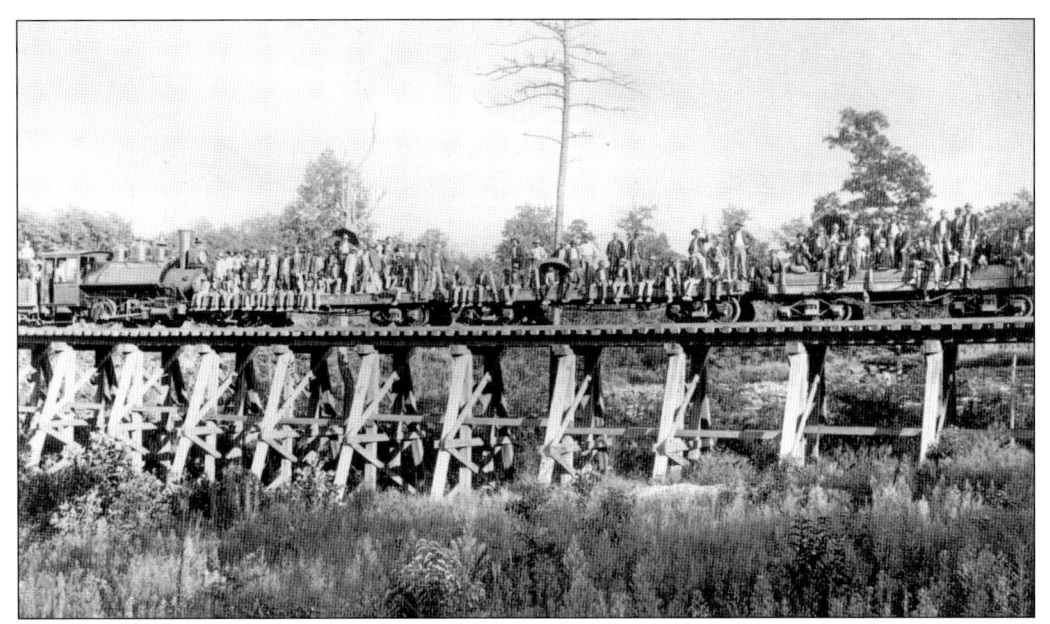

THEY BUILT THIS CITY. A train is on a trestle of the railroad line built to the Biltmore Estate, c. 1890–1895. Some workers are sitting and standing on the train cars.

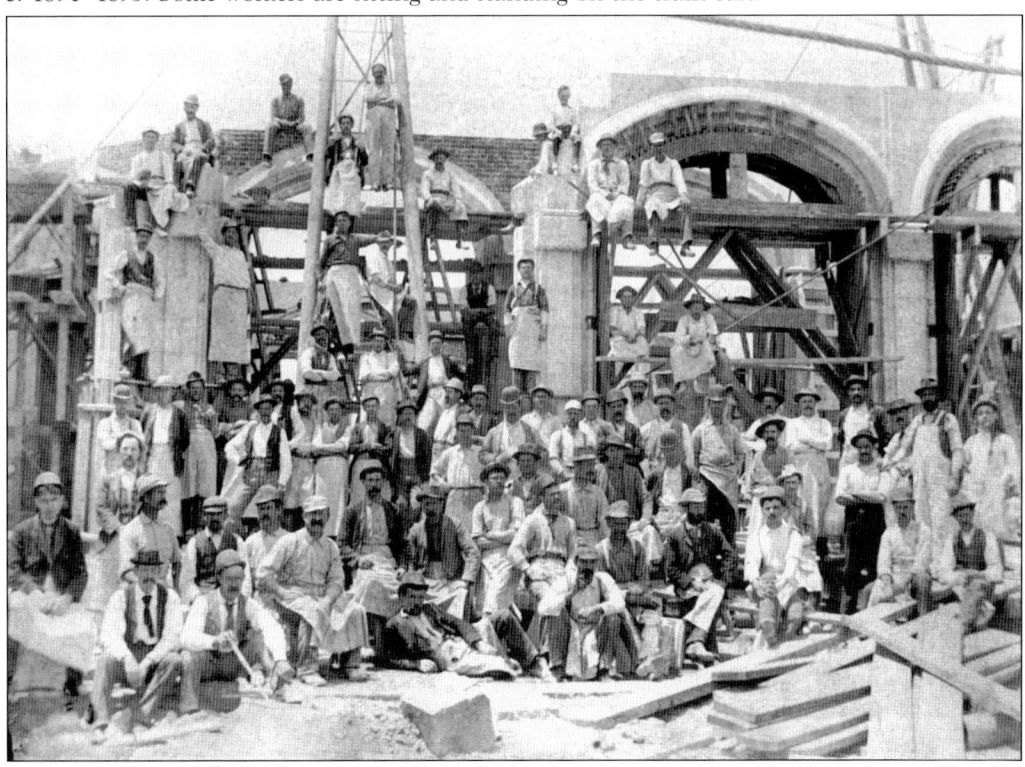

THE STONECUTTERS. These stonecutters who worked on the Biltmore House stand in front of one partially completed section of the house, including columns and arches. Wooden ladders, scaffolds, and framework are visible. The photo indicates that the group was employed by Sinclair of New York.

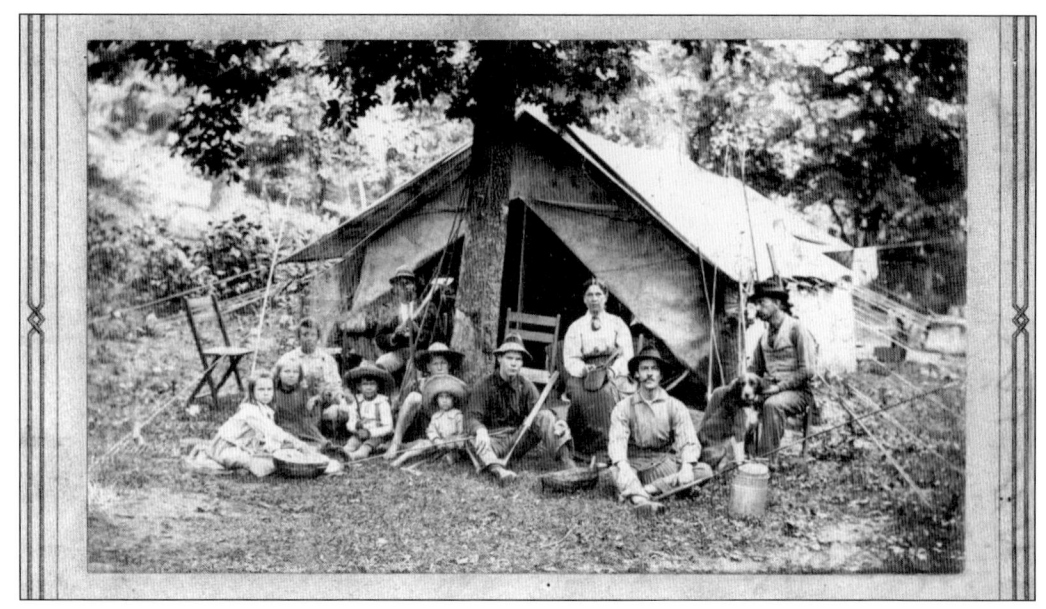

THE DOE FAMILY CAMPING PARTY SEATED IN FRONT OF THEIR TENT, 1895. The location noted on reverse—"Waterworks, 5 miles from Asheville"—may refer to either Waterfall Creek in northeast Buncombe County or to Watershed Ridge in Buncombe County near North Knob and Wildcat Mountain. The family members include, from left to right, Mr. and Mrs. Doe and Thomas, Jennie, Dora, Willie, and Wildon Doe. Also identified are Pearl the servant girl; John the servant man; George Williamson of Newville, Pennsylvania; Galloway Williamson; and the old dog Dandy.

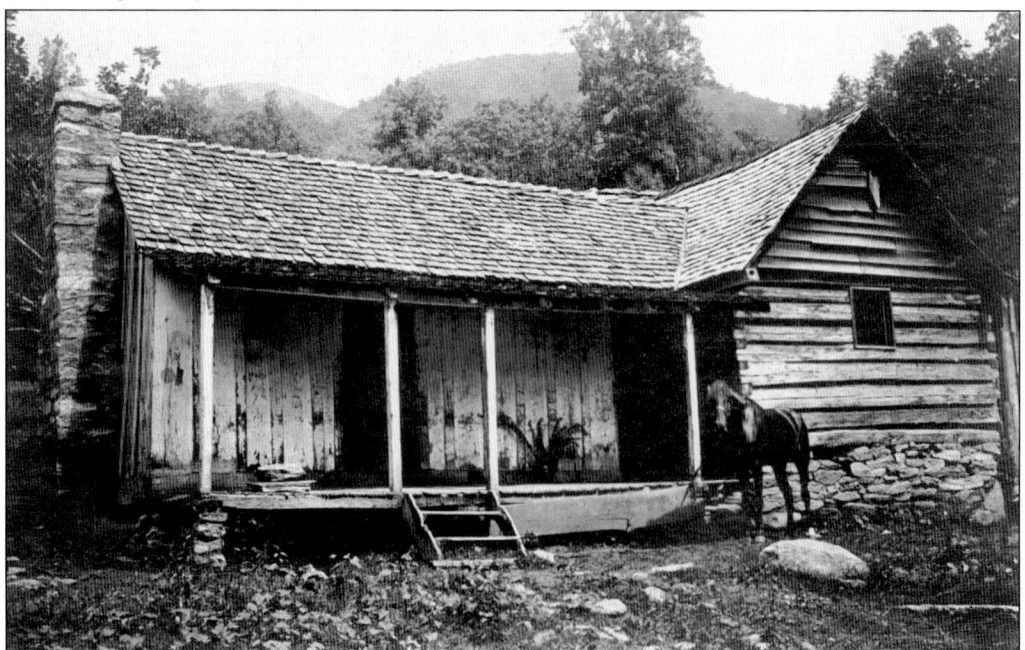

PINK BEDS. Modern forestry was an integral part of Asheville's development. This is Dr. Clifton D. Howe's cabin in the Pink Beds of Pisgah Forest/Biltmore Forest School, c. 1905–1906. Dr. Howe was assistant forester of Biltmore from 1904 to 1919.

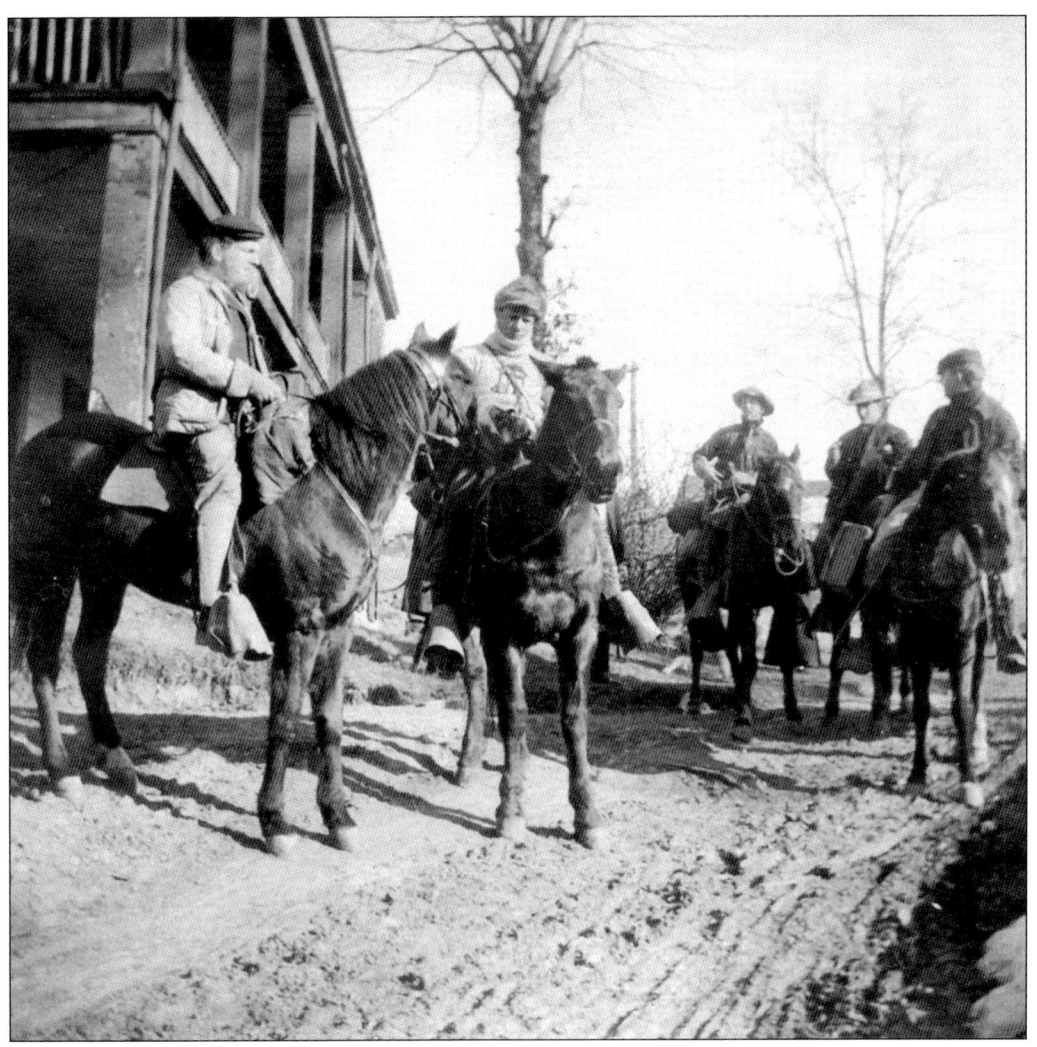

THE BILTMORE FOREST SCHOOL. The people in the picture are, from left to right, Dr. Howe on horseback, Perry Emigh?, Guy K. Gooding, Jack D. Mylrea, and Perry M. Wilson at the Forest Hill Inn in Asheville *c.* 1905–1906. Dr. Howe's horse may have been named Silverthorn.

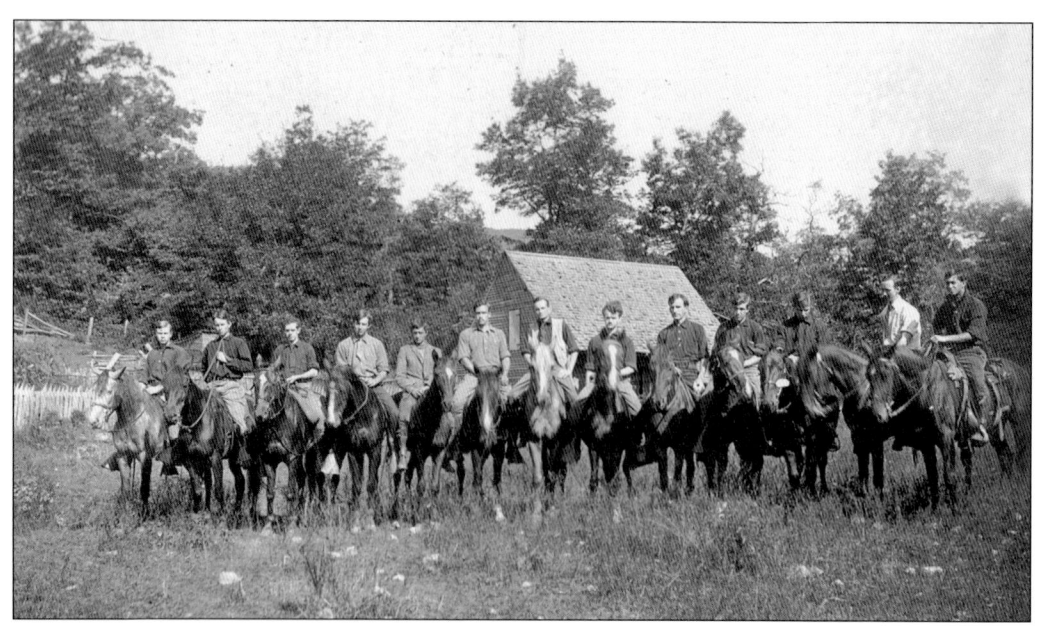

DISTINGUISHED STUDENTS OF FORESTRY. These Biltmore Forest School students, from left to right, are unidentified; Russell G. Pond, class of 1905, from New England; Roger B. Sherman from Cincinnati; Perry M. Wilson, from Wausau, Wisconsin; Ralph G. Burton, who died around 1910 of typhoid; Howard H. Morse, class of 1906; Mr. Clancey, a "Princeton man;" Mr. Bard, from Pennsylvania; Thomas J. McDonald, class of 1905; Henry Gannett, a forester from Cincinnati; Jack D. Mylrea, from Wausau, Wisconsin; unidentified; and Guy K. Gooding, class of 1906, from Wausau, Wisconsin. The picture was taken at Gillespie's in the Pink Beds on the Biltmore Estate in the fall of 1905.

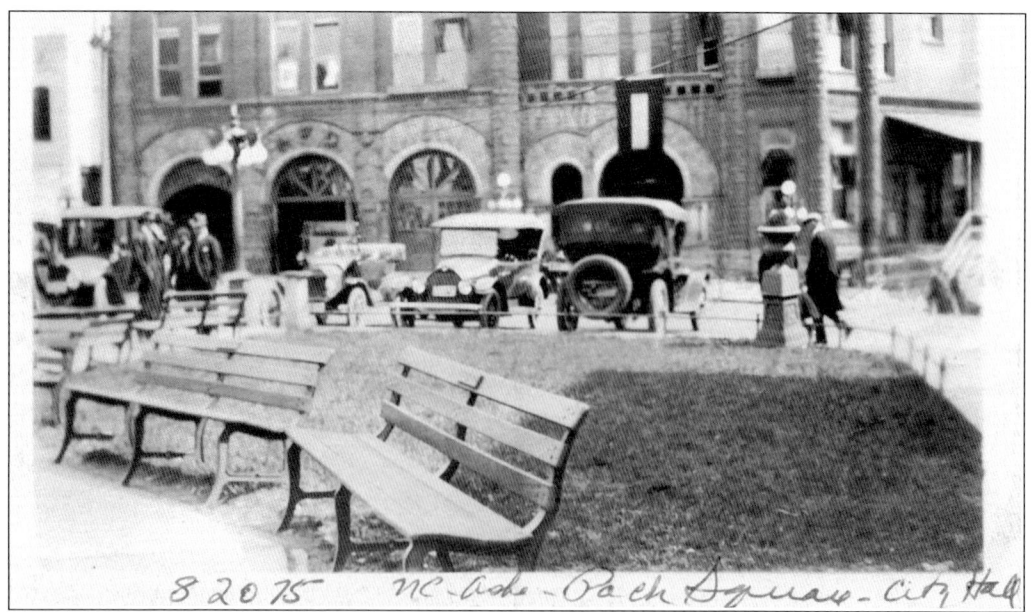

A VIEW OF CITY HALL. This view of Pack Square is from the park around Vance Monument, c. 1918. Empty park benches are visible in the foreground, and a few cars are parked in front of city hall. The flag over the door to city hall possibly honors World War I.

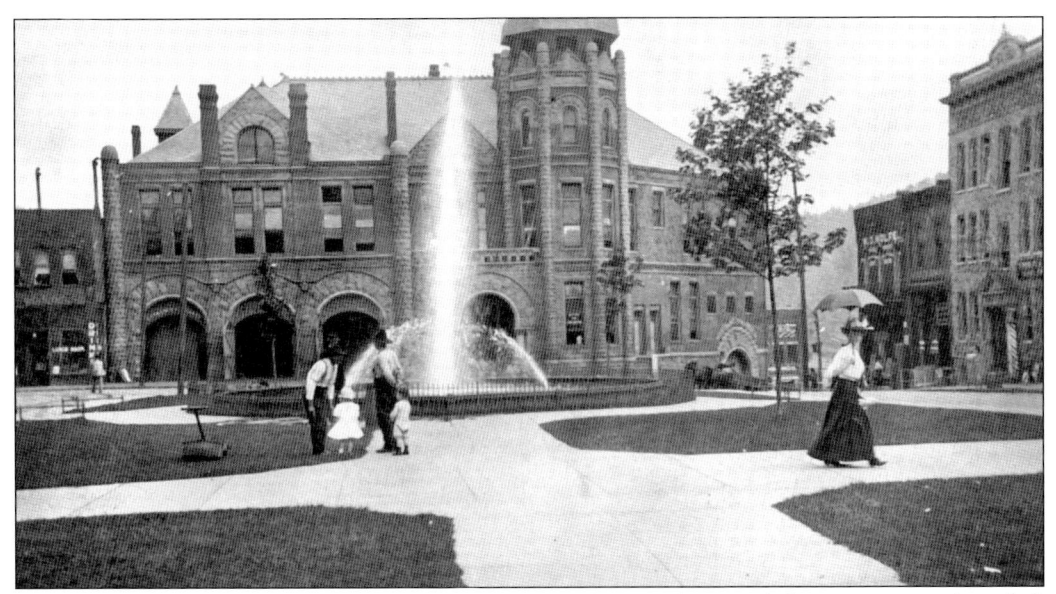

PACK SQUARE LOOKING EAST AND SOUTH, 1909. Pictured around the square are, from left to right, the Gallagher Building with the sign for David Gross's Restaurant visible, the 1892 Asheville City Hall with signs at both ends of the City Market and for the tax collector's office visible, W.H. Westall & Co. building supply store, the Wolfe Building with W.O. Wolfe's monument shop, McLean's and Guischand's shops, and the Reed Building with Lee Nichols' barber pole outside. The park fountain is in the center.

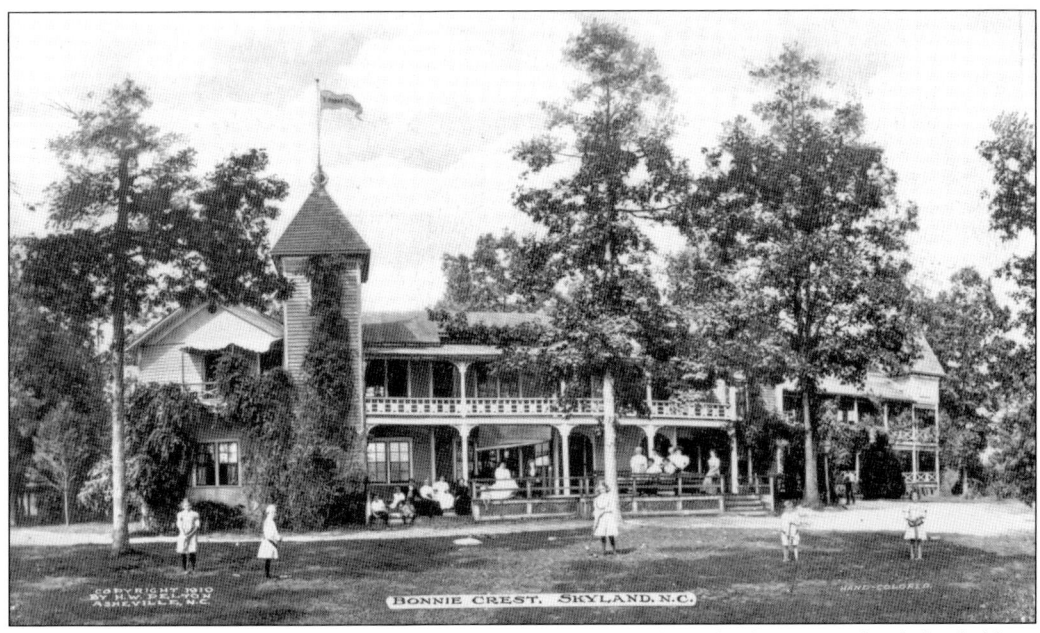

THE BONNIE CREST INN. In this c. 1910 picture ladies stand on the lower porch while children play croquet on the front lawn.

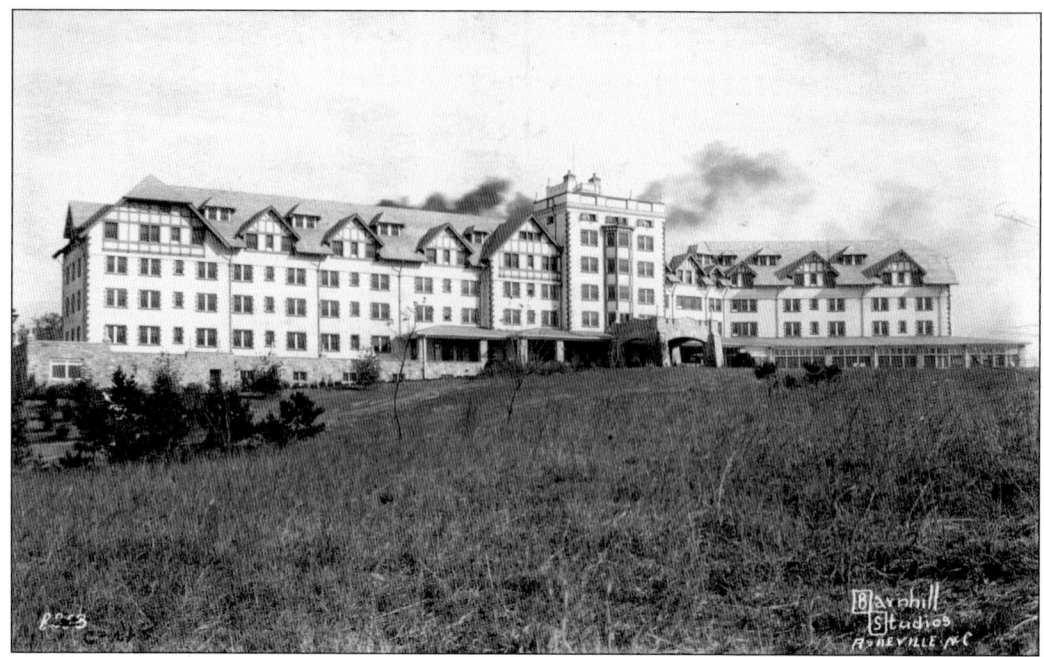

The New Kenilworth Inn, c. 1920–1922. The hotel was built to replace the original 1891 building, which was destroyed by fire in 1909. It was a psychiatric hospital known as Appalachian Hall from 1931 until recently, when it was converted into apartment condominiums and returned to its original name.

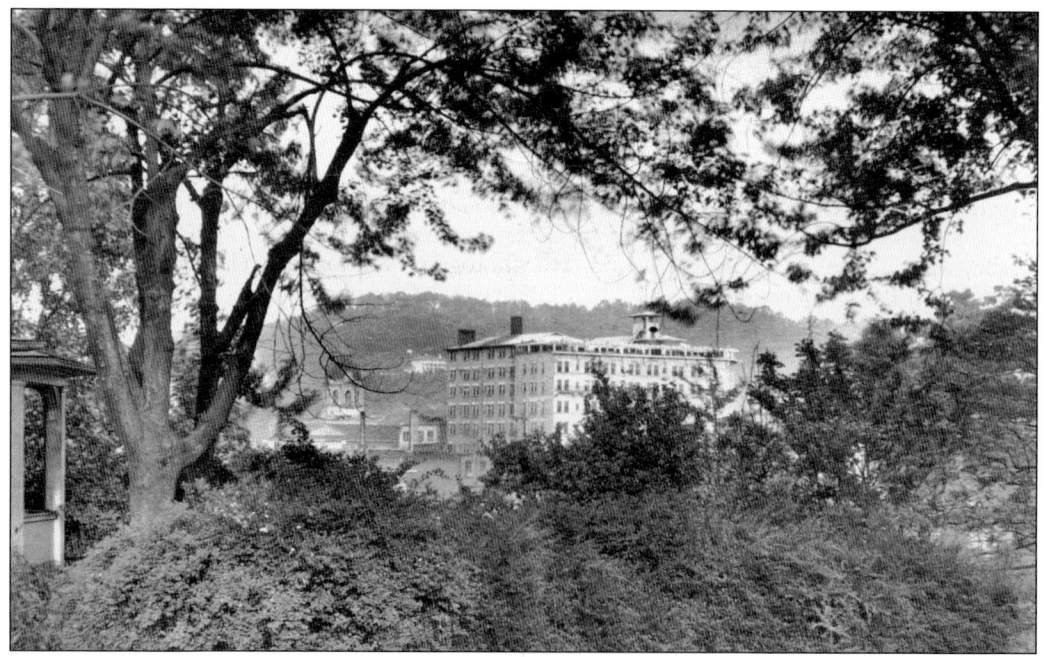

A View from the Northwest of Downtown Asheville, Possibly from Battery Park Hill. In the center, framed by trees, are the Langren Hotel on the right and the 1903 courthouse dome on the left. The Langren was on the northeast corner of Broadway and College Streets.

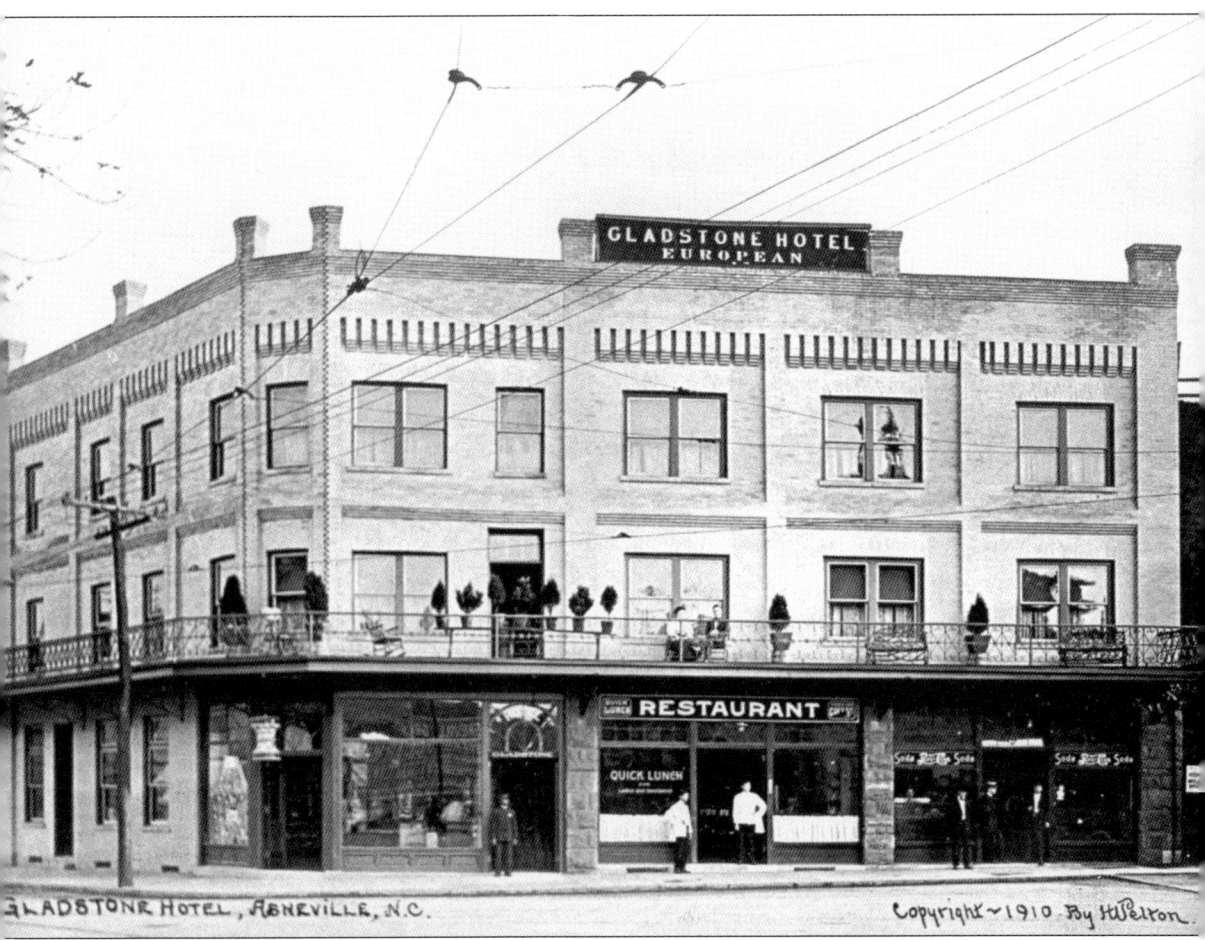

The Gladstone Hotel at #409 Depot Street, Near the Southern Railway Station. The hotel opened in 1910. This image shows men standing on the sidewalk in front of the hotel, which also had a restaurant and soda shop. Two people are also seated on second floor balcony. Trolley wires are visible in the foreground. The photograph was taken by Herbert W. Pelton and copyrighted 1910; it was purchased by Pack Library in 2000 from eBay.

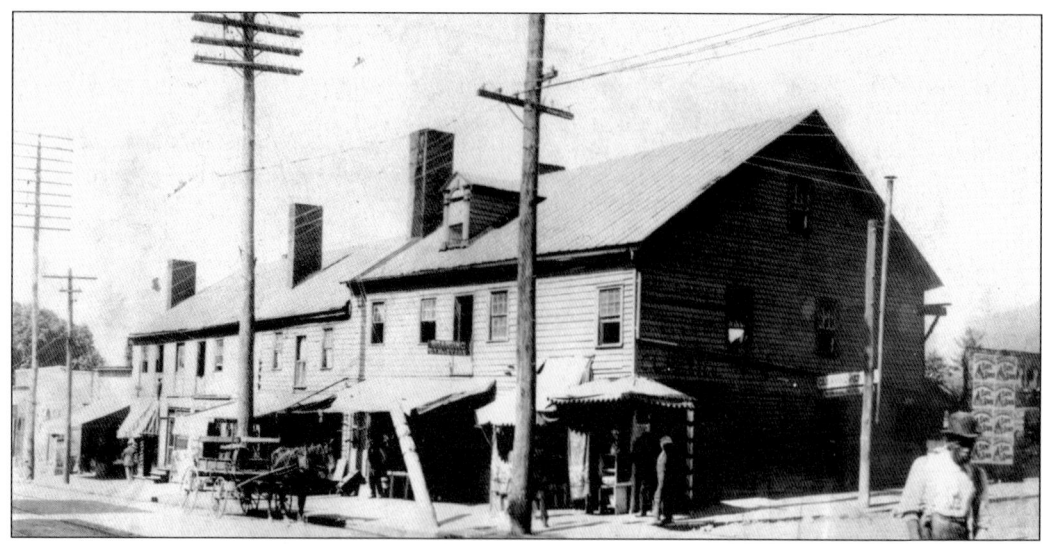

THE BUCK HOTEL. One of Asheville's first hotels, Buck Hotel was built in 1825 on North Main Street at what is now the corner of Broadway and College Streets. It was originally owned and operated by James McConnell Smith. While the south end is original, the north end was added onto twice. The sign of the Buck was a large buck's head hanging up high. The Buck Hotel became Mrs. Evans's boarding house in the 1890s, near the time of this photo. The hotel was demolished 1907 and replaced in 1912 by the Langren Hotel.

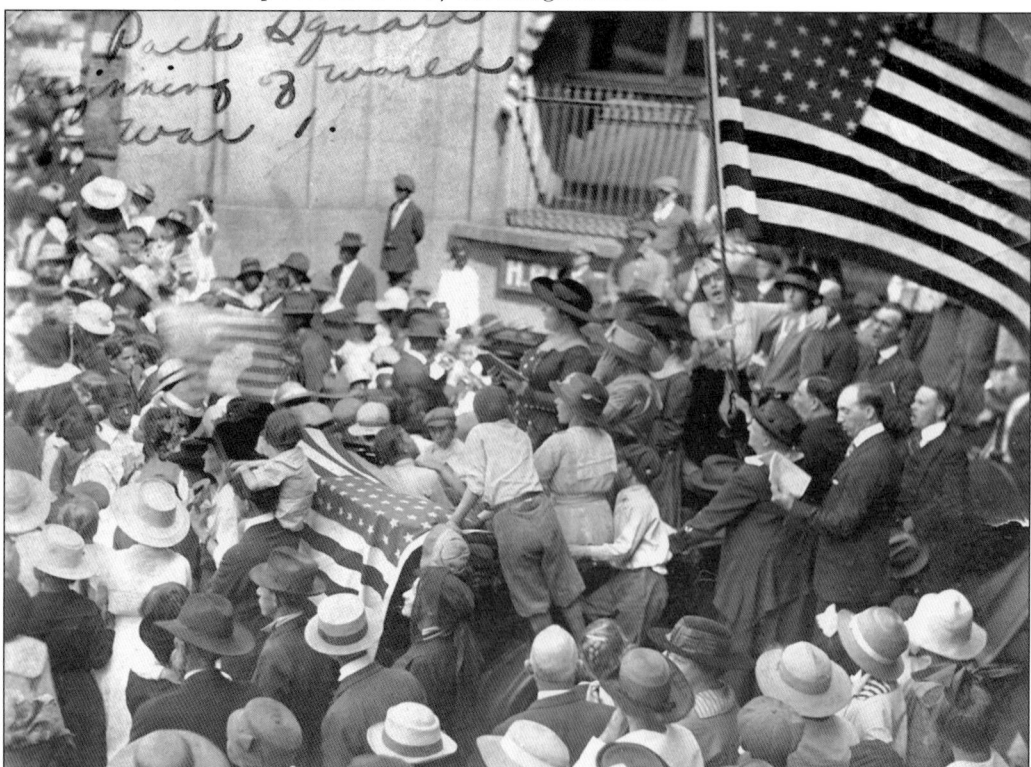

A RED CROSS MEETING, C. WWI. The meeting took place in front of the Library Building on Pack Square. "Pack Square beginning of World War I" is written across the top left in blue ink.

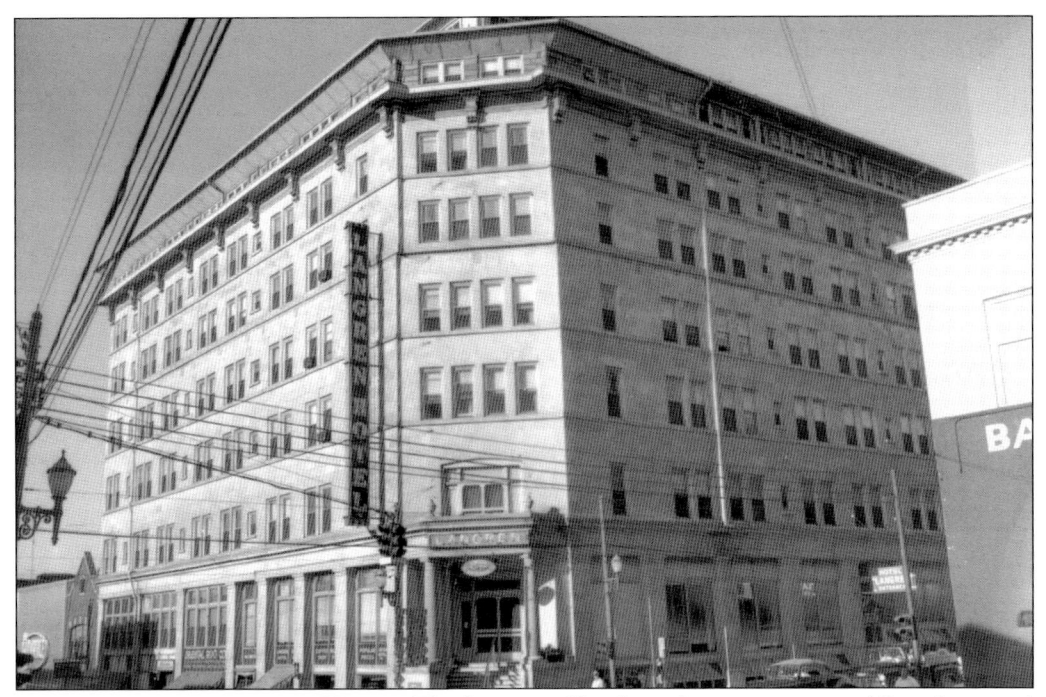

A VIEW OF THE LANGREN HOTEL. The Langren Hotel, at the intersection of Broadway and College Streets, was begun in 1908 but stood unfinished until it was bought by Gay Green and John H. Lange; the hotel took its title from their combined names. The hotel opened in 1912. Green and Lange operated the hotel until 1933, after which it was leased. It was sold in 1957 to the Claude L. Leach Hotel Co. of Norfolk, Virginia, and again in 1964 to Northwestern Bank, who planned to raze the hotel, in a three-way arrangement with Asheville City and the Goodyear Mortgage Co.

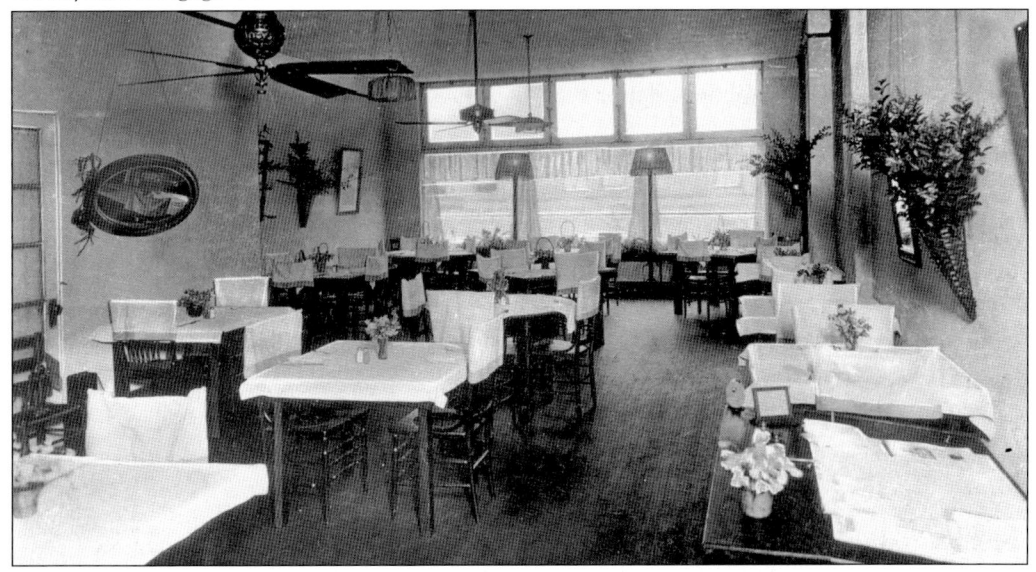

AN INTERIOR VIEW OF THE PLAZA CAFE AT 7 PACK SQUARE SW, DATED 1920. This photo shows a narrow room, with a view towards upper-floor windows. The café had small wooden tables with two or four chairs, electric lights, and ceiling fans.

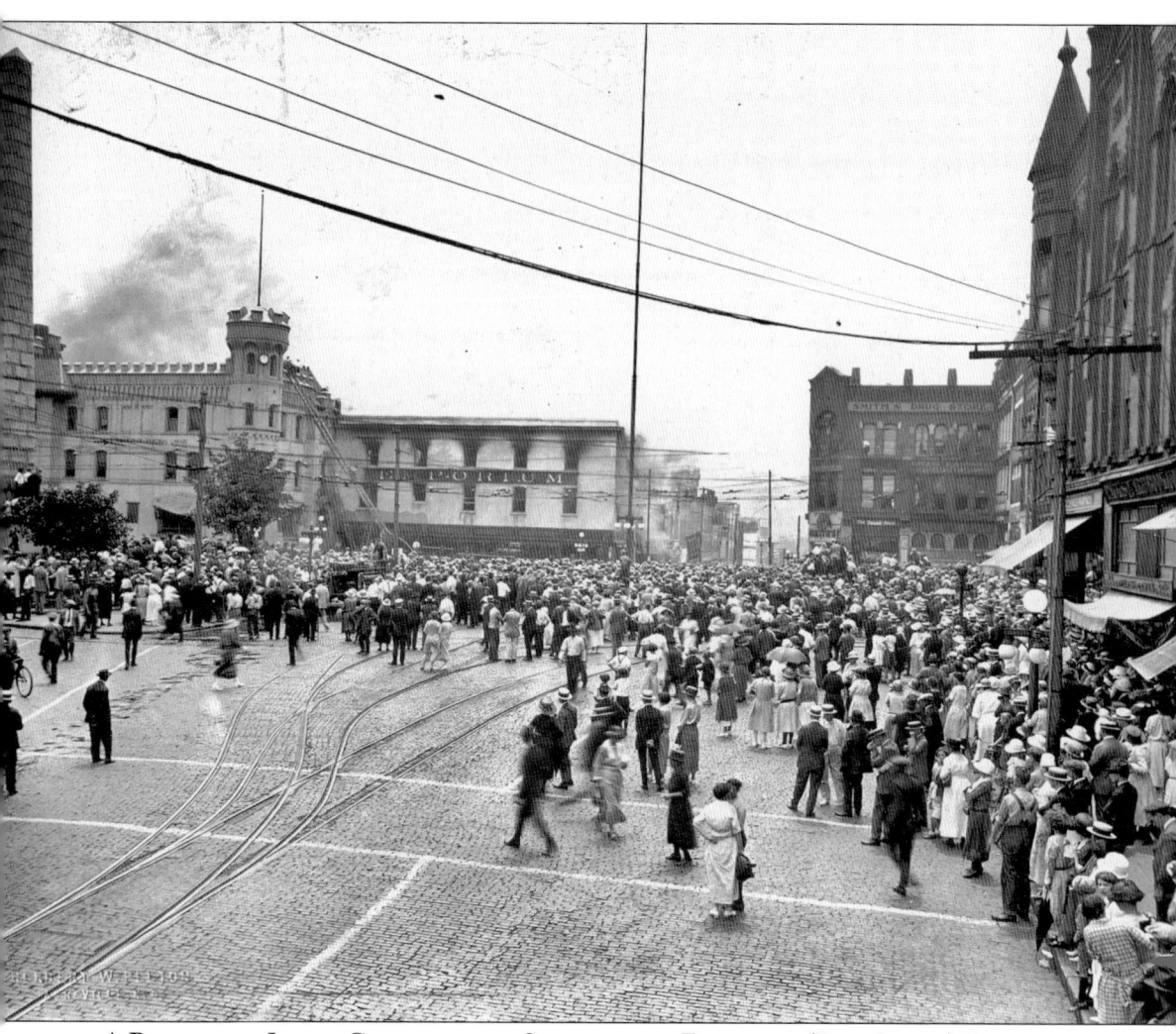

A Photo of a Large Crowd at the Scene of the Emporium (Dry Goods) Department Store Fire on July 25, 1923, at 2 Biltmore Avenue. Firemen can be seen battling the blaze from the roof of the Pack Memorial Library Building. The building had housed the First Nations Bank and was purchased by Pack and given to the library in 1899. The Vance Monument is visible in the left foreground. There is a good view of 1 Biltmore Avenue, which housed Smith's Drug Store, with its gabled parapets over the entrance in the right background. Also on the right side of photo is the turret of the Revell Building at 3 1/2 Pack Square NW, which was replaced in 1964 by the North Western (BB&T) Bank Building. (Pelton photo embossed in lower left corner. "Davis" is written on back in pencil and in other photos is Russell C. Davis and may refer to donor.)

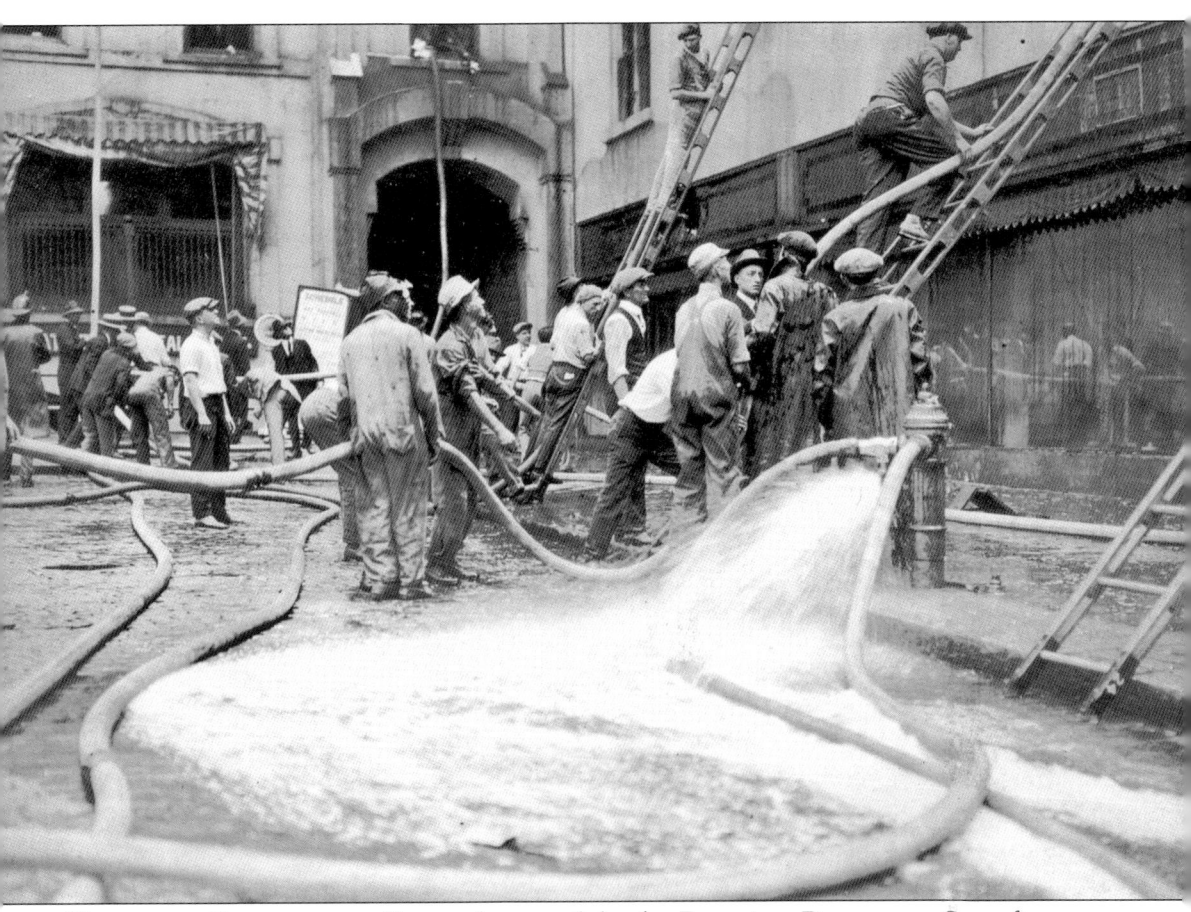

VOLUNTEER FIREFIGHTERS. Here, volunteers fight the Emporium Department Store fire on July 25, 1923.

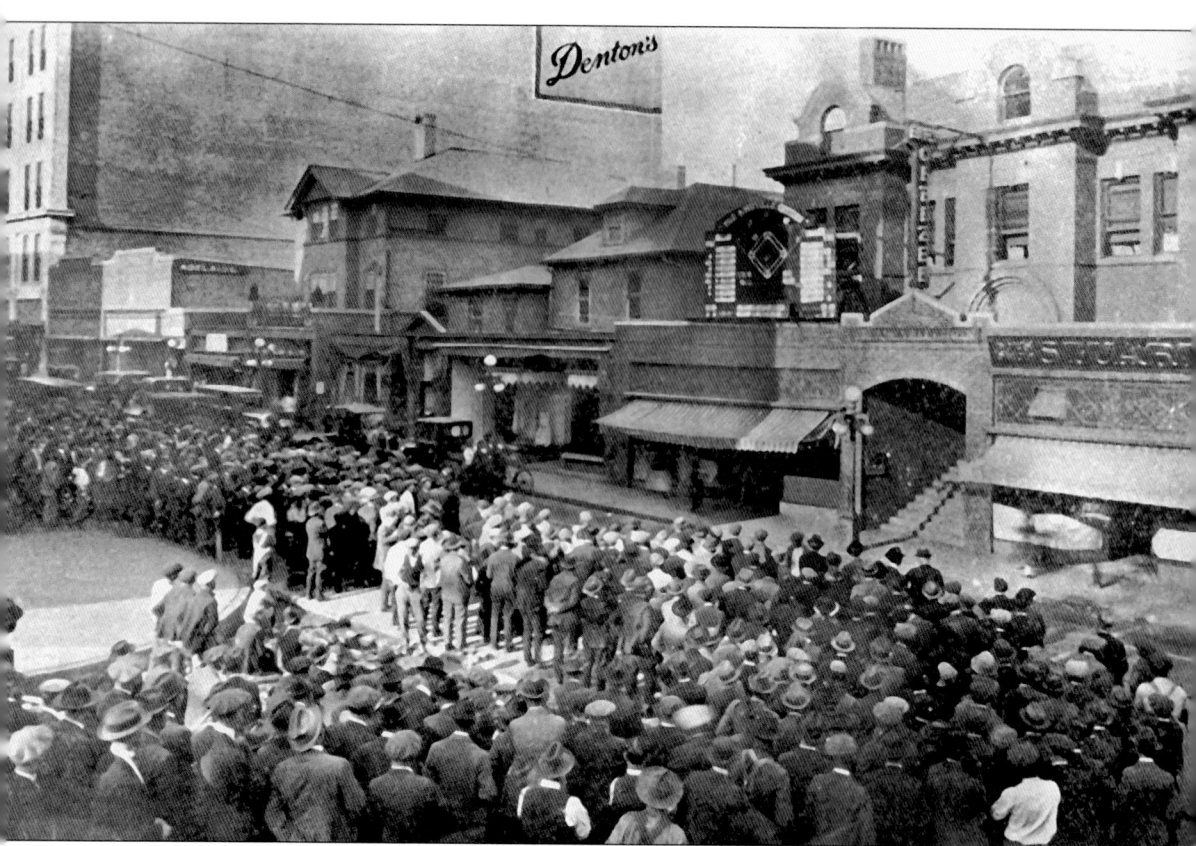

THE 1923 WORLD SERIES. This crowd watches the 1923 World Series scoreboard on the Citizen Building at 25 Haywood Street. The view is from the upper floor of the Miles Building. The buildings along the east side of Haywood from Battery Park Avenue to Walnut Street include Stuart's Inc.; the Boys Shop, located in the Citizen Building; the Adelaide over Claverie's Pharmacy; the Peter Pan Candy Shop; Denton's Department Store; Austin-Vesey Co.; Haywood Tea Room; Middlemount Gardens; and Cruse-Perkinson Co.

Five

Planning and Development

Lakeview Park and Biltmore Forest were built as "residence parks" in Asheville in the 1920s. Both neighborhoods were designed around golf courses designed by Donald Ross, who also developed Pinehurst. The subdivision plan for Lakeview Park was undertaken by John Nolen, who designed one of North Carolina's first curvilinear subdivisions in 1911 with the development of Myers Park in Charlotte. In the early 1920s, lots sold briskly in both developments, but Asheville's economy was actually cooling as early as 1926. Lakeview Park, like many other Asheville neighborhoods in the 1920s, was built largely on credit and many residents lost their homes during the Depression. Because of this, the contemporary landscape is somewhat disjointed, with the 100 or so boom-era homes a striking contrast to the more modern post-war housing that resumed after World War II.

Planned communities, however, were a vital part of the development of Asheville. The city population was approaching 50,000 by the 1920s, and John Nolen was commissioned to develop a master plan to envision a future city of 200,000. Biltmore Forest was initiated soon after George Vanderbilt's widow, Edith, sold 1,500 acres to the Biltmore Estate Co. for developing "a community where persons of moderate means could build homes that would embody on a smaller scale the same ideas that had actuated Mr. Vanderbilt." Thomas Raoul, who had developed Albemarle Park in 1898, came on board, developing two-acre tracts with unprecedented restrictions, as described in newspapers of the time. While they may have targeted those of "moderate means" they were still marketing to retired barons of commerce and industry.

After completion of the railroad in 1880, streetcar neighborhoods like Montford and Chestnut Liberty began to emerge. Most of Chestnut Liberty dates between 1880 and 1929 and includes homes in the Queen Anne, Colonial Revival, and Shingle styles. Montford began a decade later, around 1890. A neighborhood of some 600 homes today, Montford Avenue is its main thoroughfare. George W. Pack helped earlier developers expand Montford, a collection of substantial homes, but also an eclectic mix of apartment buildings, boarding houses, schools, and sanitariums of the time. The Grove Park neighborhood, begun in 1905, consists primarily of Tudor Revival, Bungalow, and Colonial Revival homes. The Longchamps Apartments in the Grove Park section offer a striking fantasy of Chateau and Tudor elements against the backdrop of Sunset Mountain. Norwood Park, an extension of Grove Park, was platted in 1923 by E.W. Grove Investments of St. Louis, Missouri. Grove purchased the hillside farmland from William Farr. Grove's early documents for these developments were particularly racist. Restrictions included those preventing "persons of color" and "other disreputable persons." Fortunately, these neighborhoods around Grove Park, including Norwood Park and Albemarle Park, are today thriving in diversity and complexity. The Kenilworth neighborhood, begun in 1912, is located on the southern end of Beaucatcher Mountain. It was begun by James Madison Chiles and named for Scottish novelist and poet Sir Walter Scott, a contemporary and rival of Lord Byron. Kenilworth was one in his Elizabethan series, The Waverley Novels. The neighborhood was built primarily in the Tudor and "English cottage" style, although Bungalow and Prairie style homes are also found.

West Asheville has recently enjoyed resurgence and newfound real estate speculation. The development of West Asheville reflects the importance of what was then known as the Western Turnpike. Haywood Road follows this path to Haywood County. In 1885 Edwin Carrier began developing Haywood road as part of the West Asheville Improvement Company. As the owner of the Sulfur Springs Hotel, near current-day Malvern Hills, Carrier developed an electric railway system by 1891 to ferry passengers to his hotel. West Asheville grew quickly, with trolley service arriving in 1910. A classic streetcar neighborhood with a fairly consistent grid pattern of streets, West Asheville was built with an eclectic mix of late Victorian, Queen Anne, Craftsman, and Bungalow inspired homes. Haywood Road was paved in 1914, and while West Asheville was incorporated as a separate town, it was merged with the City of Asheville in 1917.

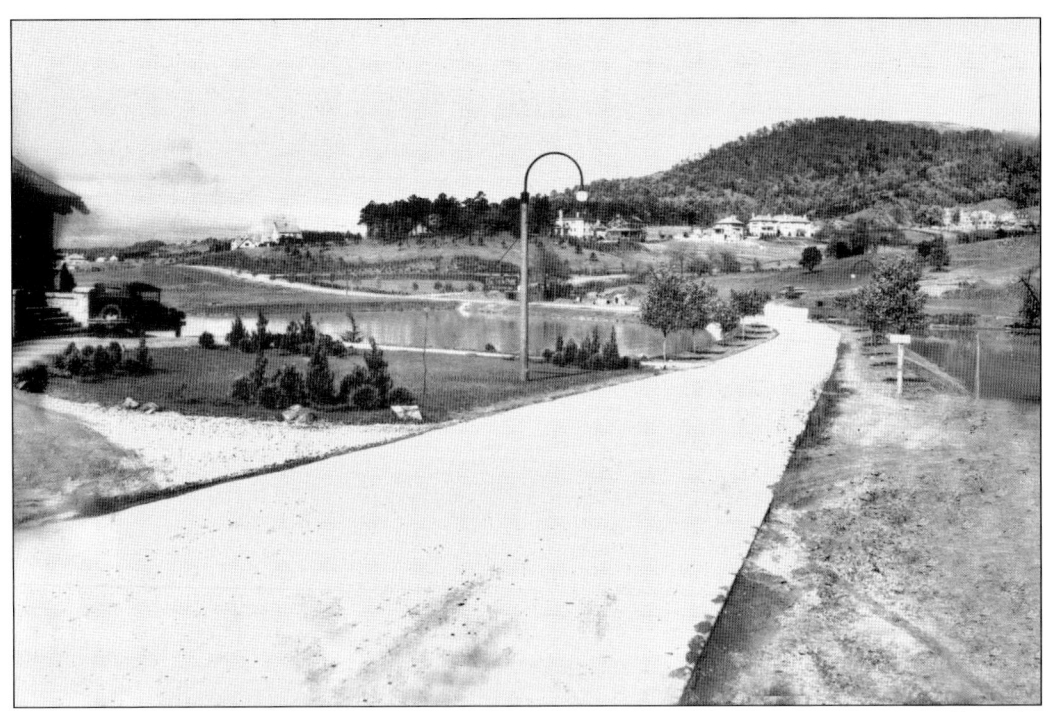

A VIEW OF MERRIMON AVENUE THROUGH LAKEVIEW PARK. Houses, some still under construction, line Edgelawn Road to the right. Lakeview Park was developed in 1922 by J.D. Murphy and Fred Sale. Beaver Creek flooded Baird's Bottoms creating Beaver Lake, at left.

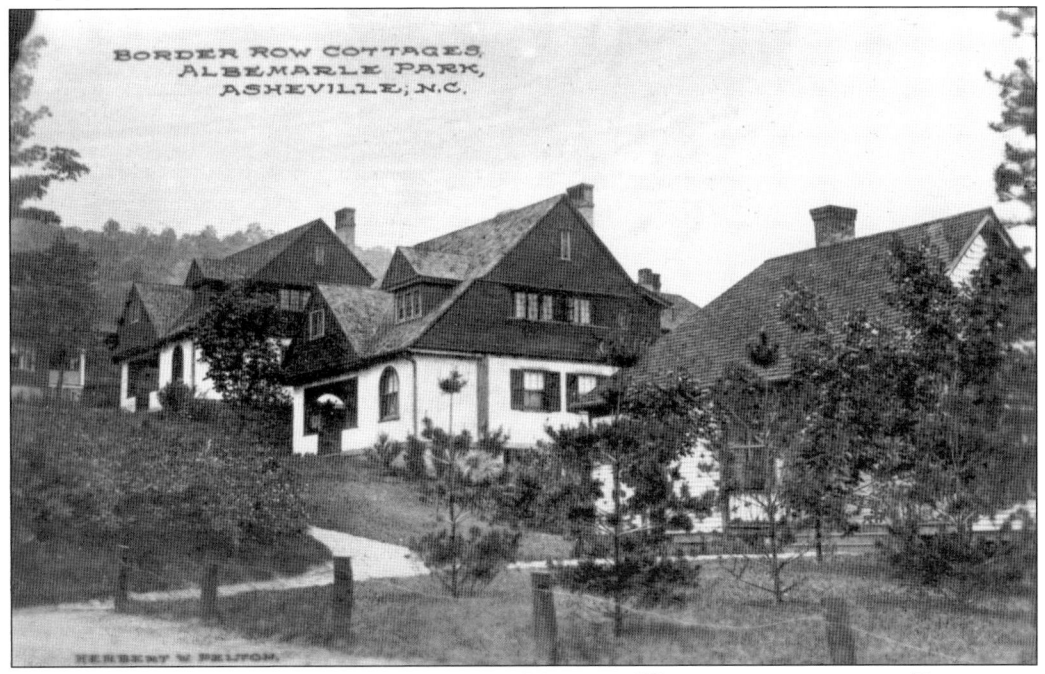

THE THREE BORDER ROW COTTAGES ALONG HILLSIDE WALK, AS VIEWED FROM ROSEBANK. The cottages are, from left to right, Hollyhock, Marigold, and Larkspur. (Original to the Albemarle Park Development, Pelton, 1910. Obtained via North Carolina Collection.)

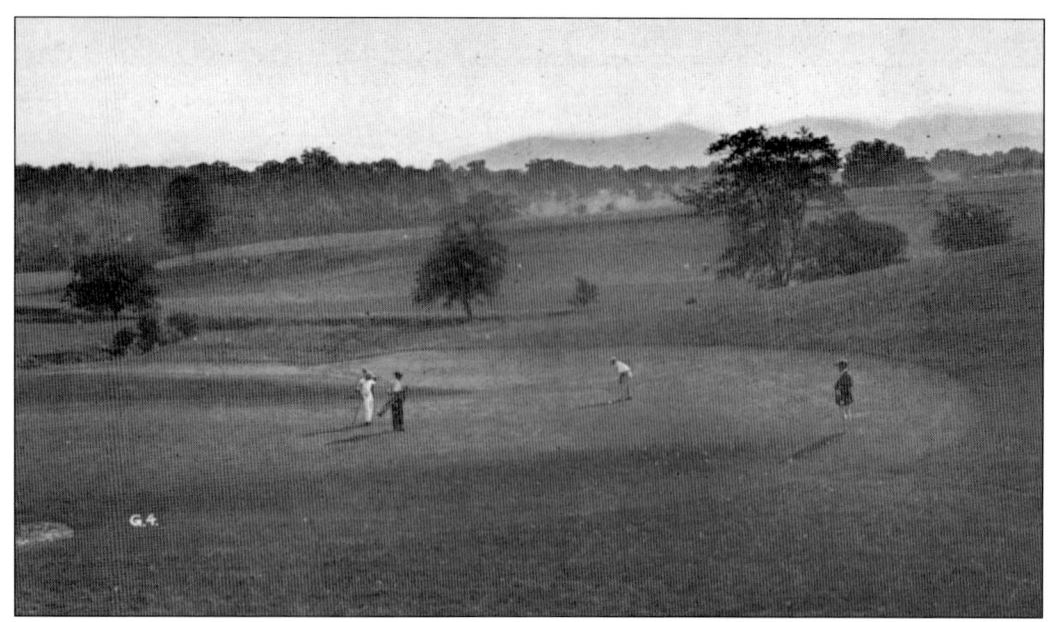

A GOLFER PUTTING ON THE 13TH GREEN AT ASHEVILLE COUNTRY CLUB. This photo is taken from *Golf In Asheville: The Golfer's Record and Diary, c.* 1914.

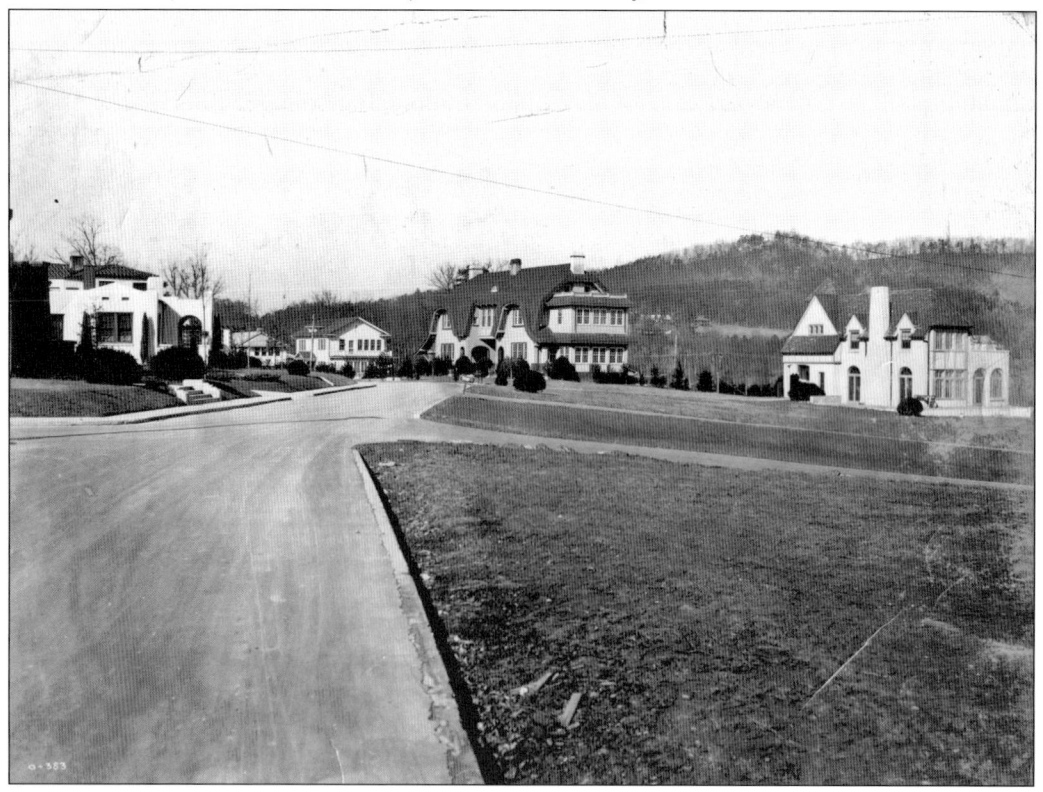

KENILWORTH PARK. The residential area of Kenilworth Park was developed by James "Jake" Madison Chiles. The houses, from left to right, are Holland House, the top of Brennen House, Self House, English House, and Lon Pollock.

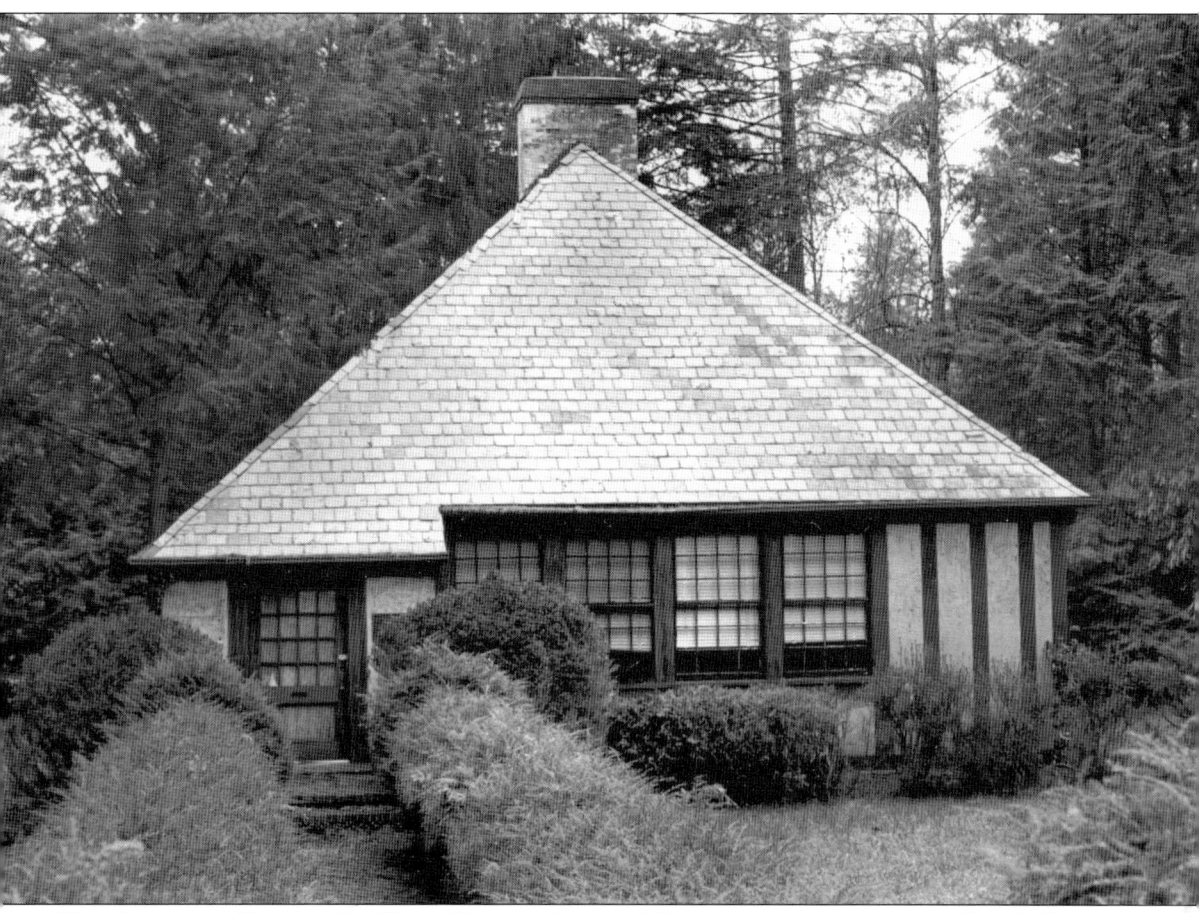

THE BILTMORE ESTATE CO. REAL ESTATE OFFICE. The realty company, pictured c. 1921, is located on Vanderbilt Road at Busbee Road. The company was later known as the Biltmore Forest Co. The office is housed in a small square Tudor cottage with a pyramidal slate roof, a central chimney, and vertical half-timbering and rough stucco. The building later served as the Biltmore Forest Town Hall.

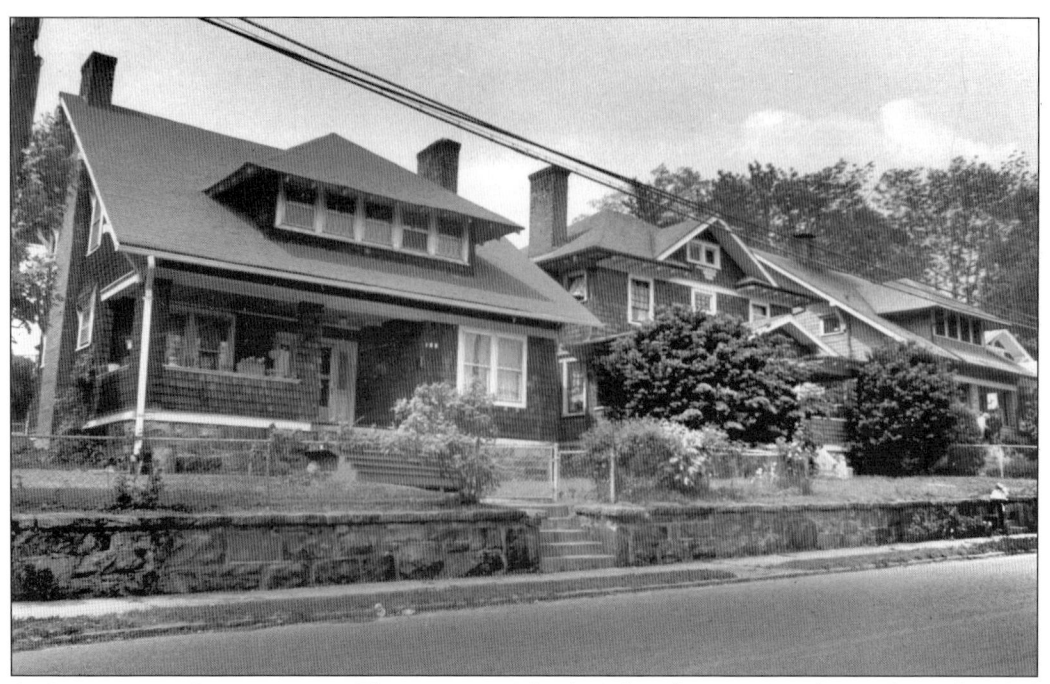

A CRAFTSMAN STREETSCAPE. This scene in North Asheville, c. 1920, shows three shingled houses, two of which are grand bungalows and one of which is a box plan. All three have shallow front yards built up behind a stone wall at the sidewalk.

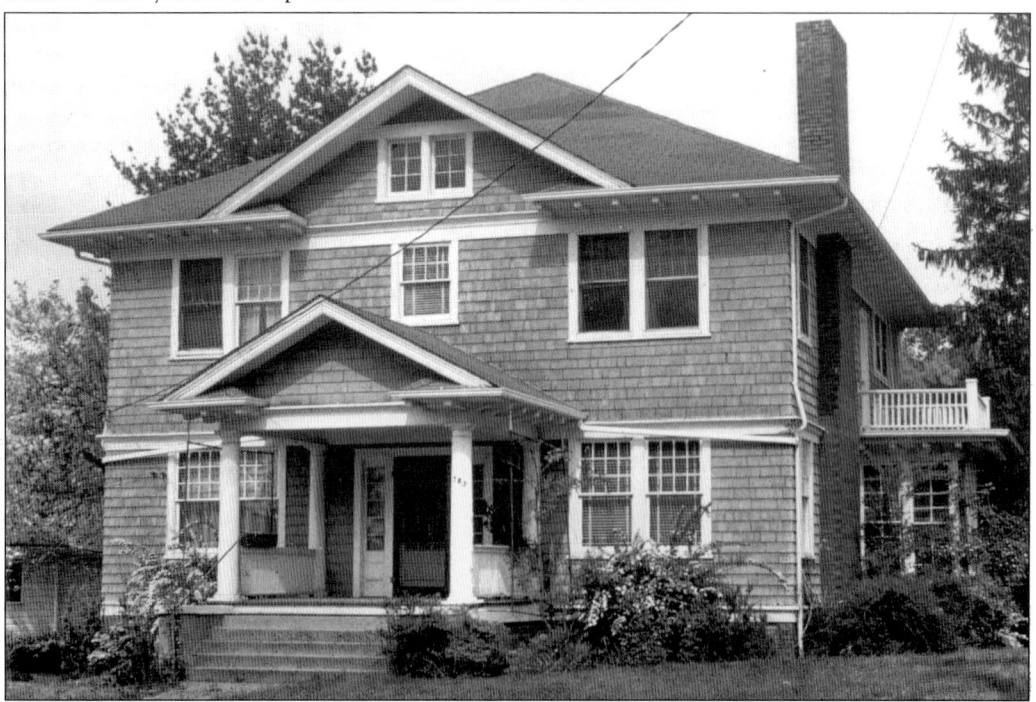

A CLASSIC CRAFTSMAN. Pictured in North Asheville c.1910 is a two-and-a-half–story shingled house with returns on its roof and entrance gables, two circular columns, an exterior brick chimney, and an upstairs deck above a sunroom on the right.

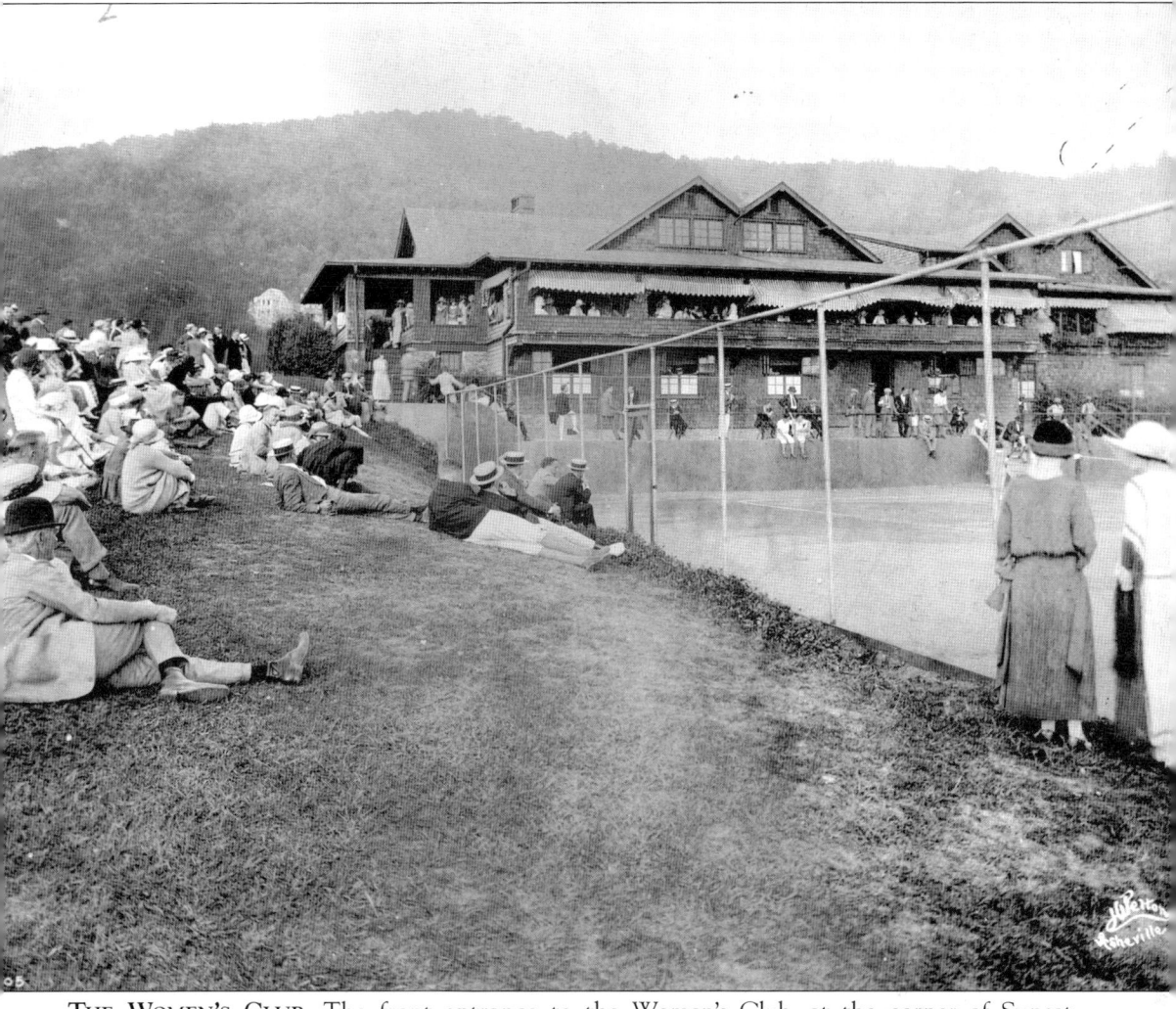

THE WOMEN'S CLUB. The front entrance to the Women's Club, at the corner of Sunset Parkway and Charlotte Street, is pictured c. 1910–1920.

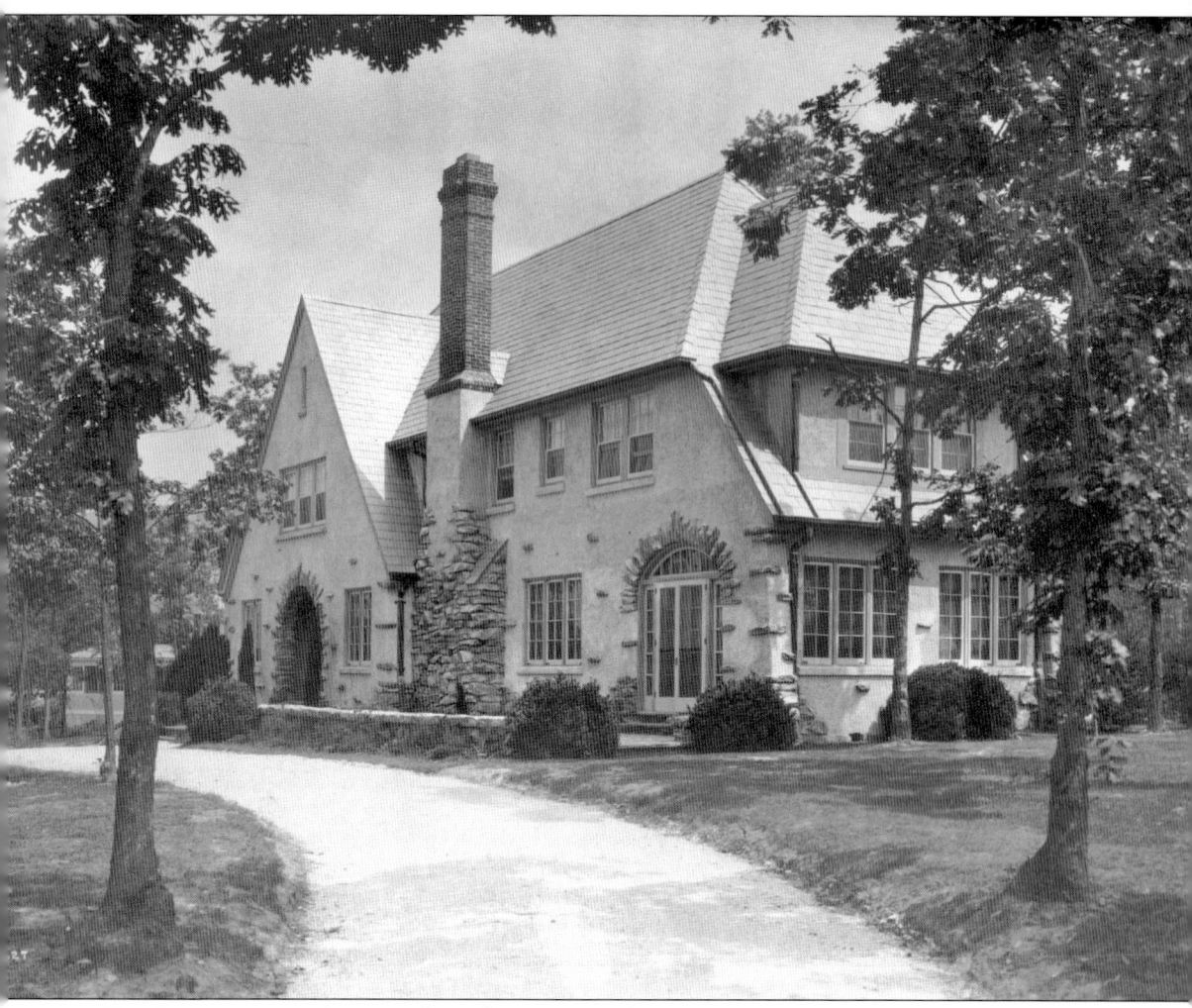

THE SCENE OF THE CRASH. This Biltmore Forest home, pictured in 1929, was owned by Herbert O. Miller, president of Dorian Music Co. Some grand homes, like this one, were built and occupied for less than a year before the Great Depression hit Asheville with a vengeance.

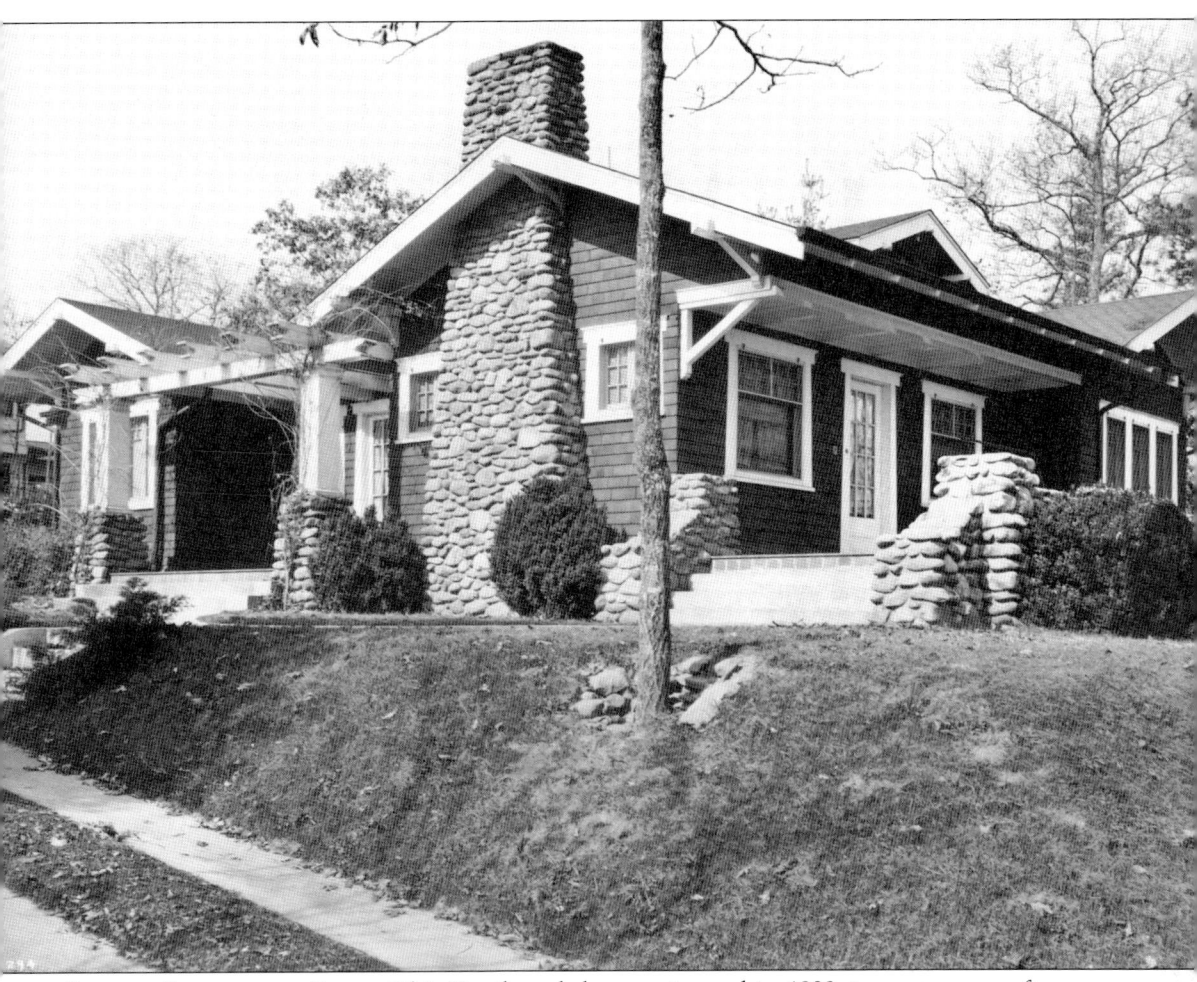

IN THE CRAFTSMAN STYLE. This Kenilworth home, pictured in 1929, is an ornate craftsman bungalow with stone porch piers and chimney.

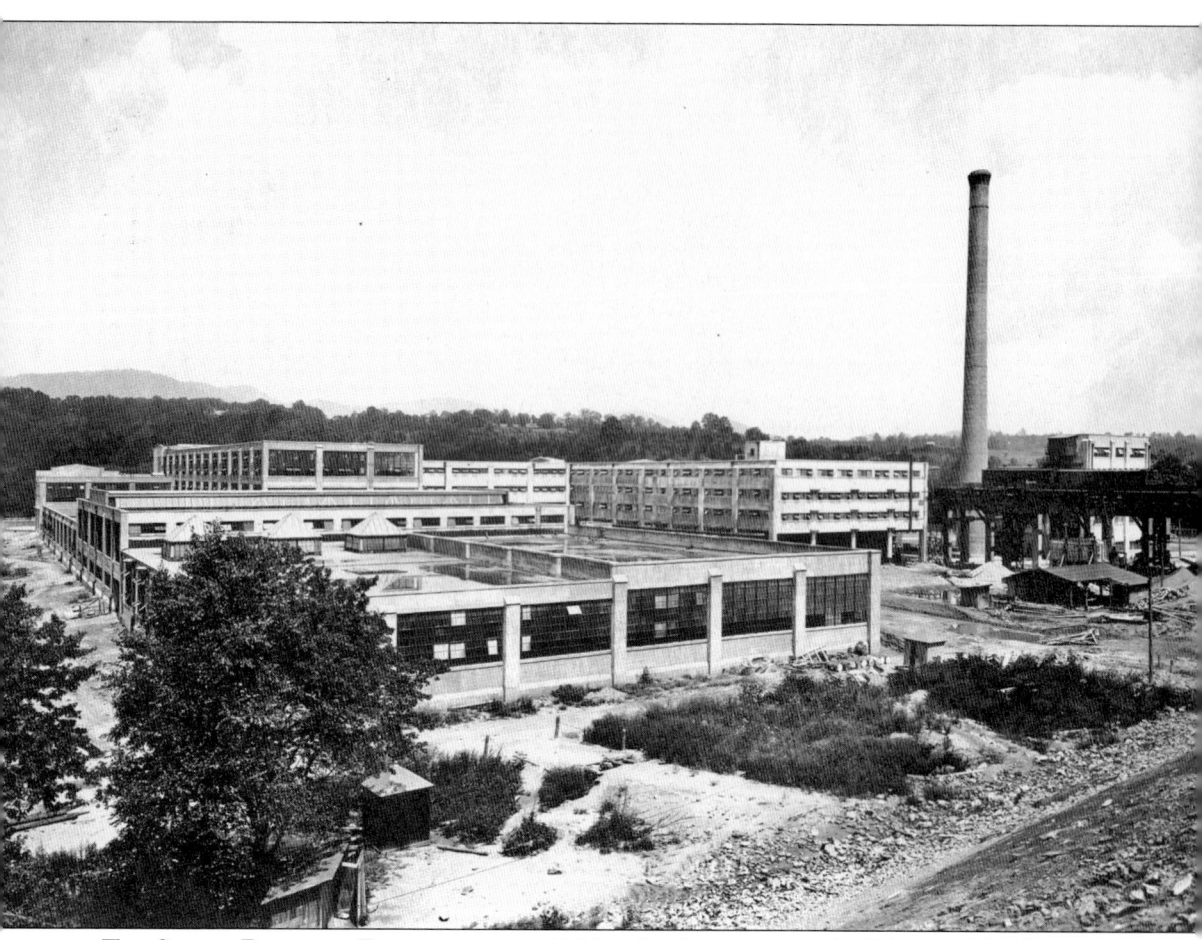

THE SAYLES-BILTMORE BLEACHERIES IN 1929. After long service, the Biltmore Bleacheries are being demolished in 2004.

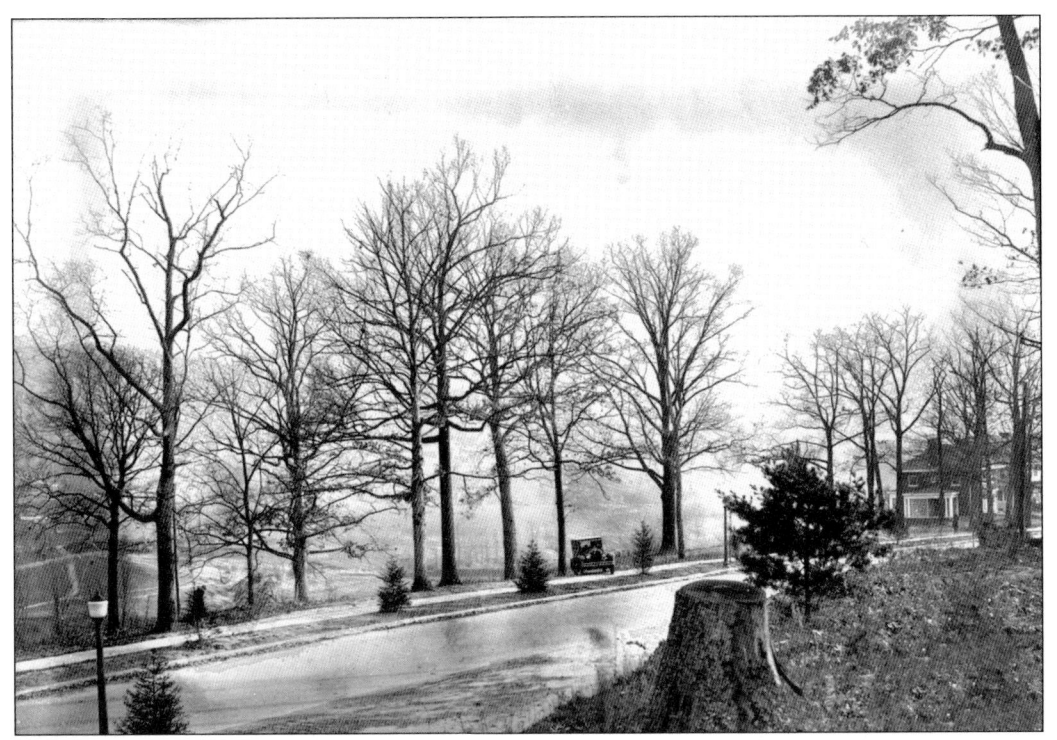

THE GROVE PARK SECTION, POSSIBLY MACON AVENUE.

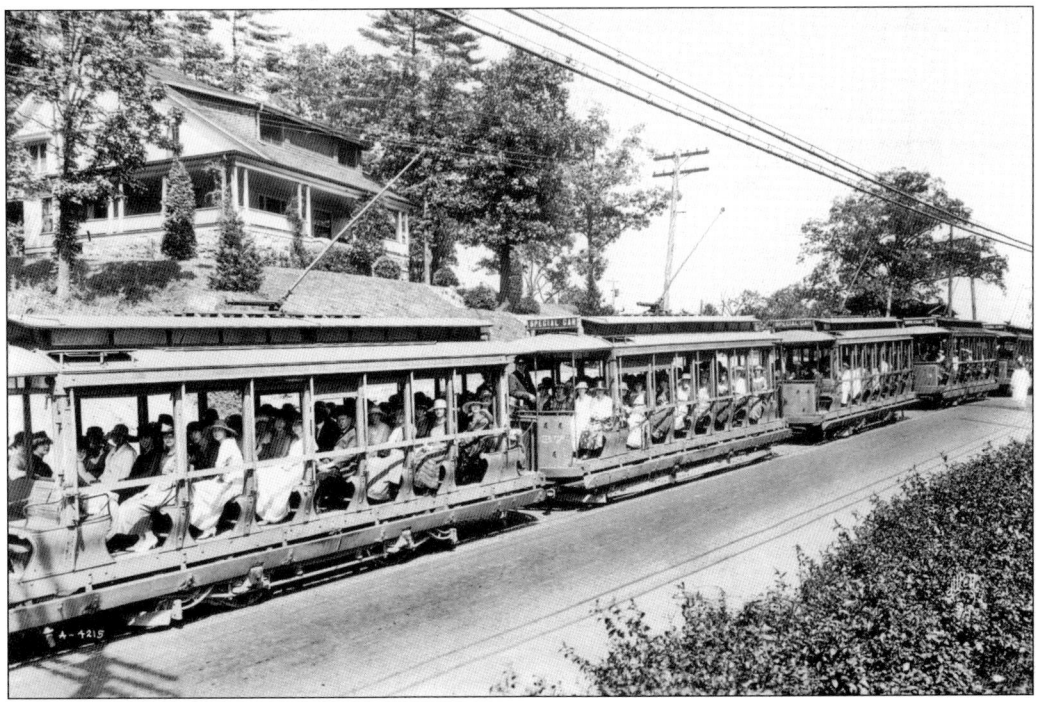

TEACHERS AT ASHEVILLE NORMAL SCHOOL. A string of five streetcars loaded with teachers attends the summer school session at Asheville Normal School, c. 1919. There is a good view of a house on a hill behind the streetcars, but the location is unidentified.

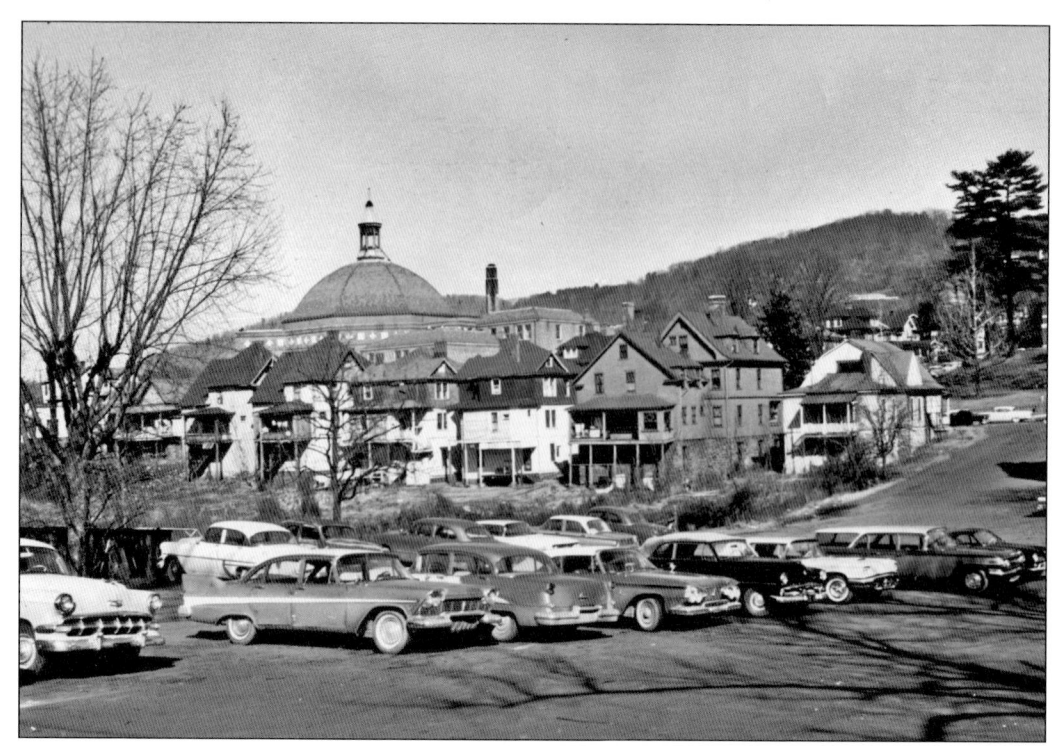

A LATER VIEW OF AN OLDER NEIGHBORHOOD. This view toward the First Baptist Church shows the backs of houses facing Oak Street, behind a parking lot, c. 1950.

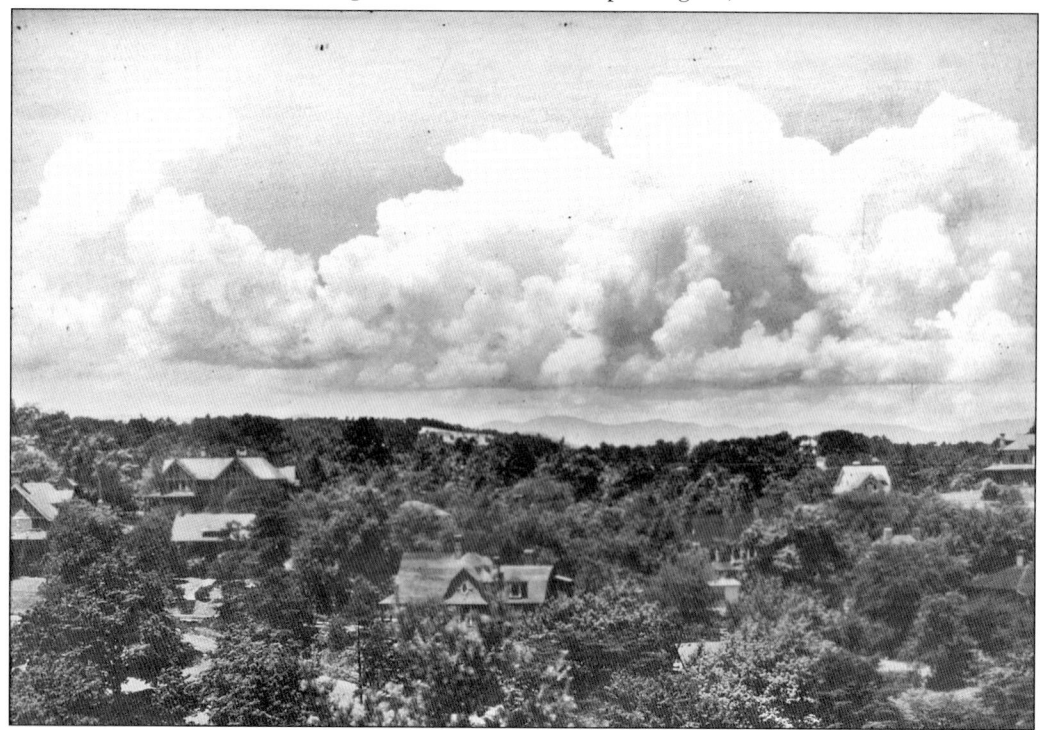

AN EARLY VIEW OF HISTORIC MONTFORD. This view is from the west of the Montford area.

Six

A CITY EMERGES

The land-boom gold-rush days of the 1920s ended as quickly as they began. Some of the images in this chapter attempt to "freeze" the moment in 1929 when it all came crashing down. So much of Asheville's boom was heavily financed with both private credit and public debt. On November 20, 1930, Asheville's Central Bank and Trust Company, with assets of over $52 million, closed. Dozens of banks all over Western North Carolina followed suit. Buncombe County, the City of Asheville, and the public school system lost nearly $8 million. Bank officers were arrested. Asheville's mayor committed suicide.

Leo Finkelstein, born in Asheville in 1903, inherited his pawn shop from his father. In an oral history recorded for "Voices of Asheville" he said that during the Depression, he knew most of his customers and made about 100 loans a day—half to African Americans, half to whites. The customers had no credit and could not borrow from the bank. They needed cash for doctor bills, to buy drugs, and to eat. His father gave loans on practically nothing. The most reliable were the prostitutes. He gave $5 with no collateral to a man who bought a portable stove and chestnuts, which he roasted. The man later opened a restaurant with two sections, one African-American, one white. Finkelstein had money in the American National Bank and, when he got a tip that the bank was going to close, asked his sister Rosa to withdraw all but $100. She did as asked but came home with a cashier's check, which was worthless.

Dr. Russell Norburn was born in Danville, Virginia, and came to Asheville in 1901. He attended the Montford Avenue School and the Orange Street School until the fourth grade, when his father's failing health forced the family to move out of the city to West Asheville, where he attended Sand Hill High School. He went to the University of North Carolina and Vanderbilt University, where he obtained his medical degree. After graduation in 1921, he came back to Asheville and opened a private practice with his brother, Dr. Charles Norburn. Together they opened the Norburn Hospital in 1928 at 346 Montford Avenue. Despite doubling their capacity and taking care of over 33,000 bed patients, the hospital struggled to survive through the Depression, when few of their patients could afford to pay their medical expenses.

Despite these many hardships, Asheville not only survived, but because it did not have the ability to finance large public projects in the 1950s and 1960s, it did not embark on massive public building projects that would have decimated both the central downtown business district and nearby neighborhoods. The most significant public works projects of the 1960s and 1970s was probably only the cross-town expressway linking downtown to West Asheville and I-240 slicing through downtown. A photo on page 74 indicates part of what might have been lost. While so many other cities in America seemed to recover within a decade or more after the Great Depression, aided greatly by the boon of economic infusion from World War II, Asheville seemed trapped in time. From 1966 to 1980, Asheville's population declined from 65,000 to a paltry 53,708. Preservation by neglect is neither desirable nor wise, but it happened in the case of Asheville to hold demolition at bay, allowing a better day to arise when those who would be able to better preserve and restore would still have commercial and residential buildings of such significance. The "Program for Progress" of the 1920s became an *overbearing recipe for stagnation until the 1970s. The $50 million debt, which Asheville did not walk away from but paid off in refinanced bonds, served to preserve much of Asheville. The debt was finally retired in 1976. Less than a year later, the Asheville Revitalization Commission was created and developed a plan—"A Revitalized Downtown."*

It is important to note that much of what visitors to Asheville see today was largely constructed within a 20-to-30–year time-span, and while there has been more contemporary building since then, from such landmarks as the Northwestern Bank Building in 1964 and the Akzona-Biltmore Building in 1978, designed by I.M. Pei, much of the early 20th-century cityscape has been uniquely preserved. And since 1976, when the debt was finally repaid, it has taken roughly the same time span to renovate many, if not most of, Asheville's commercial and residential architectural gems, as it took to build them. There are still probably more opportunities for preservation and renovation on the residential side, as commercial downtown today appears almost ready to split at the seams.

Even the author's parents, John and Betsy McDaniel, perhaps unknowingly, were reinvesting in downtown, leasing an office above a restaurant called Gatsby's in a new redevelopment called Lexington Park by developer John Lantzius in the early 1980s. This was an early mixed-use development with apartments, offices, and parks that many cities today are just beginning to get their arms around. This project set the tone for the future possibility of Asheville's revitalization. Lantzius, and others like him, stayed in Asheville, and restored the city you see today. A pioneer in preserving Asheville, Lantzius opposed plans to tear down a huge swath of downtown and build a self-contained mall. Because of his role in the preservation of downtown Asheville, October 10, 2001, was declared "John Lantzius Day" by the city. These battles of preservation versus "progress" will always be a part of Asheville. In 2003, the Grove Park Inn sought to put a new high rise on Pack Square, in what is now public green space. Opposition mounted quickly. On December 31, 2003, the Grove Park Inn caved in, withdrawing its plan for luxury condominiums.

In 2000, Asheville's population was 68,889. Buncombe County had reached 206,330.

Guess we'll have to wait and see what happens next.

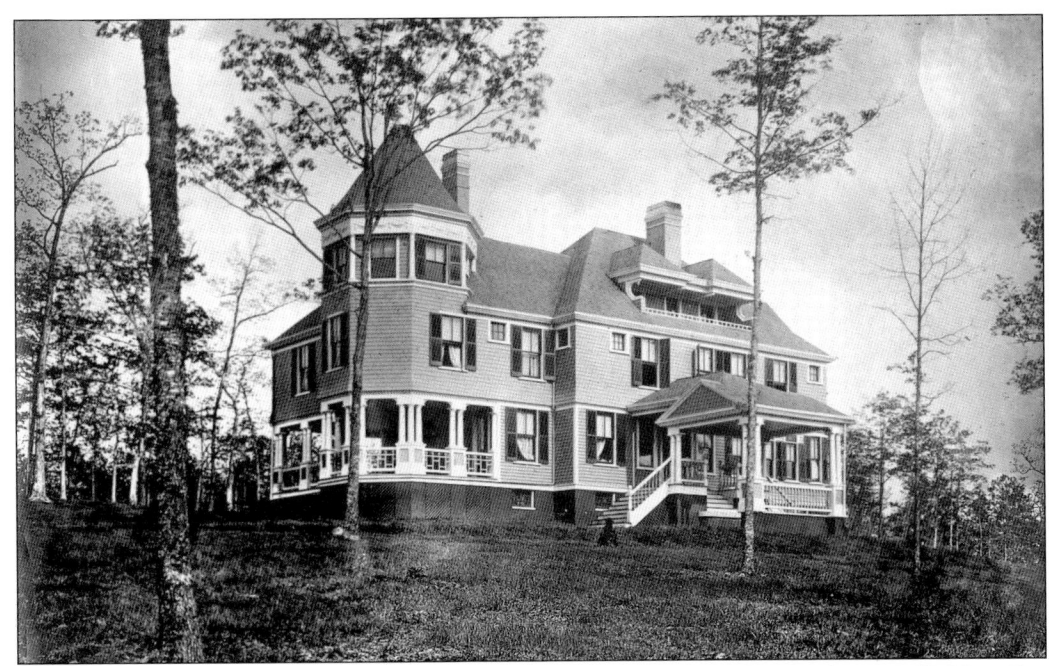

INSIDE OUT. Shown is the exterior of Buck Shoals, owned by Edgar Wilson "Bill" Nye. See below for an interior view.

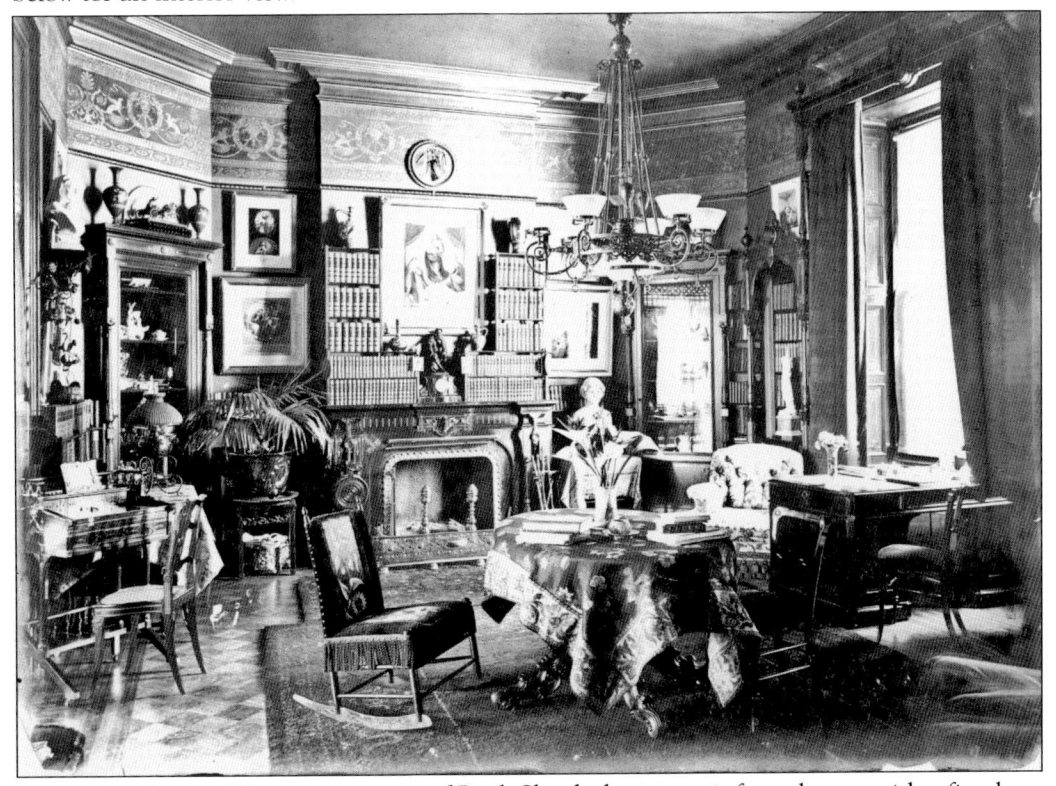

HOW THEY LIVED. This interior view of Buck Shoals depicts an informal room with a fireplace, a chandelier, several desks, and a small table with two small chairs in the center.

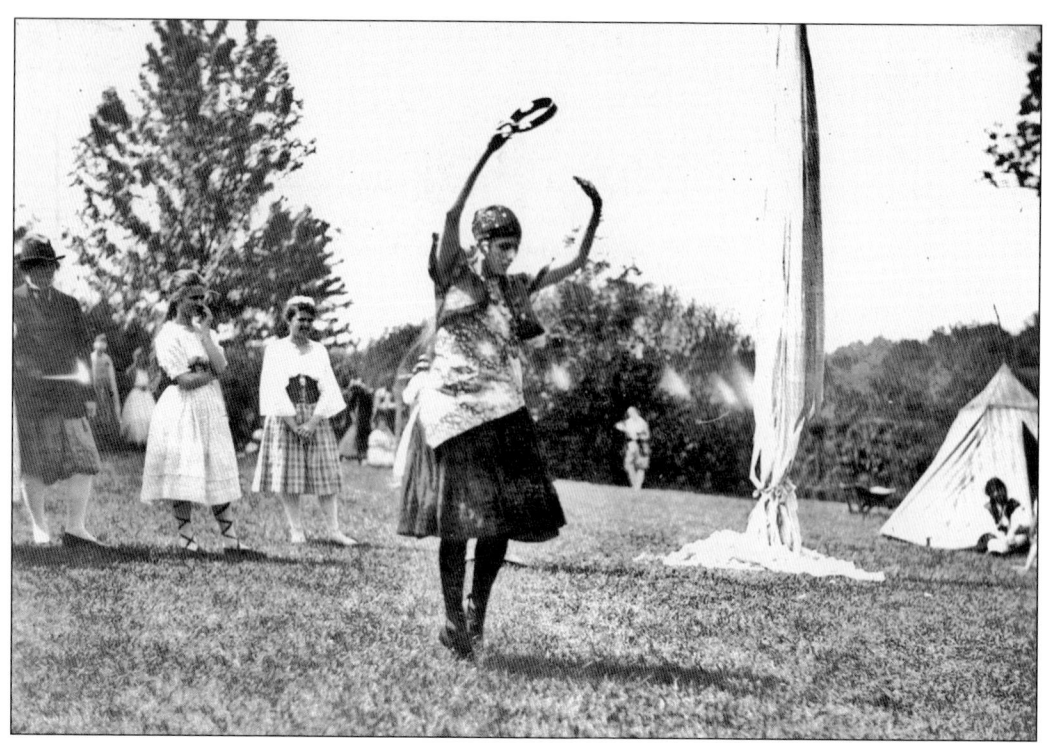

A MAY DAY CELEBRATION. This photo of a dancer in ethnic-looking "gypsy" costume and holding a tambourine, was taken at a May Day celebration on the campus of Asheville Normal School, c. 1920.

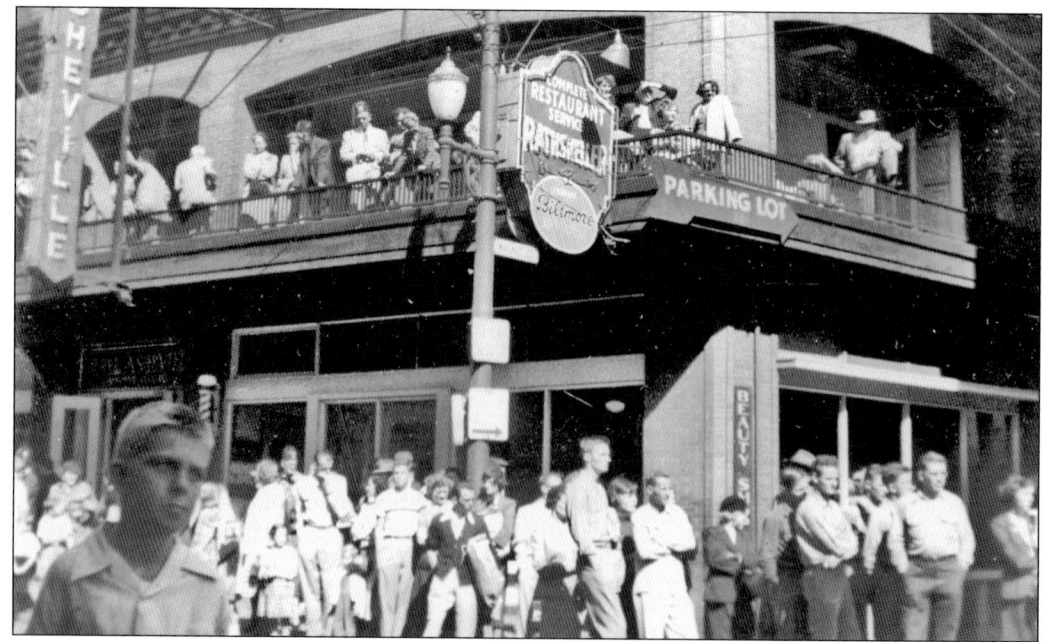

THE HOTEL ASHEVILLE. This photo shows a parade passing in front of the Hotel Asheville, at the corner of Haywood and Walnut Streets. A sign is visible at the corner for the Rathskeller Restaurant, which was in the back of the hotel building.

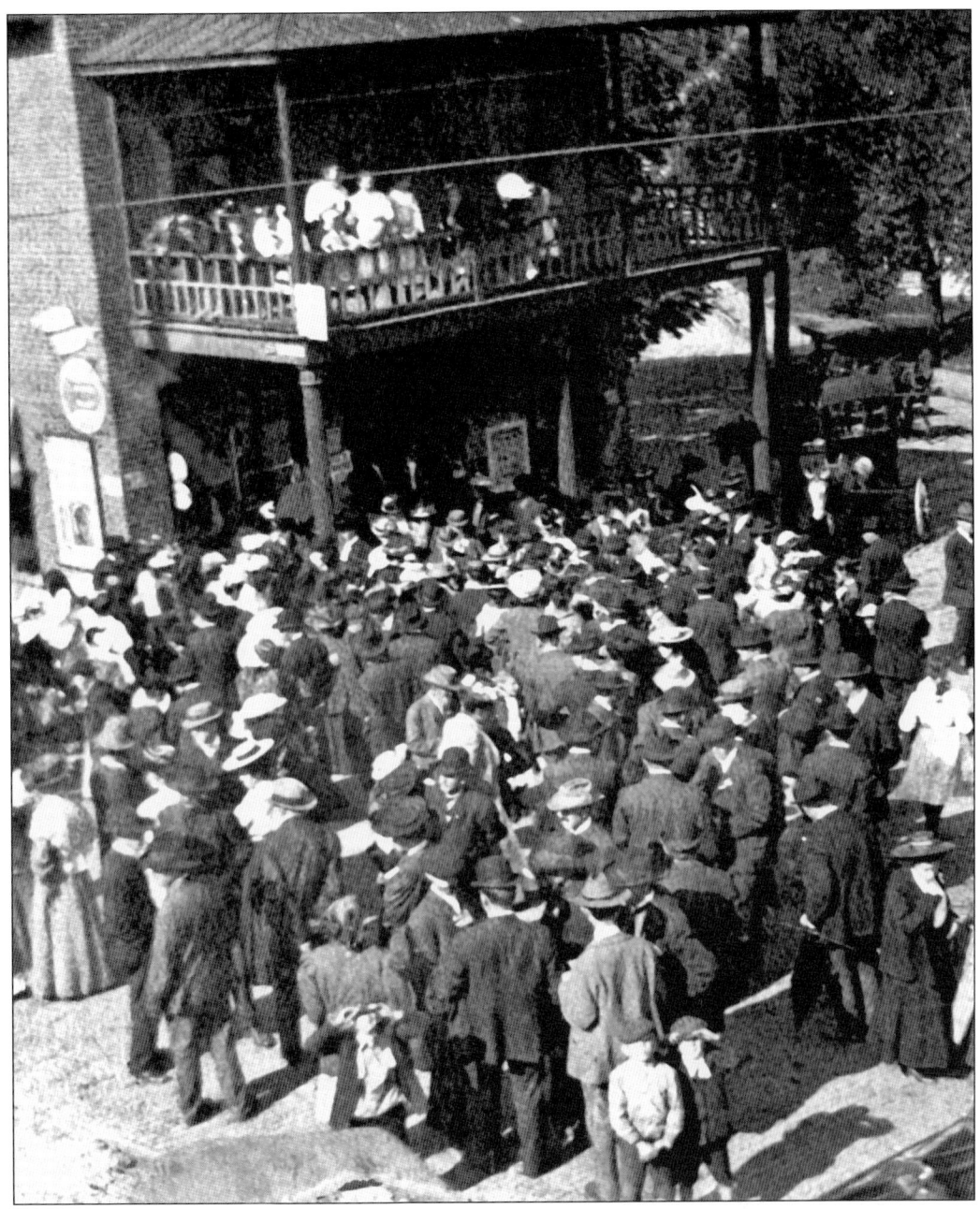

GET OUT THE VOTE. Men and women gathered in front of Chedester's Grocery Store at 130 Main Street N to vote on Prohibition in 1907. Although women could not vote, they were there to be sure their husbands voted against alcohol. Horse-drawn carriages are on the right side of store.

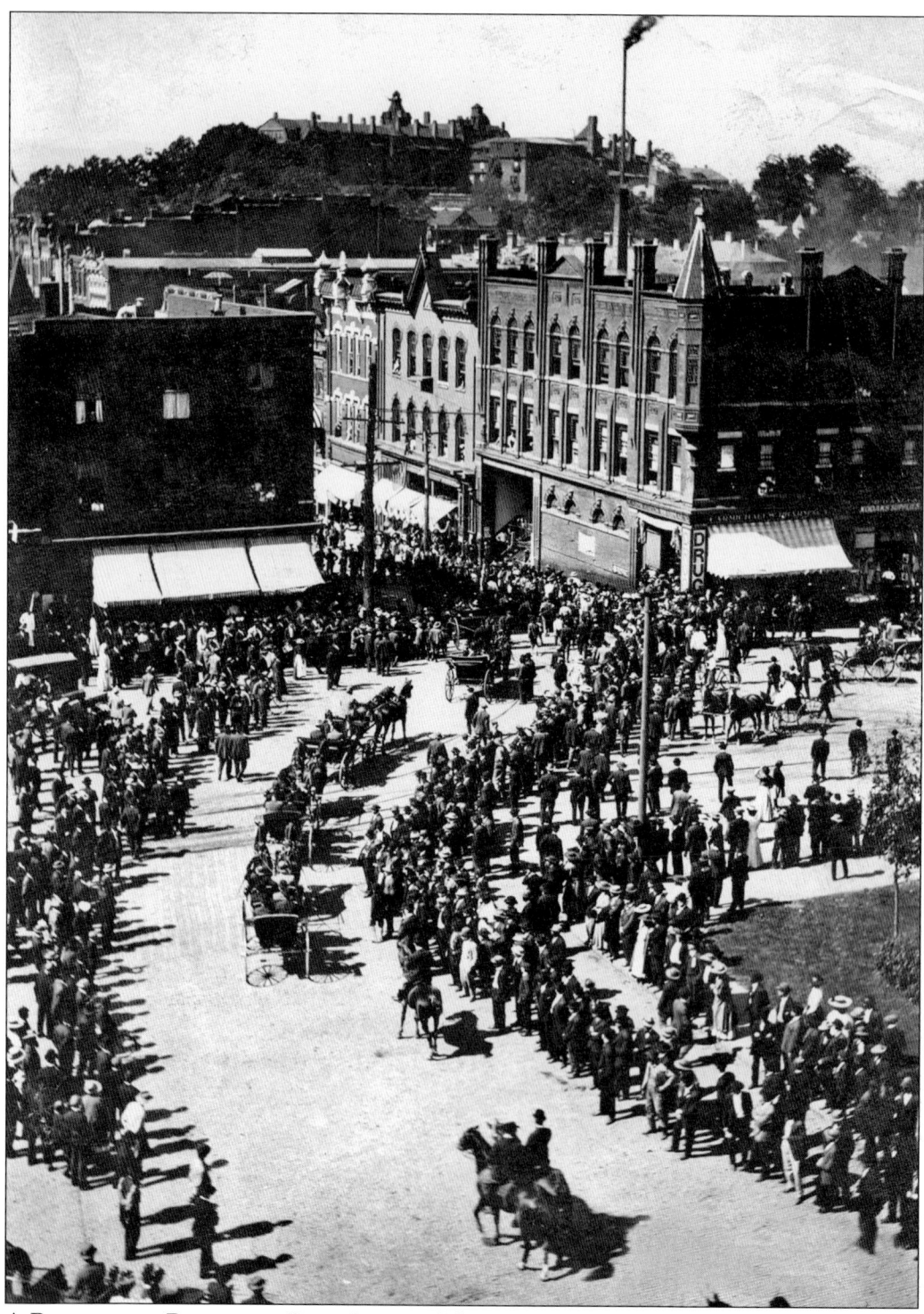

A PROHIBITION PARADE ON PACK SQUARE. The 1886 Battery Park Hotel is on top of the hill in the background, and the buildings on right side of Patton Avenue can be seen, beginning with the Revell Building, which housed Carmichael's Pharmacy, c. 1900.

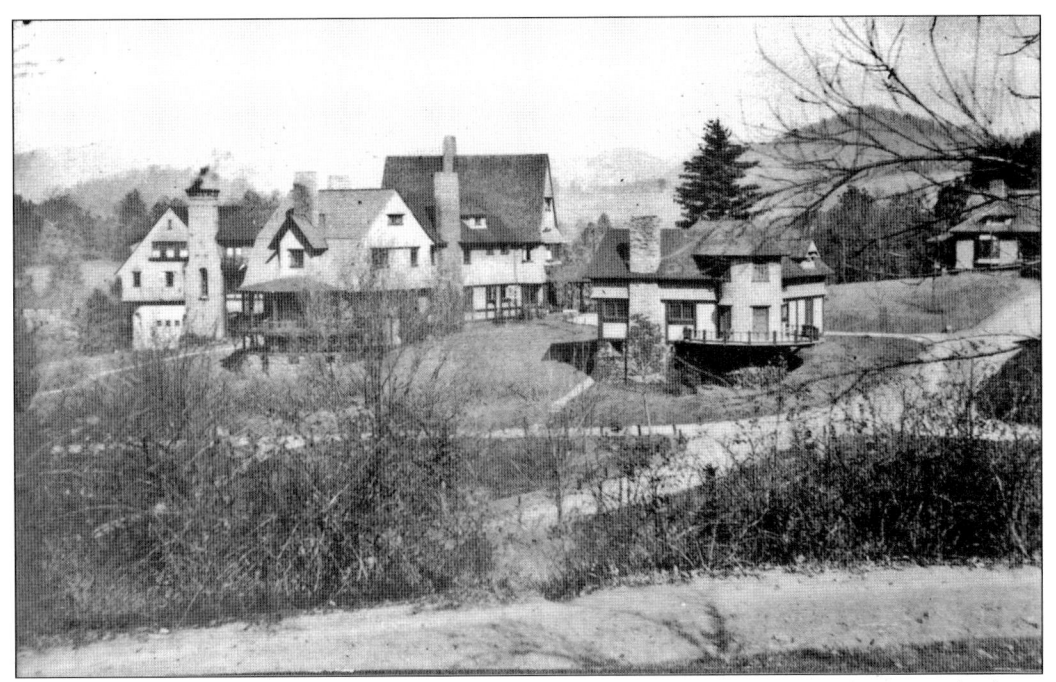

THE MANOR, WITH CLOVER COTTAGE TO THE RIGHT. The Lodge, the Gatehouse, and Clover Cottage were all built in 1898 as part of the Albemarle Park Development.

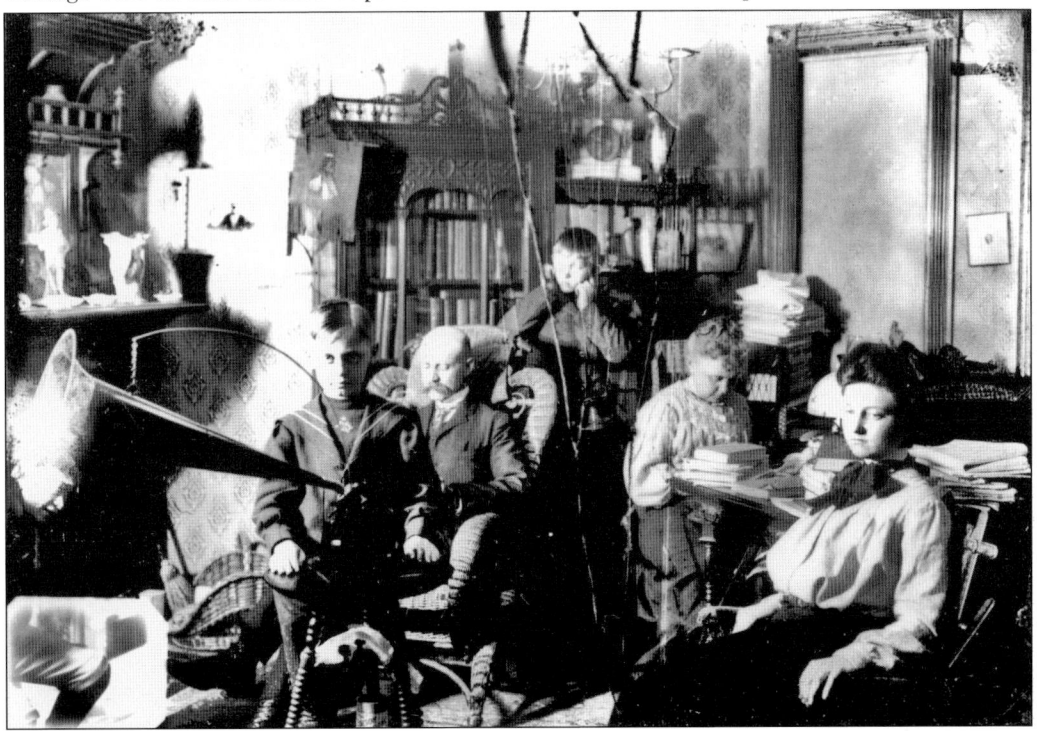

AN INTERIOR VIEW OF A GROVE STREET BOARDING HOUSE. This photo, c. 1903, is possibly of the Stephen J. Cain House, or of Three Oaks, which was operated by Mrs. Charles W. "Bessie" Carr. They were both listed in 1902–1903 city directories.

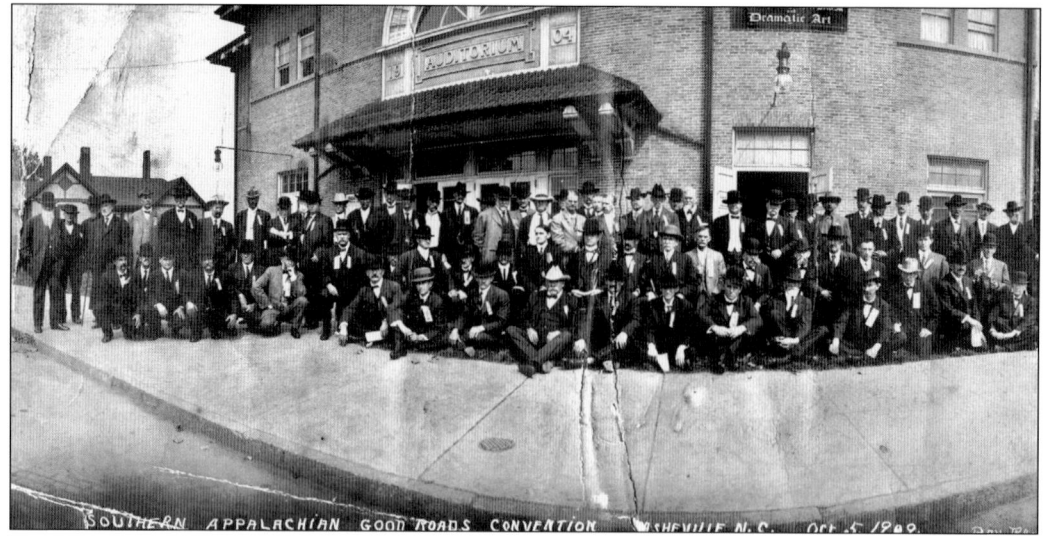

They Were Serious About Making North Carolina the Good Roads State. This portrait from the Southern Appalachian Good Roads Convention was taken on October 5, 1909, in front of the Asheville Auditorium, which also housed the Asheville School of Music and Dramatic Art. William J. Cocke is identified "on back row with large hat" and an arrow in the top margin.

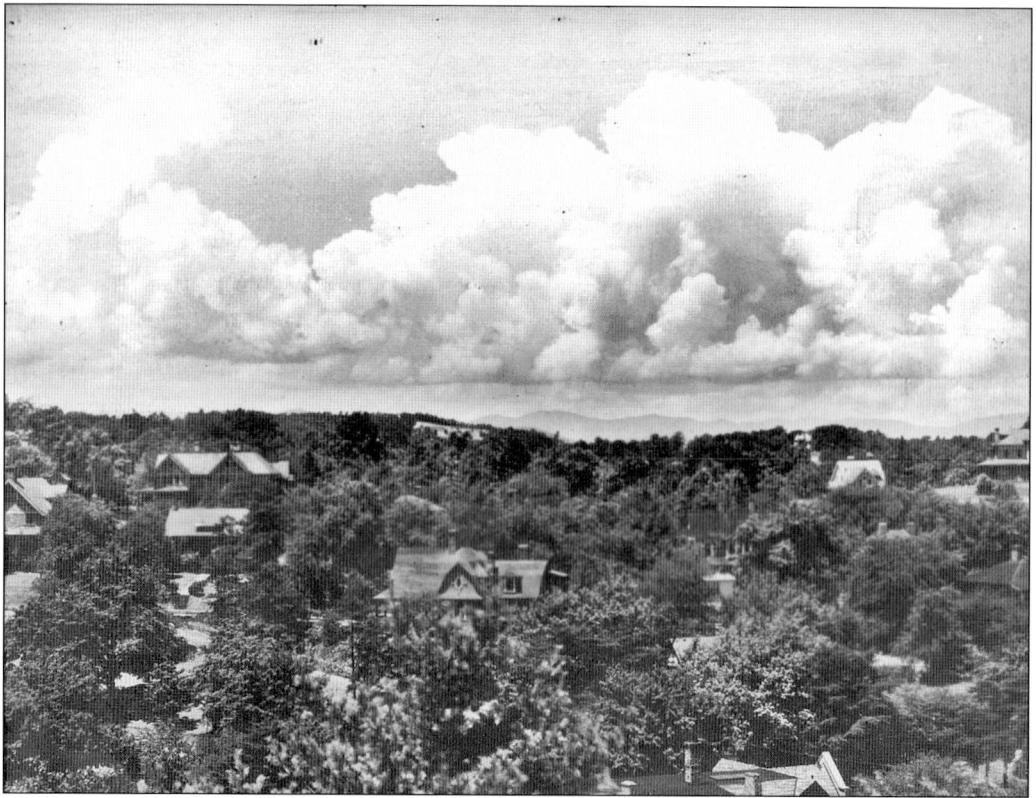

A View from the West of Montford Area. Today Montford is coming back as a popular and desirable late Victorian neighborhood.

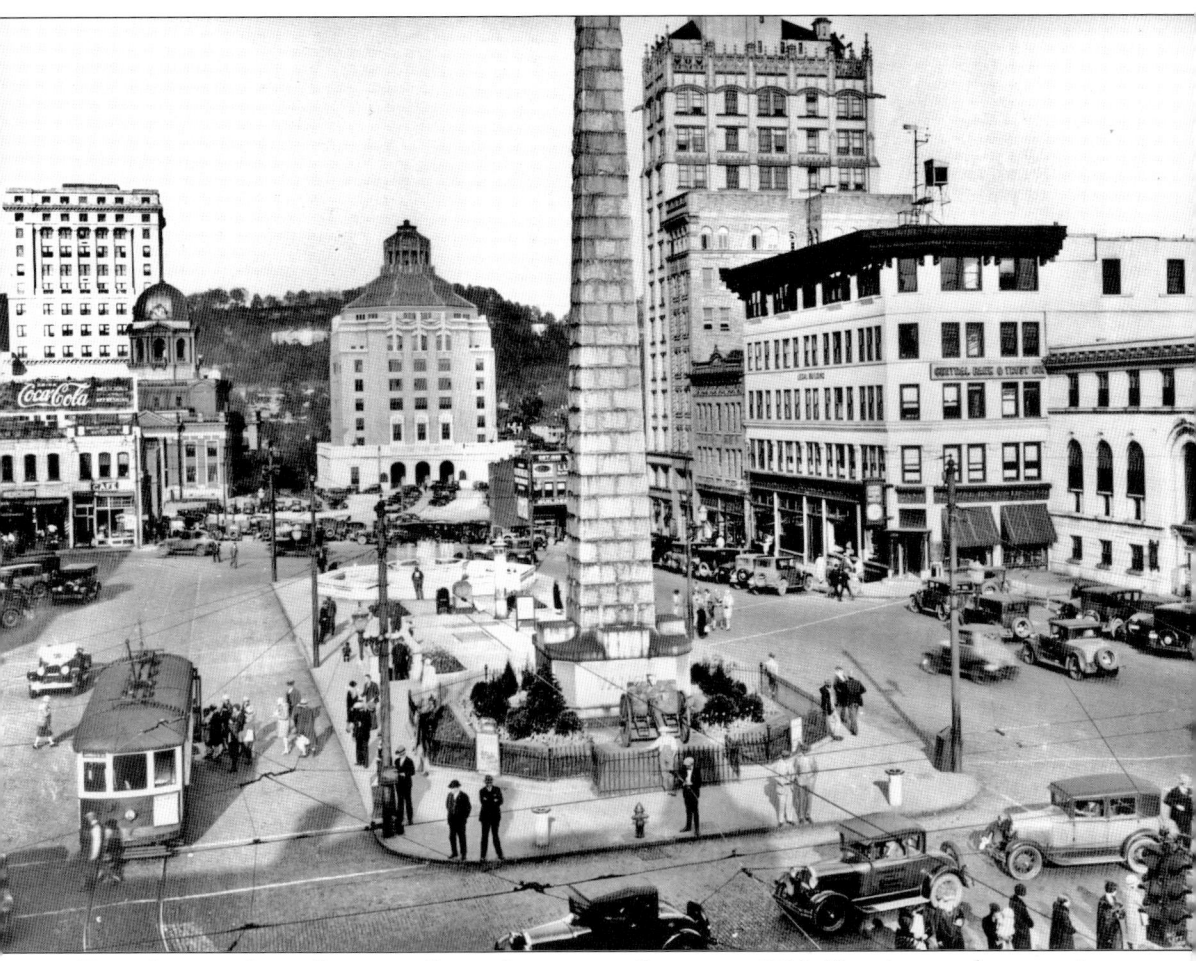

Pack Square Still Bustles, Even After the Crash of 1929. Here is a good perspective of the location of the 1903 courthouse in relation to the "new" City County Plaza, *c.* 1930. Steps between the monument and the fountain went to underground restrooms. The east end of Pack Square N is at left, with the Oates Building on the end. The 1926 Asheville City Hall and both the 1903 the 1928 Buncombe County Courthouses are to the left of Vance Monument. The older courthouse was probably demolished by the end of 1929. Pack Square S is to the right of monument; other buildings are, from right to left, the Pack Memorial Library; the Legal Building, with Central Bank & Trust and with weather bureau equipment on the roof; the Commerce Building; the Westall Building; and the Jackson Building. W.H. Westall Lumber Co. is behind the monument. The McIntyre Building, at NE Pack Square, houses the Central Cafe, Mercurio's Fruits, and Busse Pleating & Button Co.

83

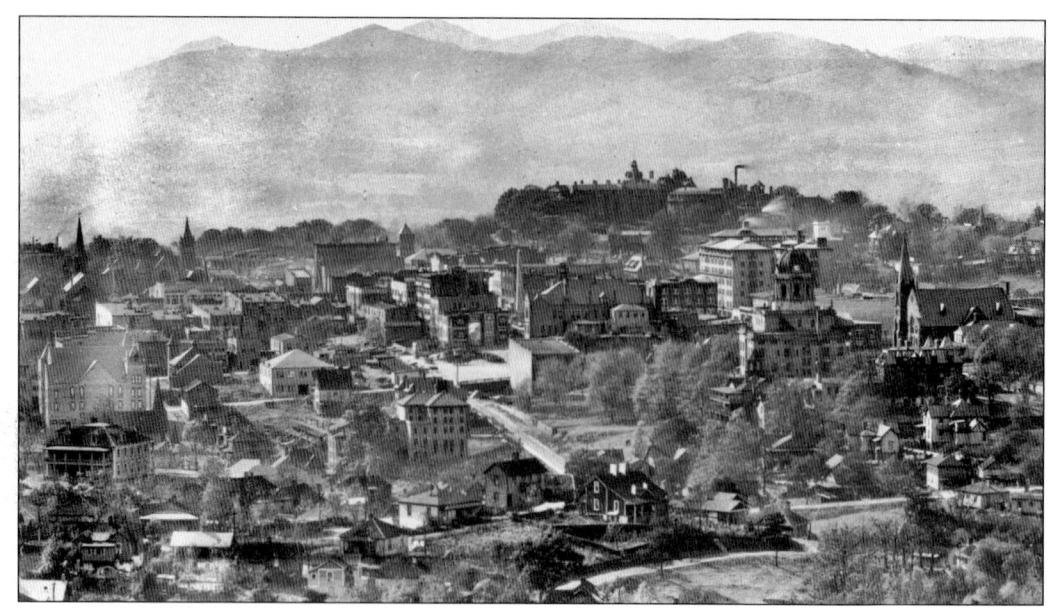

A 1920 View of Asheville from Beaucatcher Mountain. The 1886 Battery Park Hotel is on the hill in front of the mountain. The Valley Street area, including Davidson Street and Velvet/Short Velvet/Dixon Street, is in the foreground. The twin towers of St. Lawrence Catholic Church are at the right margin, behind Dr. Briggs's house and the Asheville Auditorium, built in 1904, on Haywood Street. The church at right middleground is First Baptist, on Spruce Street, with the 1903 courthouse to its left. Vance Monument is in the center, between Pack Square S and the 1892 city hall. The church spires at top left are First Presbyterian and Central Methodist. The buildings to the lower left are Mount Zion Baptist, St. Matthias Episcopal, the Masonic Temple, and the Seventh Day Adventist Church.

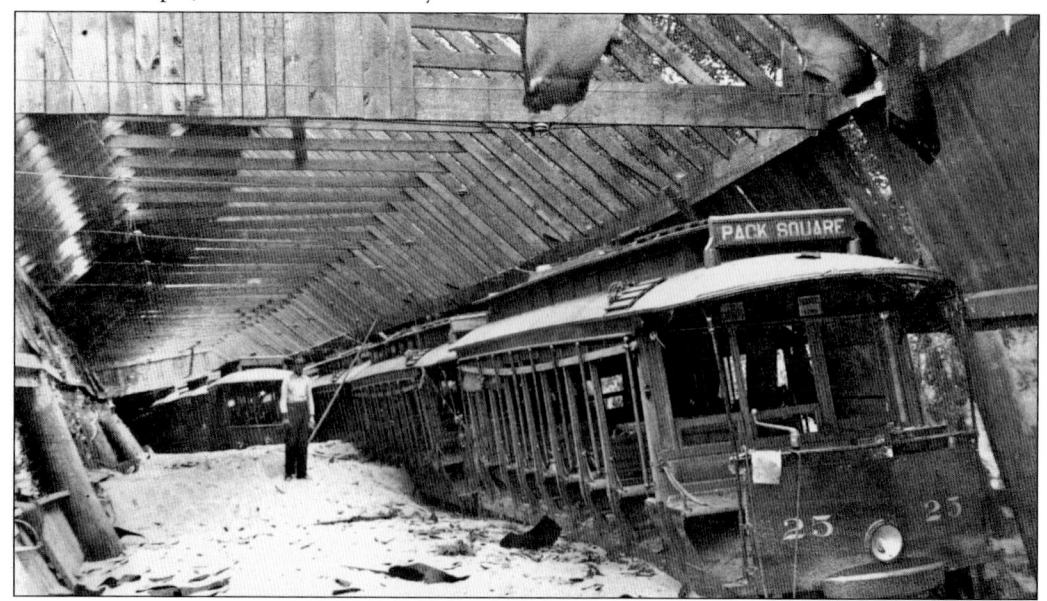

The 1916 Flood. This view is of the inside of a heavily damaged streetcar barn at Riverside Park after the 1916 flood; the entire building is leaning left and a large portion of roof is missing. At least five streetcars are parked inside; the one in front is the "Pack Square" no. 25.

84

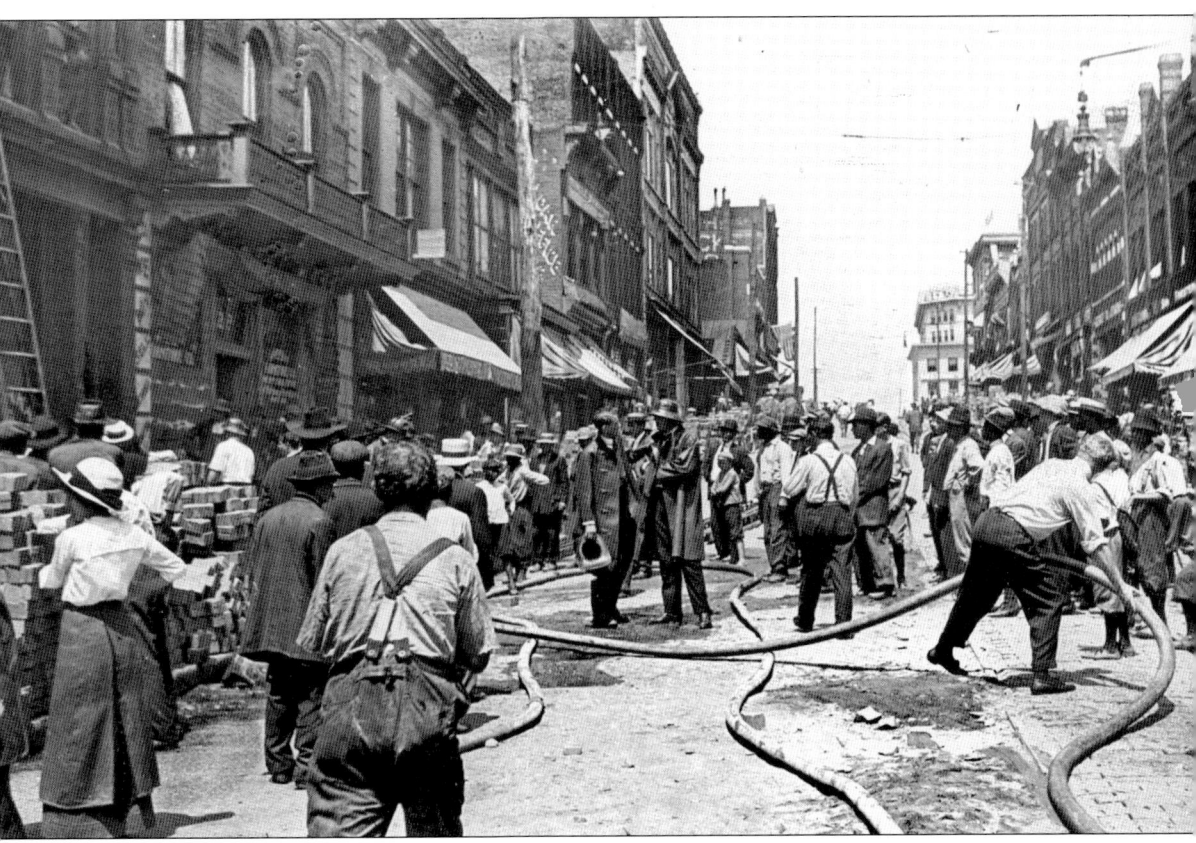

A FIRE AT THE SWANNANOA-BERKELEY HOTEL. This is the first photograph that William Barnhill sold to Eastman Kodak, supposedly of the scene in the street in front of the Swannanoa-Berkley Hotel as a minor fire burned in the summer of 1914. Asheville Fire Department records tell of a fire at the hotel on May 19, 1914, but no newspaper coverage has been found. The building to the left is two stories tall and does not match the images of the three-story Swannanoa-Berkeley Hotel; therefore, the view is believed to be a block north of the hotel, with the Asheville Furniture Co. sign at right. The building with the ladder, according to the city directory, would be N.S. Trakas & Co. Wholesale Fruits at #31 South Main; the directory places it at #29, but the window appears to read #22. The hotel sign on right may be for the Paxton Hotel. The view toward the square shows the top of the Langren Hotel. Other buildings on the west side of the street are, from left to right, Asheville Furniture Co., Beaumont Furniture Co., Finkelstein's Pawn Shop (#23–25), and others up to the Johnston Building. The Paxton Hotel is on the right side of the street. Notice the dirt street, with only area between the streetcar tracks bricked in, and the stack of bricks on the sidewalk at left.

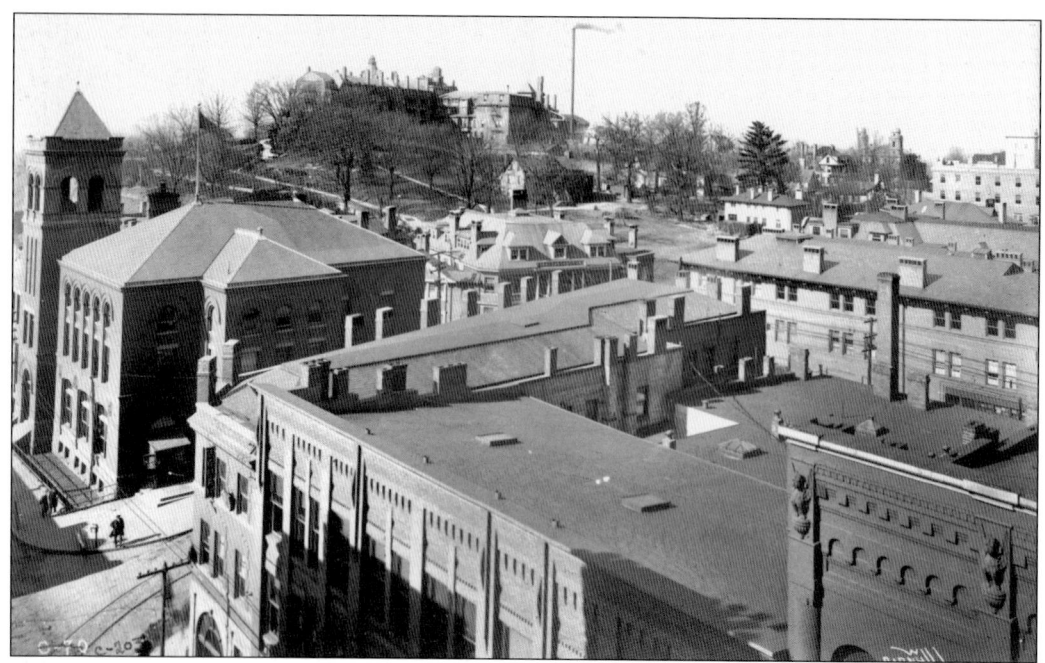

A VIEW FROM THE ROOF OF THE AMERICAN BANK BUILDING TOWARD BATTERY PARK HILL. The Patton Avenue intersection with Haywood Street is in the foreground, with the 1892 post office on the left and the Paragon/Citizens Bank Building on the right. The 1886 Battery Park Hotel is on the hill, with the Medical Building, on the corner of College and Haywood Streets, in front of it. The New Sondley Building is at right, on the opposite corner of Haywood Street. The tall building at right is the Elk's Home Building, with the St. Lawrence Tower to its left. (Photo by Barnhill, c. 1920.)

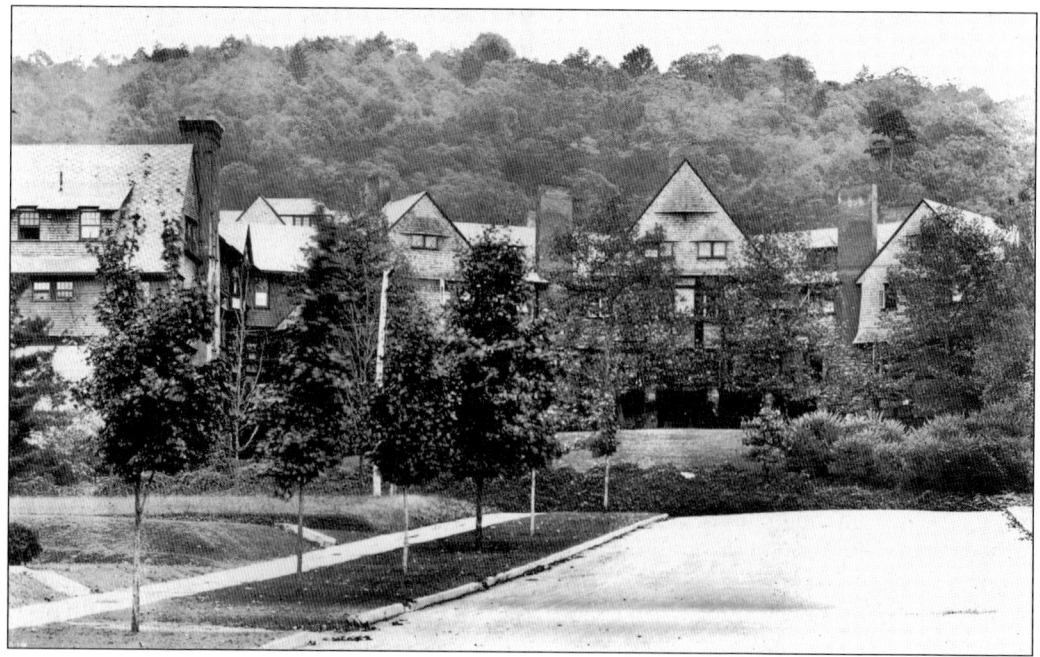

THE MANOR. This view of the Manor is taken from Edwin Place across Charlotte Street.

SEELY'S CASTLE. This view through trees is of Fred L. Seely's castle, which he named Overlook, profiled on top of Sunset Mountain. (Photo by Barnhill, c. 1920.)

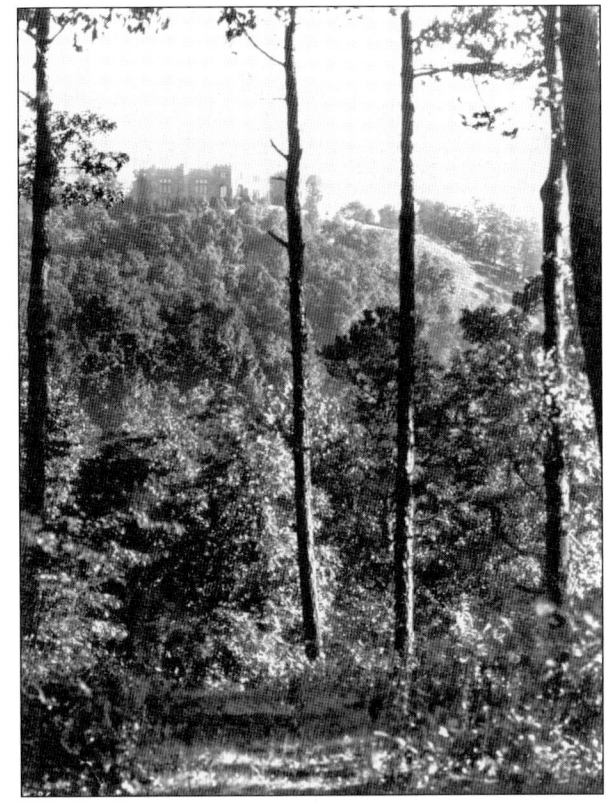

A VIEW OF THE LIVING ROOM OF SEELY'S CASTLE ON SUNSET MOUNTAIN. The living room features a high ceiling with exposed beams, two chandeliers, wood panel wainscoting, a stone fireplace, and a monochromatic rug over stone tile flooring. Fred Seely was the son-in-law of E.W. Grove.

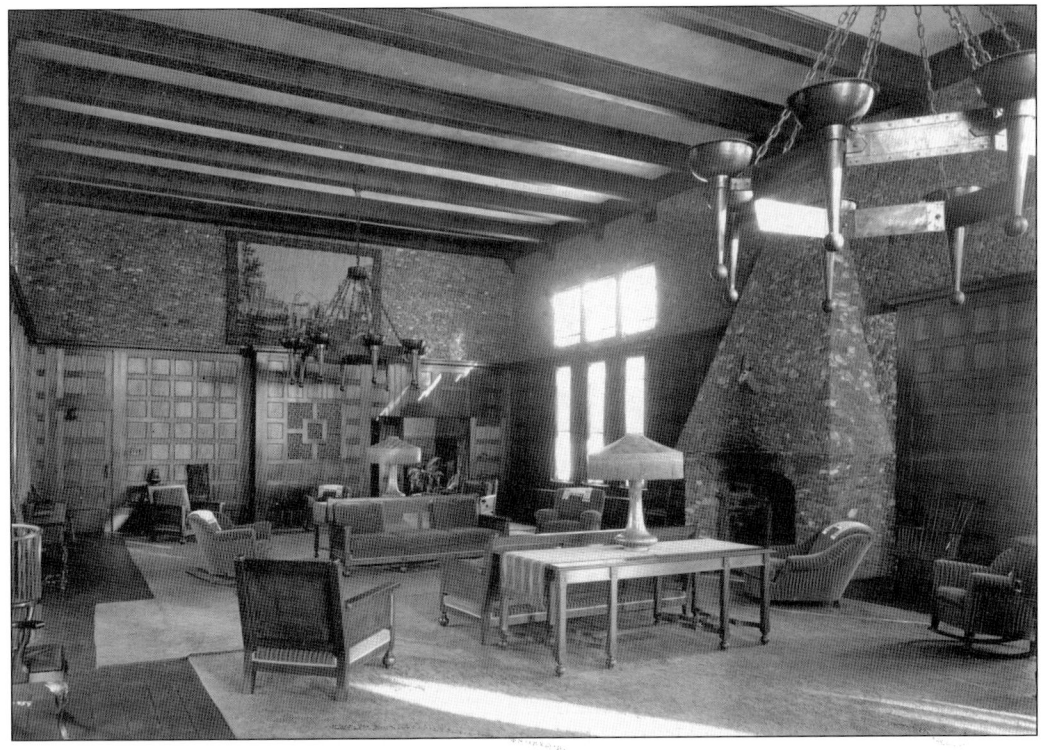

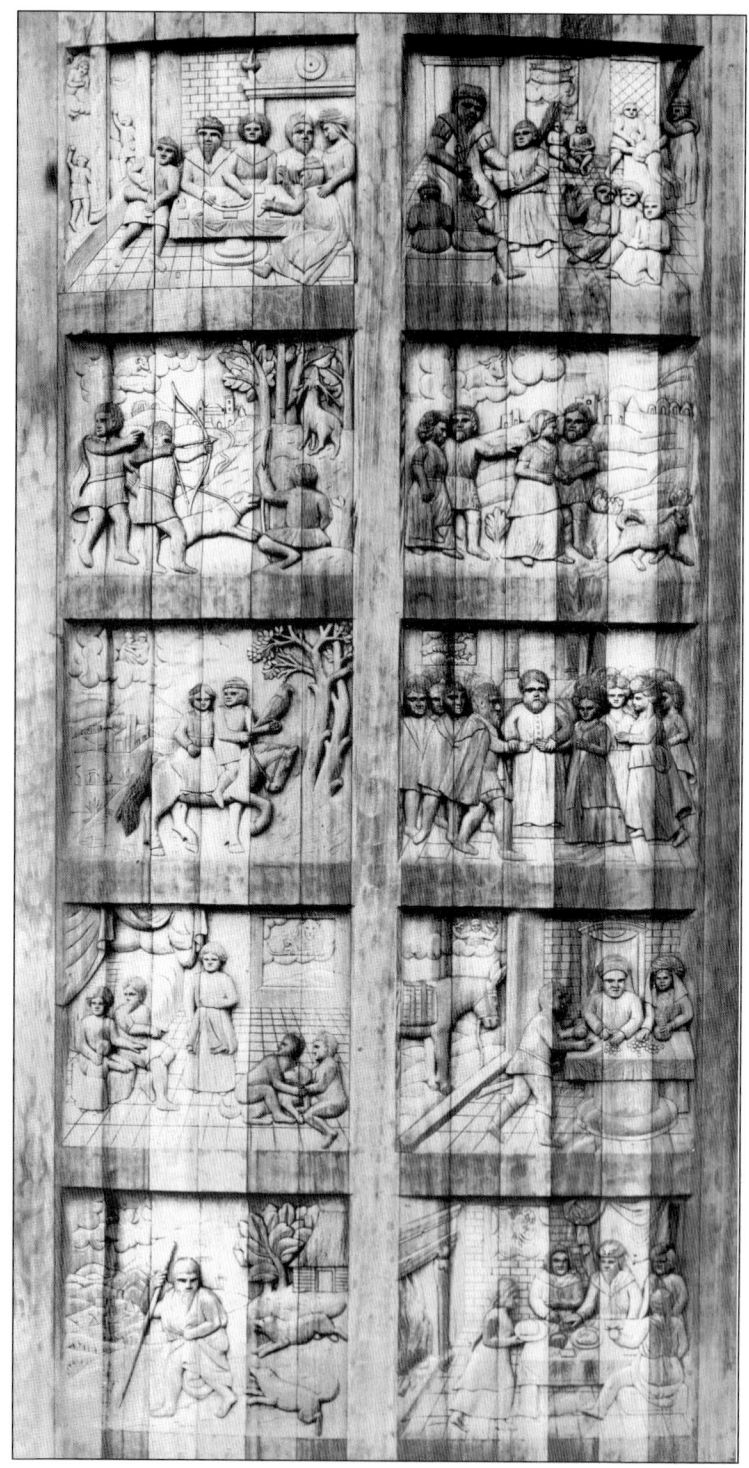

The Canterbury Tales. This is a detail of a door designed and carved by Eleanor P. Vance for Fred Seely's castle on Sunset Mountain. The panels show scenes from the *Canterbury Tales*. The door is now in a private home in Memphis, Tennessee.

OF CASTLES AND TURRETS. This view of Seely's castle, Overlook, shows the base of a stone turret, with the door designed and carved by Eleanor P. Vance in place.

THE MALVERN HILLS GOLF CLUBHOUSE. The clubhouse was designed by Ronald Greene and built at a cost of $27,000. It was constructed before 1926 in the Malvern Hill subdivision, an area formerly known as Sulfur Springs, adjacent to the grounds of The Asheville School. The head of the sulfur springs was enclosed in the open cellar of the clubhouse. A nine-hole course, designed by Carl R. Frye of Columbus, Ohio, accompanied the clubhouse.

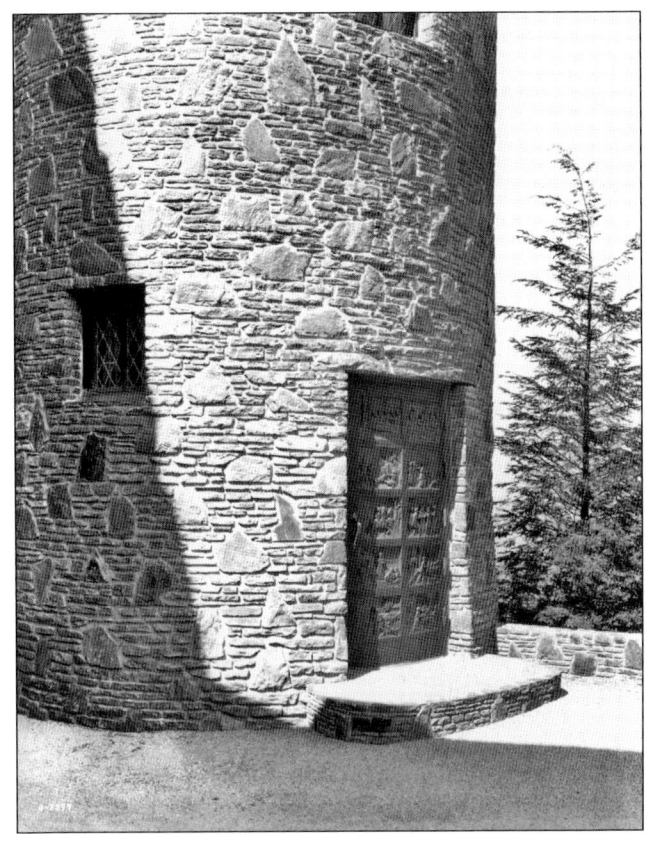

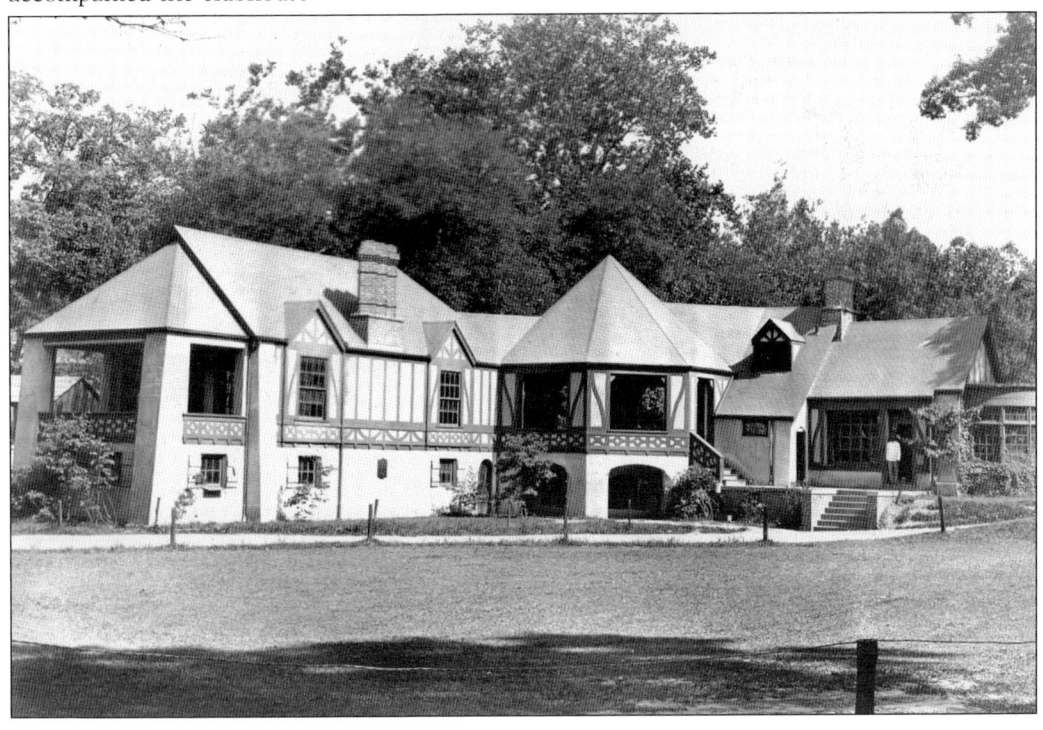

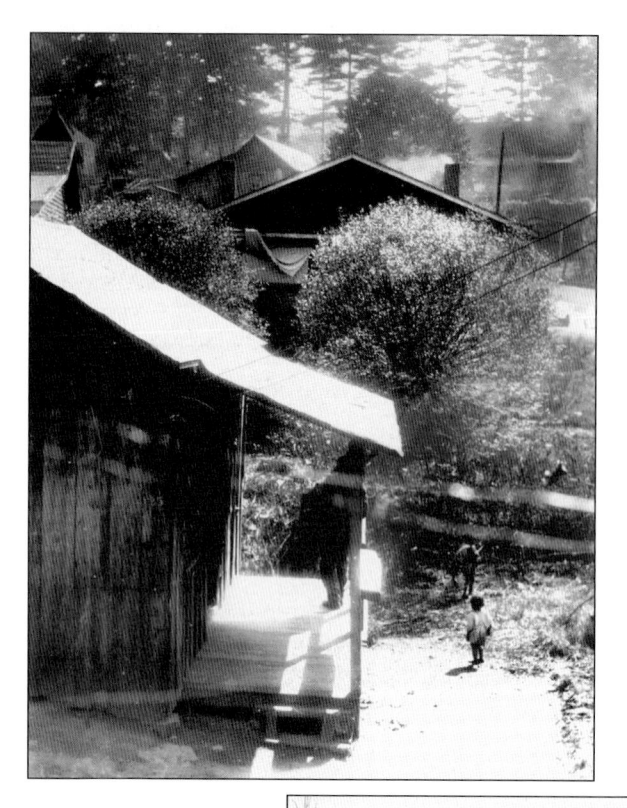

A View of the Valley Street Area. Valley Street was a historically African-American area of Asheville, shown here c. 1949, from one hill to another. The Valley Street area was reportedly part of Thomas Wolfe's newspaper route.

A Street Scene: Eagle Street at the Intersection of Valley Street. Eagle Street Cut Rate Market is at the far left corner; the Ever Ready Café is across the street in the center of the photo. The pedestrian at right may be Frank Wolfe.

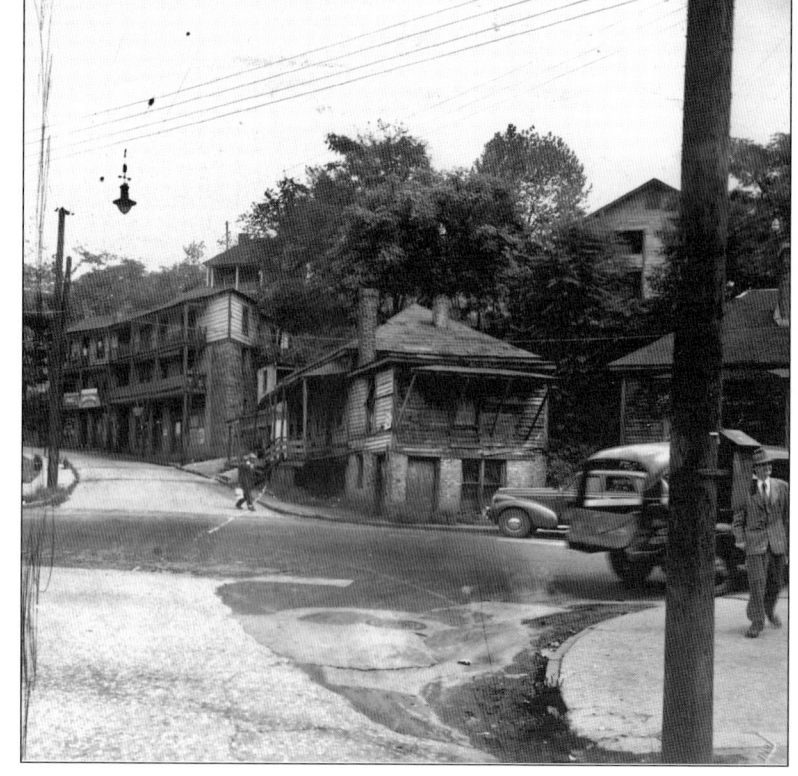

DOUBLE EXPOSURE. This little boy is riding a pedal-car in the Valley Street section of Asheville, c. 1949.

THE ISAAC DICKSON HOUSE. Isaac Dickson, a businessman of growing importance in early Asheville, was the son of a Dutch landowner and a freed slave from Shelby, North Carolina. The Valley Street area was known for some time as "Dickson Town." Dickson co-founded the Young Men's Institute and was the first African-American man to serve on a North Carolina school board. The house served as a funeral home for many years. Downtown buildings are visible, including the Jackson Building.

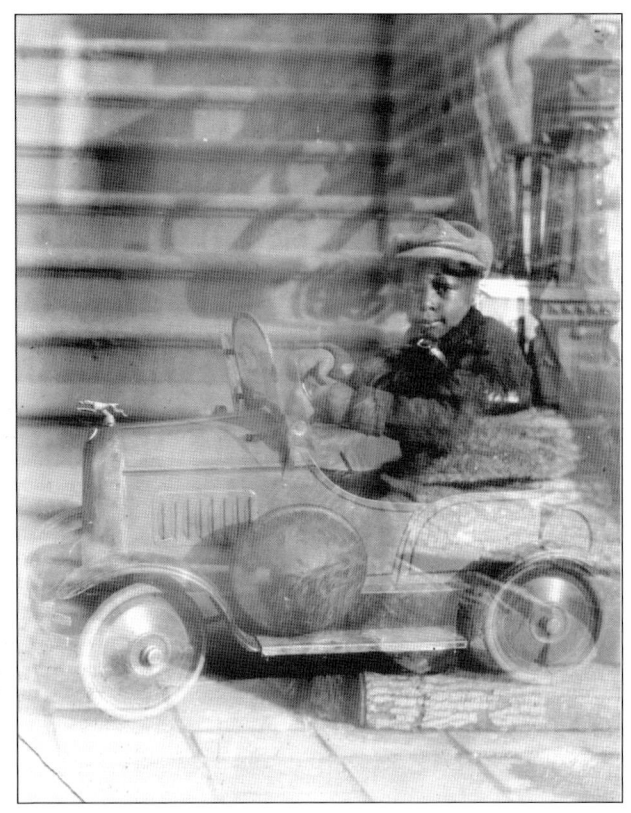

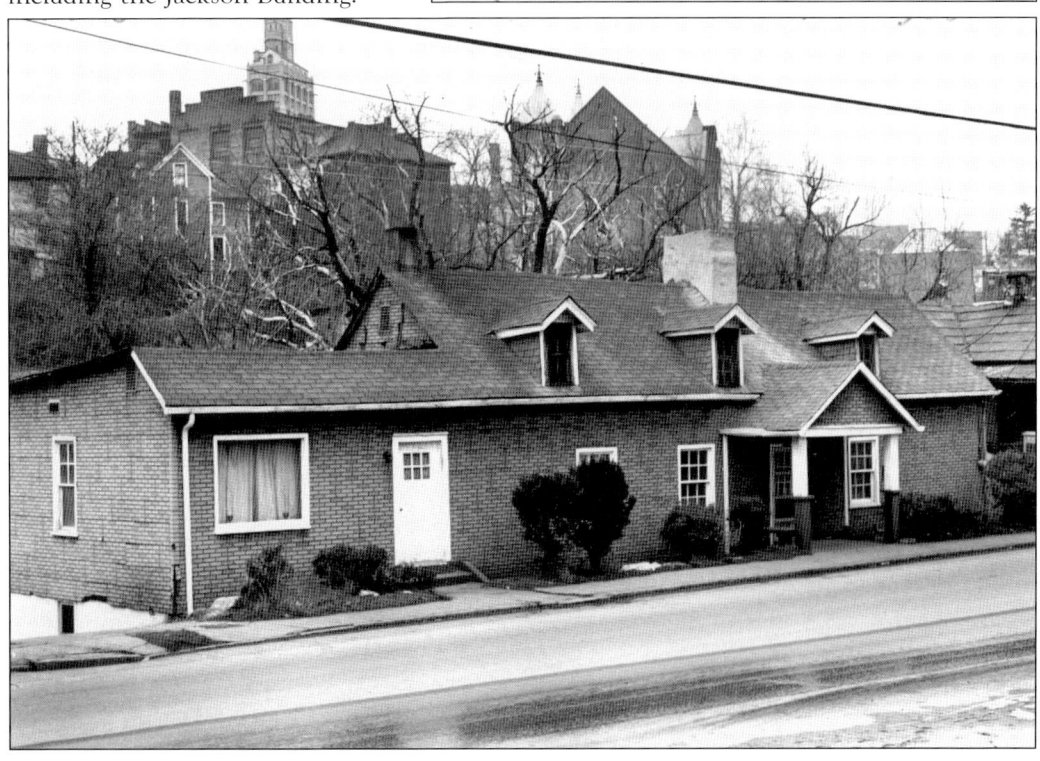

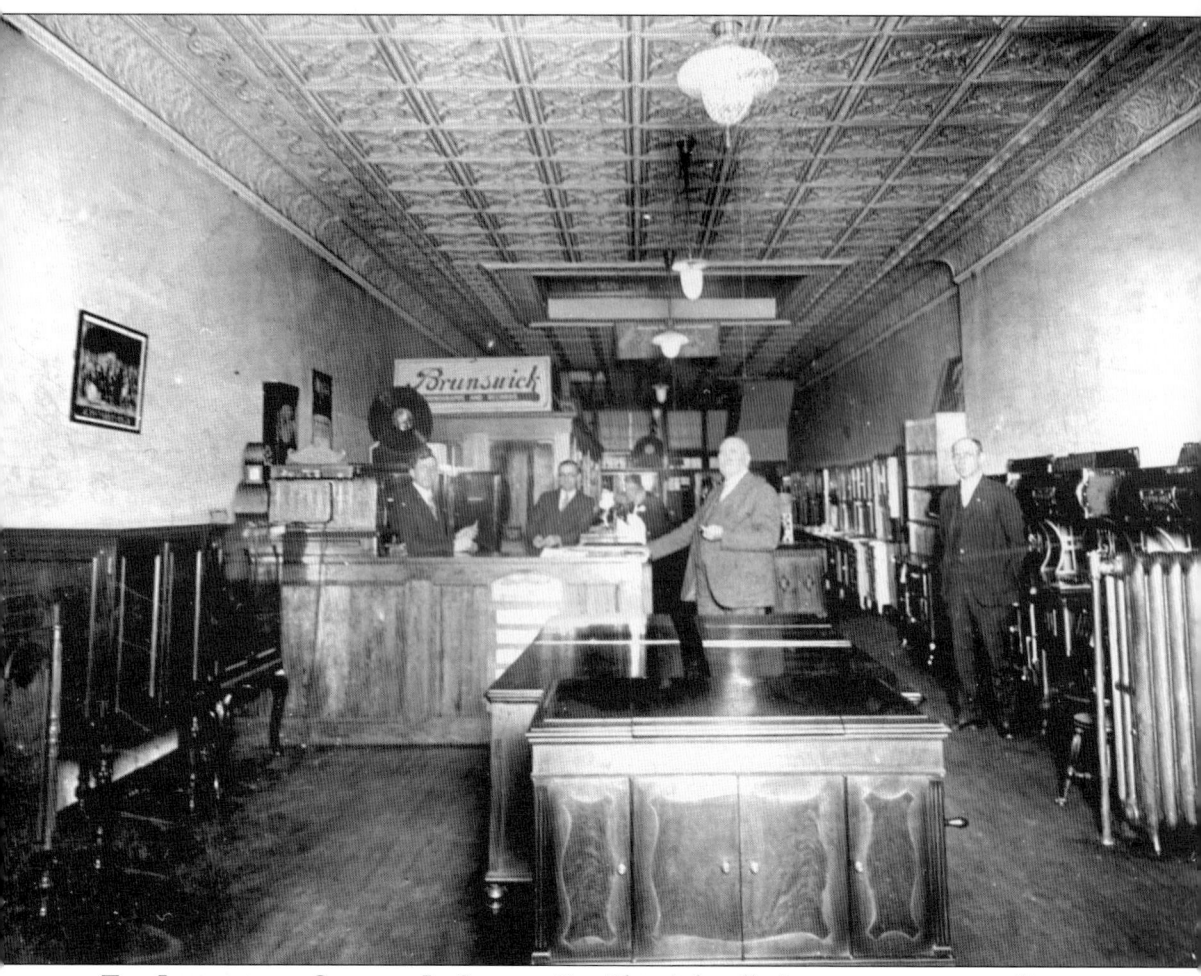

The Interior of Charles L. Sluder Co. This Asheville furniture company still survives today. The large man in center is Charles Sluder, who opened his first store in 1905 at 62 South Main Street. This store opened in 1936 at 19 Broadway Avenue, and moved into 25 Broadway Avenue in 1938. Sluder died in the early 1950s. The store features Brunswick phonographs and records along with large pieces of furniture.

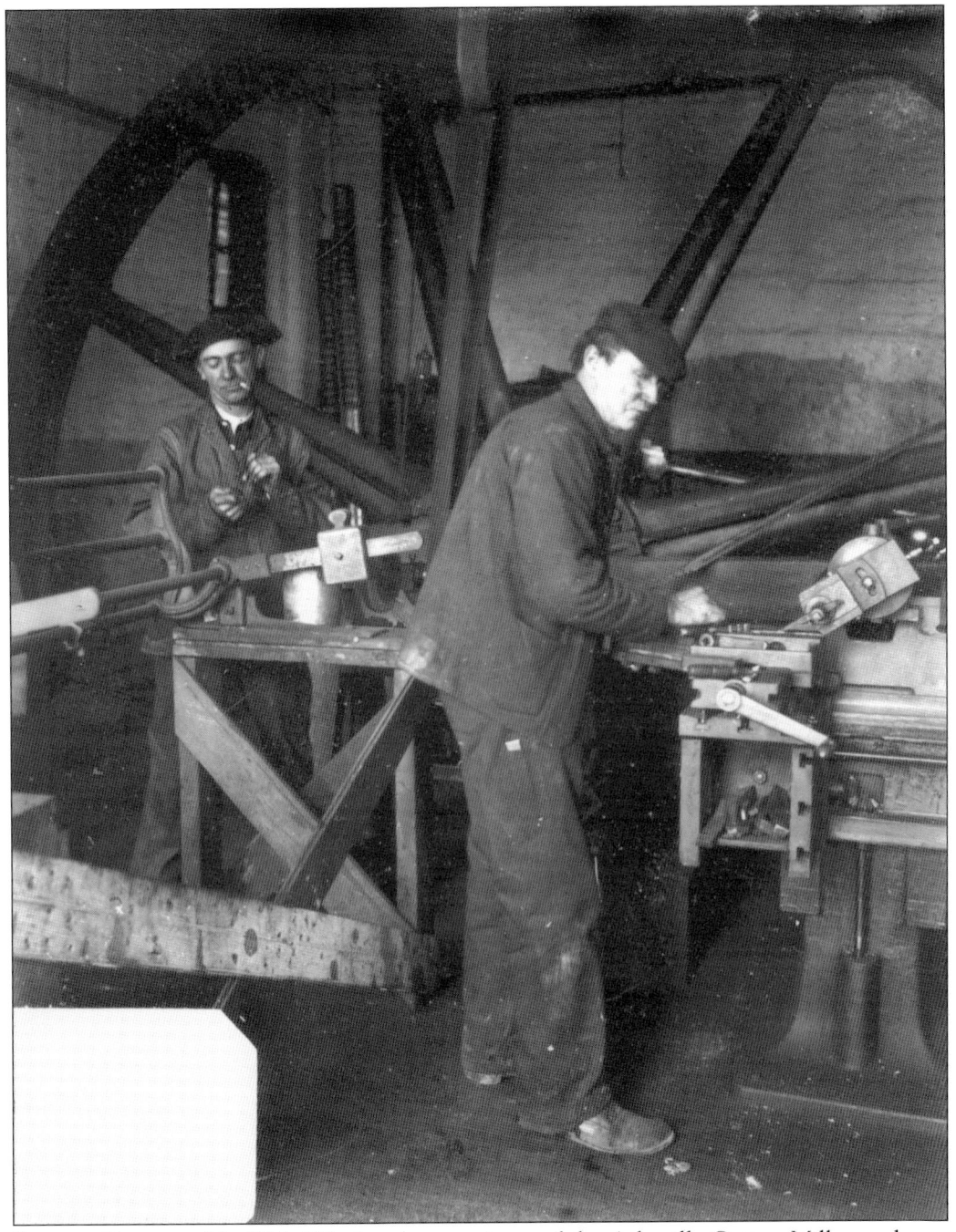

SUNDAY REPAIRS. Mr. W.A. Ward and an engineer of the Asheville Cotton Mills are shown doing "Sunday repairs," c. 1905–1910.

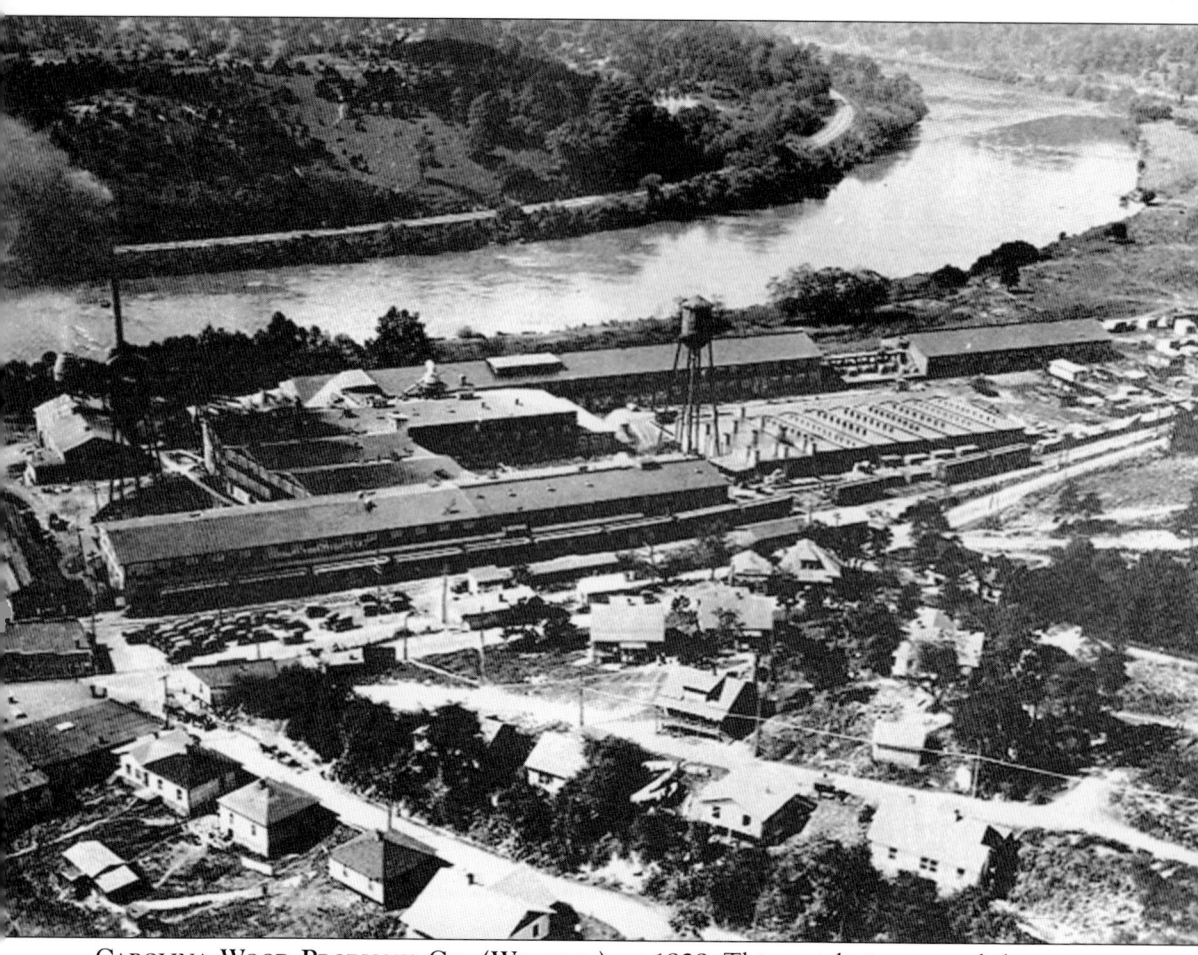

CAROLINA WOOD PRODUCTS CO. (WOODFIN) IN 1929. This aerial view toward the river, at top, shows a residential area in foreground. Expansion of Asheville included both residential and commercial development on the northern edge of the city in adjacent Woodfin.

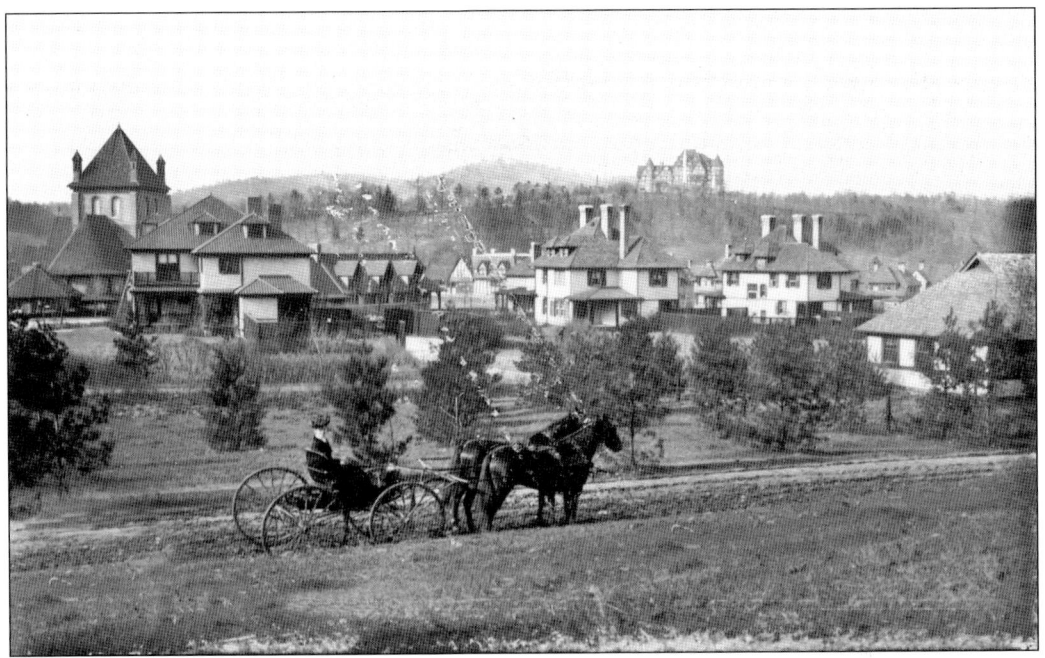

BILTMORE BY HORSE-AND-BUGGY. A woman rides a two-horse carriage in the foreground; Kenilworth Inn is on the hill at top right. Biltmore Village runs across the middle of the photo, with All Souls Episcopal Church on the left, c. 1903.

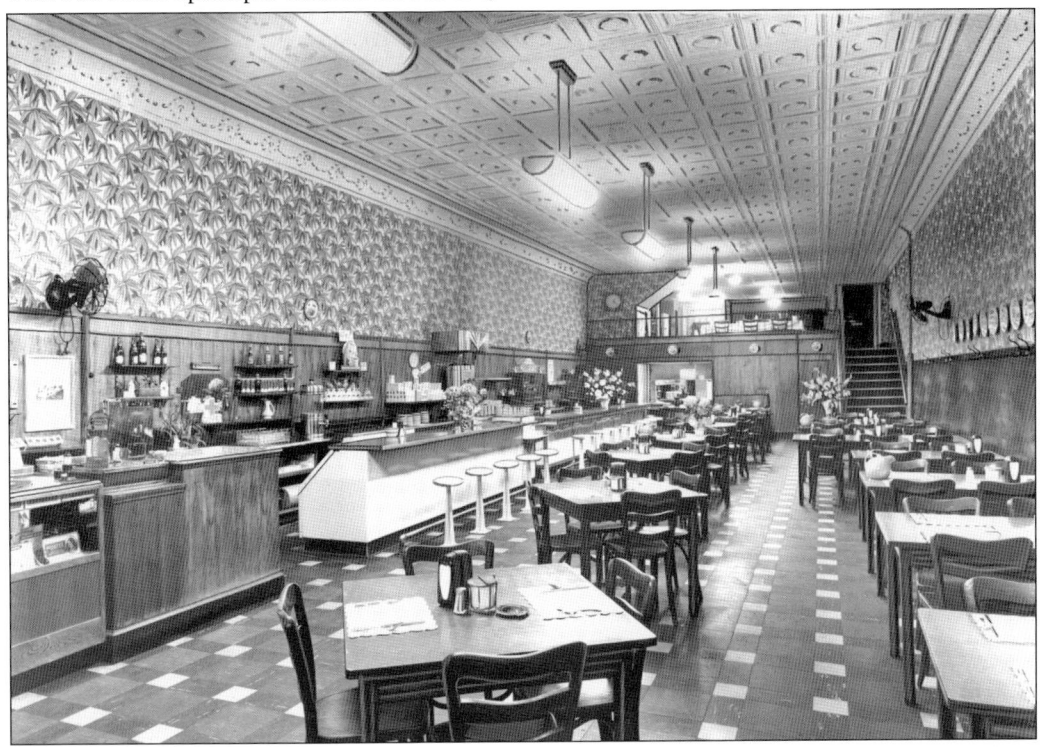

A RECENT PACK LIBRARY ACQUISITION. This photo of the popular Tingle's Cafe on Broadway Street was recently donated to the Pack Library's North Carolina Collection.

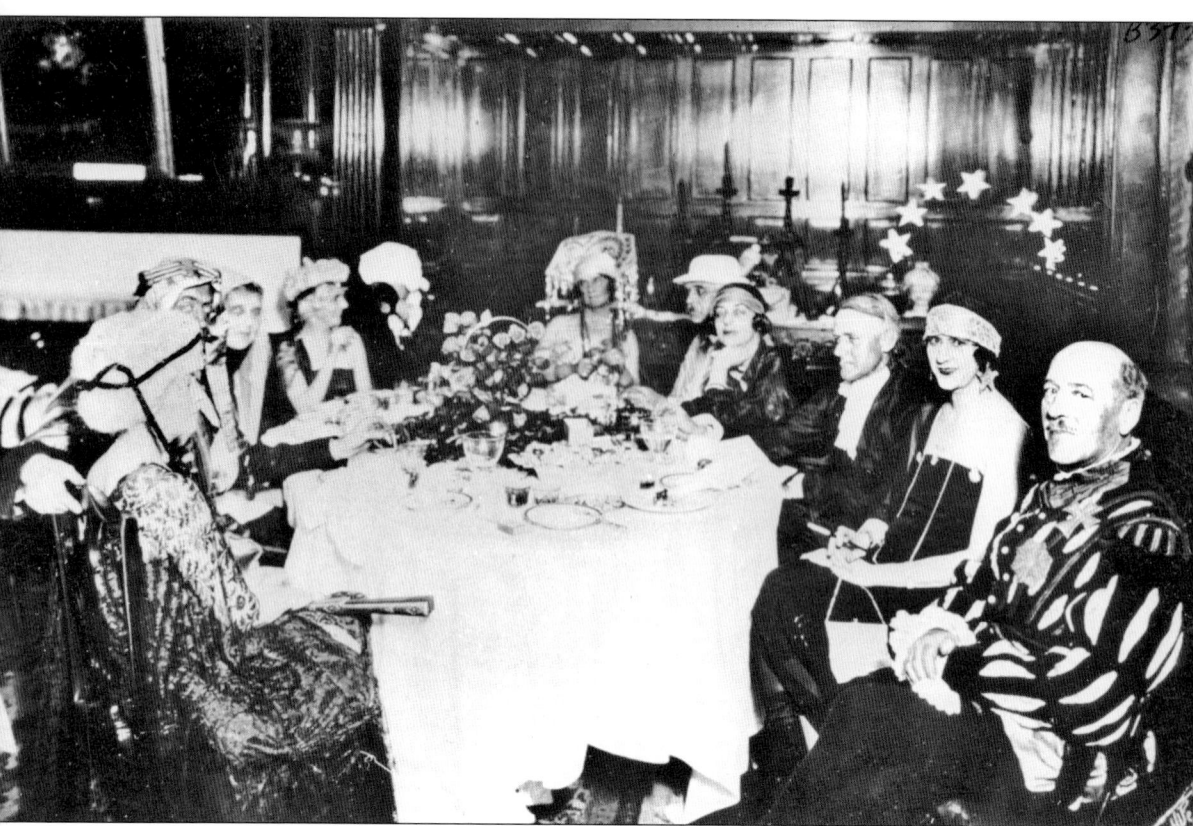

A Festive Gathering at Zealandia. Eleven people in costume are shown seated at the round table. Sir Philip Henry is at far right, seated next to Edith (Mrs. George) Vanderbilt. Mrs. Vanderbilt is wearing a hat with seven stars suspended on a wire above it and star earrings. Philip S. Henry, a businessman whose art collection later became the basis of the Asheville Art Museum, commissioned the home in the English manorial Tudor style. He named the estate after his years spent in New Zealand as a diplomat.

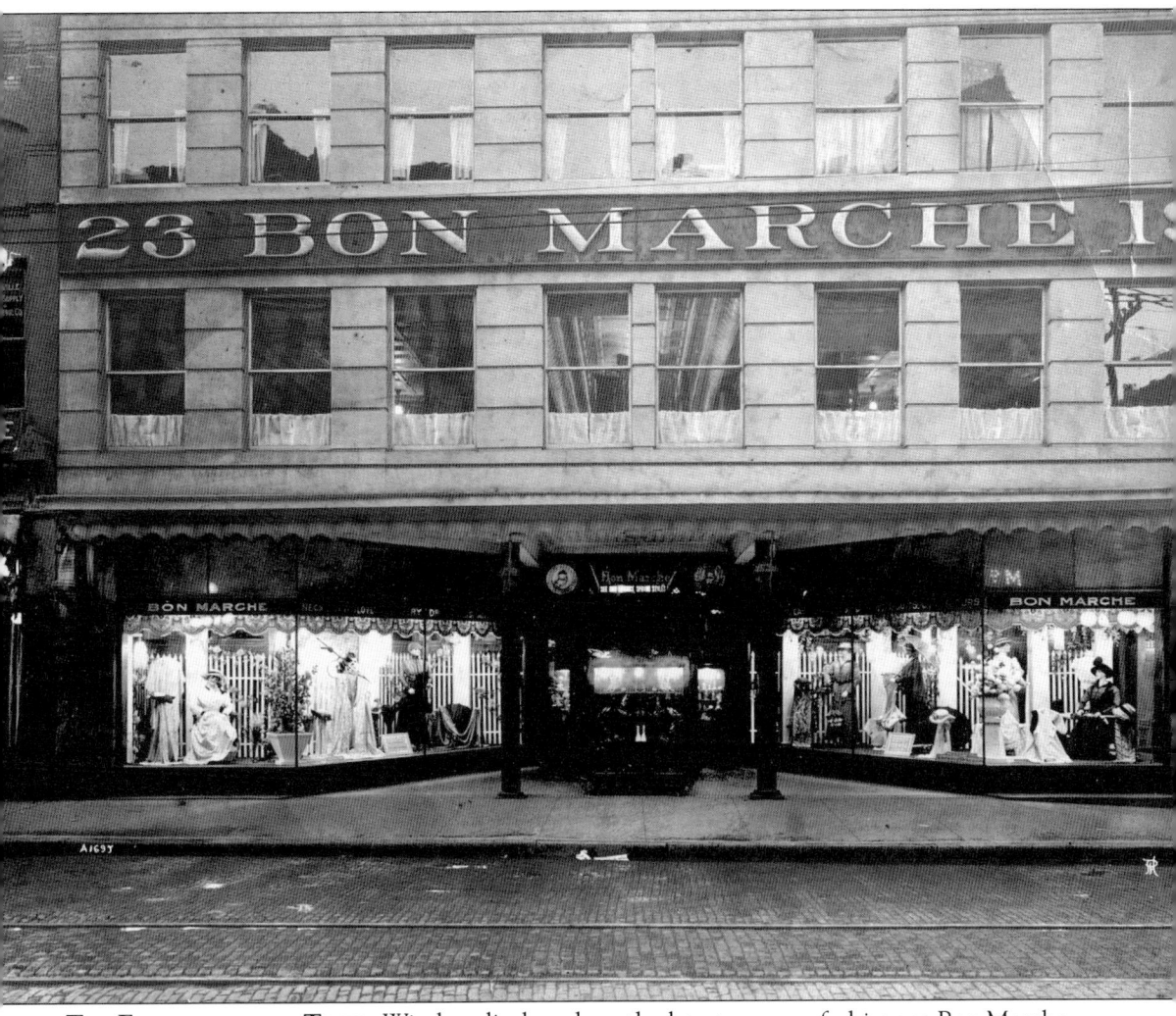

THE FASHION OF THE TIMES. Window displays show the latest summer fashions at Bon Marche, a clothing store on Patton Avenue c. 1913–1923; this would be the future site of the Kress Building.

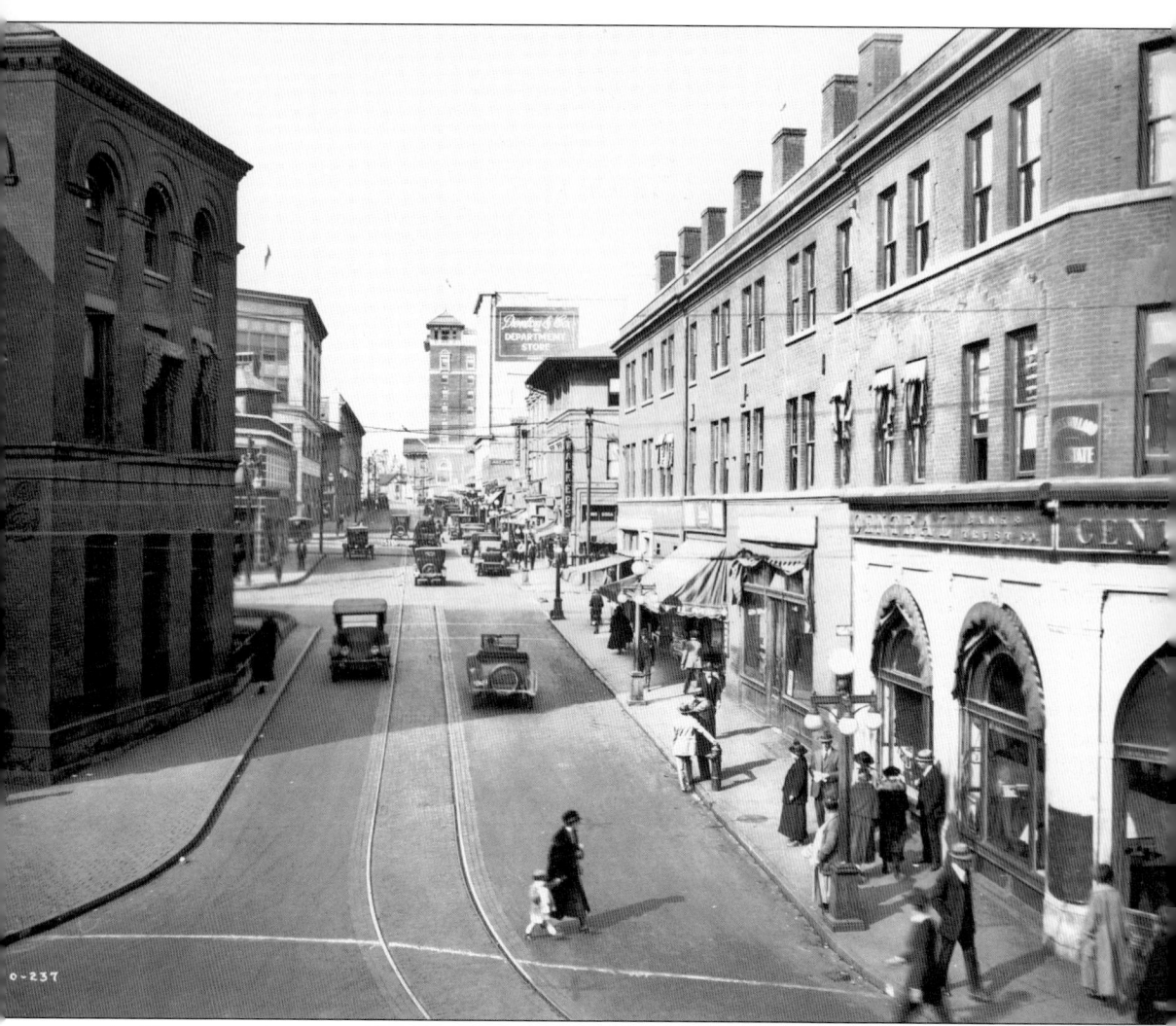

A Century Ago on Haywood Street. This view north along Haywood Street from Patton Avenue shows, on the left, the 1892 post office, the Miles Building, the Iveys Building, unidentified, and the Haywood Building. On the right are the Central Bank and Trust Co., Willard Real Estate, and others in the Paragon Building. Walker's drug store is across College Street in the New Sondley Building; signs advertise the *Daily Citizen* and The Adelaide Boarding House in front of Denton's Department Store. In the background are the Vanderbilt Hotel, the City Auditorium, and a house on Flint Street. Notice the streetcar tracks.

Seven

THE ARTISANS

Long before industrialists like the Vanderbilts or the Groves came to Asheville, mountain men and women were crafting many artistic forms, including carving, pottery, weaving, and glassmaking. Early local businesses included the Treasure Chest, the Log Cabin, Brown Brothers Pottery, and Noncannah Pottery. The Treasure Chest flourished as a retail outlet for local craftspeople in the Asheville area from approximately 1926 until about 1931 when it merged with another craft outlet, the Log Cabin. Together, they became known as the Three Mountaineers, which continued until 1992.

Even the Vanderbilts wanted to get in on some of the local craft business, founding Biltmore Estate Industries in 1901 in Biltmore Village. Crafts for many of these businesses were gathered from artisans in the Asheville and Western North Carolina area; Edith Vanderbilt recognized the value and potential of much of the weaving done by local women in "mountain cabins." Today, "mountain pottery" is a popular collectible, found in various shops and online at eBay.

Biltmore Estate Industries was founded by Charlotte Yale and Eleanor Vance, whose original purpose in coming to Asheville was missionary. However, they strongly believed in providing the local population with a trade, so they developed a craft education program. They encouraged the development of homespun and wool creations, which was inspired from a previous trip to Scotland; they returned from that trip with a model of the loom they would mass-produce for Biltmore Estate Industries. Much of their work was subsidized by the Vanderbilt family, specifically George W. Vanderbilt and Edith Vanderbilt, who were strong supporters of mountain arts and crafts.

George Vanderbilt died in 1914, and Fred L. Seely purchased Biltmore Industries from Edith Vanderbilt in 1917. He built six new buildings adjacent to the Grove Park Inn. He assured Edith Vanderbilt that he would continue its educational features and develop the arts as a commercial enterprise. The business was known locally as the Homespun Shops.

Under Seely, focus shifted more to weaving than some of the other crafts, including cabinetmaking, and slowly more artisans left. Fred Seely died in 1942, but the operation continued until its purchase in 1953 by Asheville businessman Harry Blomberg.

In 1992, the legacy of Biltmore Industries continued with the opening of Grovewood Gallery, which now represents more than 400 artisans from around the country. Each of Seely's original six buildings has been restored by the Blomberg family.

Just east of Asheville in Buncombe County, the town of Black Mountain played an important part in the history of the arts of the 20th century. Founded in 1933, Black Mountain College was a reaction to the more traditional schools of the time, having formed after students and professors fled Rollins College in Winter Park, Florida. They knew that a strong liberal and fine arts education must happen simultaneously inside and outside the classroom, so the founders of Black Mountain College combined communal living with an informal class structure. Black Mountain created a learning environment that was to revolutionize the arts and sciences of its time. In 1936, the student body numbered 26, with the average age being 18–25. Many of these students chose the Black Mountain College experience over such schools as Harvard and Vassar. Students and faculty alike realized that Black Mountain

College was one of the few schools sincerely dedicated to educational and artistic experimentation; here students and faculty performed what was to become some of the first performance art in the country.

Among Black Mountain's first professors were the artists Josef and Anni Albers, who had fled Nazi Germany after the closing of the Bauhaus. Their progressive work in painting and textiles first attracted students from around the country.

By the 1940s, Black Mountain's faculty included some of the most distinguished artists and thinkers of the time: Walter Gropius, Jacob Lawrence, Willem de Kooning, Robert Motherwell, composer John Cage, Alfred Kazin, dance choreographer Merce Cunningham, and Paul Goodman. The board of directors included William Carlos Williams and Albert Einstein. One day, students might be studying drawing with Albers; another, they might find themselves working on Buckminster Fuller's geodesic dome.

In the mid-1940s, Fuller began work on a project at Black Mountain College that would not only make him famous, but it would revolutionize the field of engineering. A designer, architect, poet, educator, engineer, philosopher, and environmentalist, Fuller believed that humanity's major problems were hunger and homelessness. He dedicated his life to solving those problems through inexpensive and efficient design. Using lightweight plastics in the simple form of a tetrahedron (a triangular pyramid) he created a small dome. As his work continued it became clear that he had made the first building that could sustain its own weight with no practical limits. The U.S. government recognized the importance of the discovery and employed him to make small domes for the army. Within a few years there were thousands of these domes around the world.

By the late 1940s, word of what was happening in North Carolina had started to spread throughout the country. It was the foremost expression of American experimental education and would profoundly influence arts education at many major American institutions with its emphasis on mixing different genres in one academic experience.

By 1953, Black Mountain College had fulfilled its dream. Many of the students and faculty were leaving for San Francisco and New York. With this exodus, Black Mountain College would forever change the possibilities of American education. Realizing that they had essentially achieved their goals, they closed their doors forever.

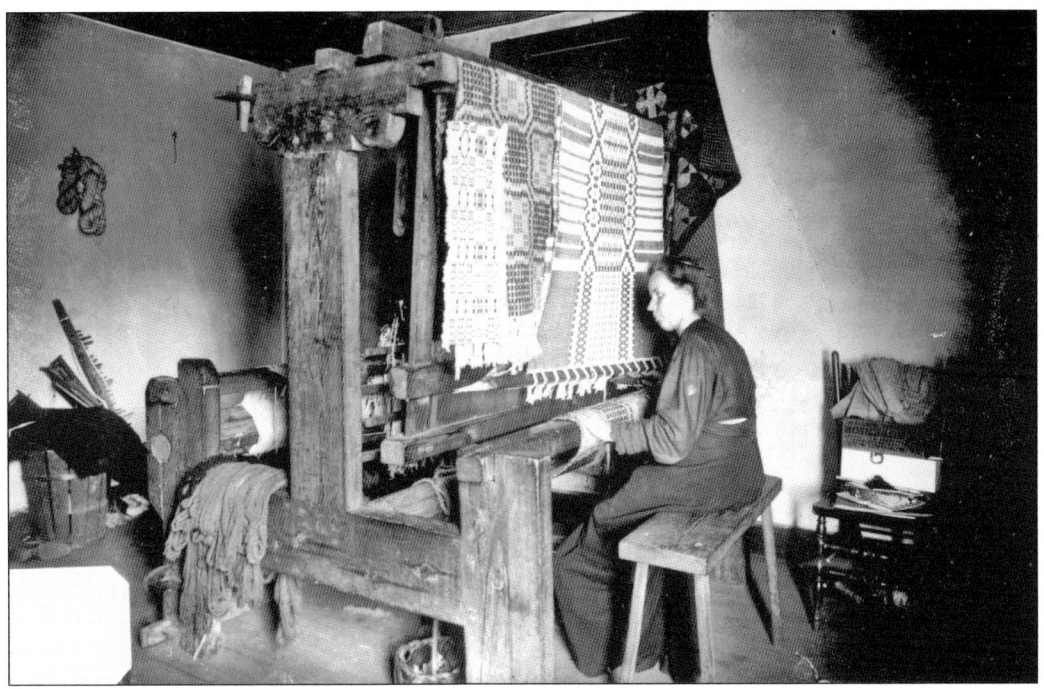

WEAVING ON BILTMORE AVENUE, 1905–1906. An unidentified woman sits at a loom at a weaving plant on Biltmore Avenue in 1905–1906.

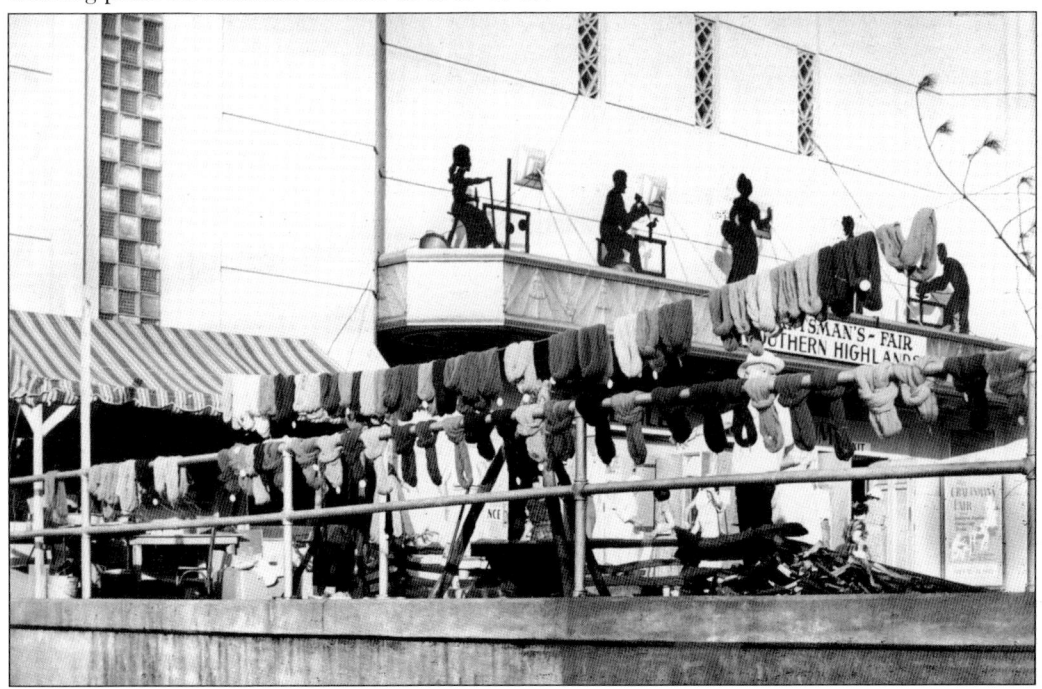

THE CRAFTSMAN'S FAIR IN 1952. This photo shows the entrance to the Craftsman's Fair, representing the Southern Highlands at the Asheville Auditorium in 1952. Carved silhouettes are visible above entrance to the auditorium; several skeins of yarn are also visible. (Photo by Edward L. Dupuy Jr.)

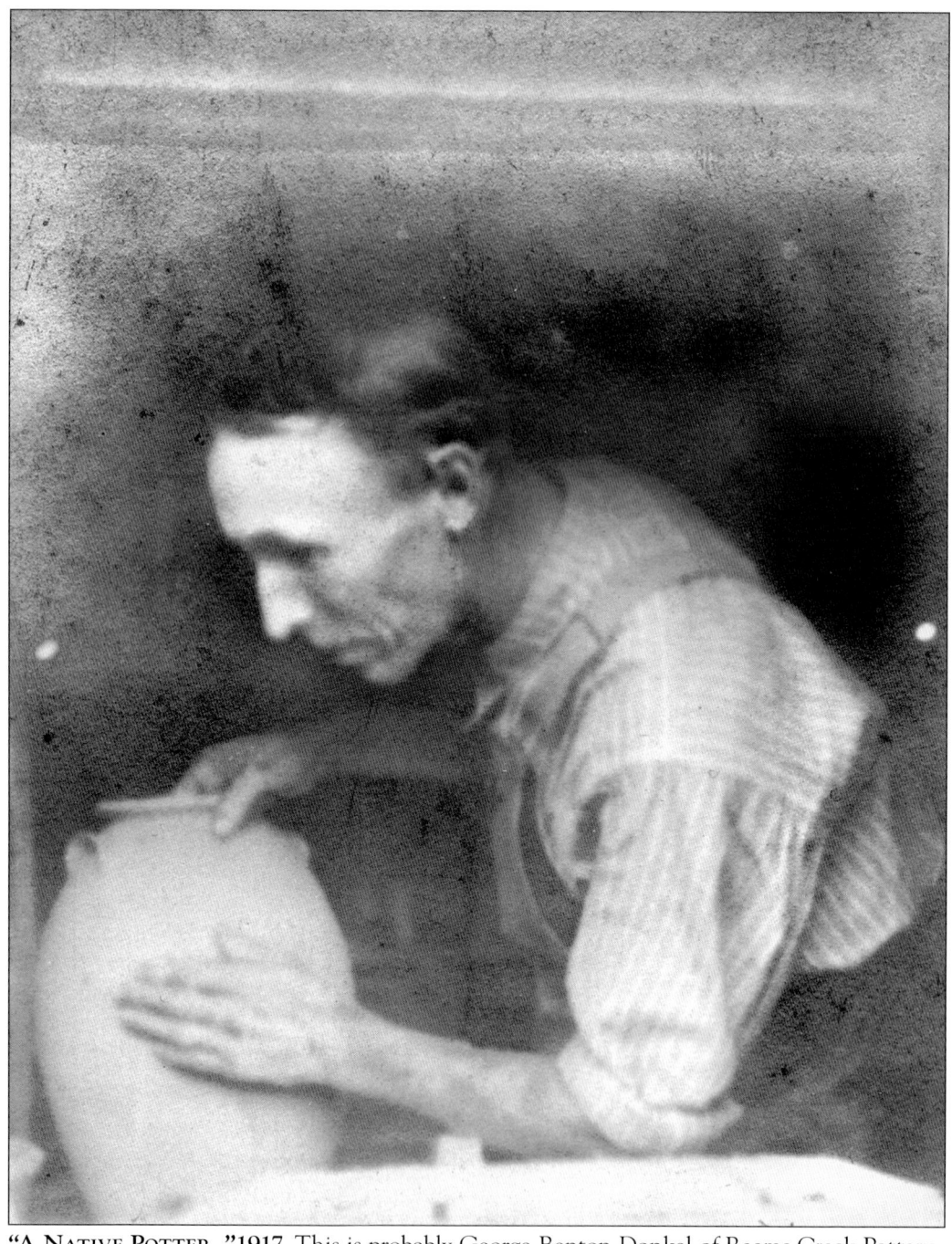

"A Native Potter," 1917. This is probably George Benton Donkel of Reems Creek Pottery.

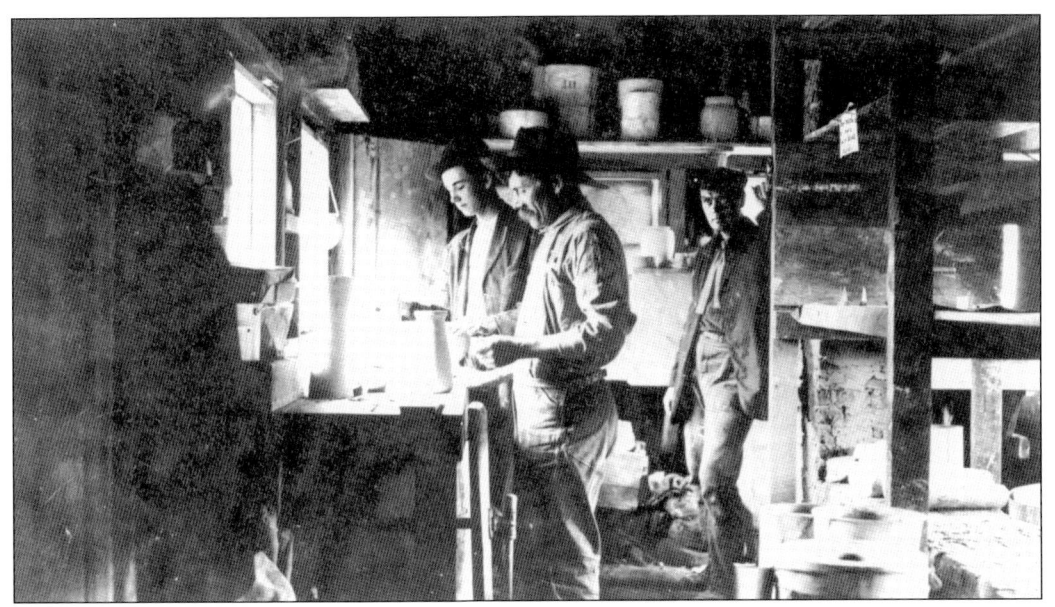

THE NONCONNAH POTTERY. This interior view of the Nonconnah Pottery in Skyland shows three men working. The Nonconnah Pottery was owned by C.P. Ryman; it operated from 1914 until sometime in the 1920s. (Gift of Mrs. James Morrison, Ryman's daughter.)

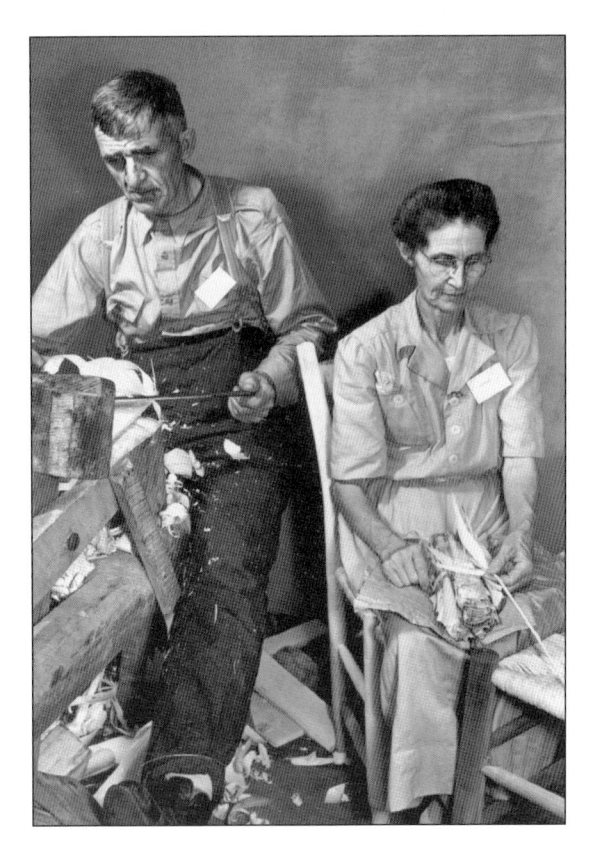

CANING CHAIRS. Mr. and Mrs. S.B. Mace of Mars Hill, pictured here at the Southern Highland Handicraft Guild Fair, c. 1953, produce cane-bottomed chairs.

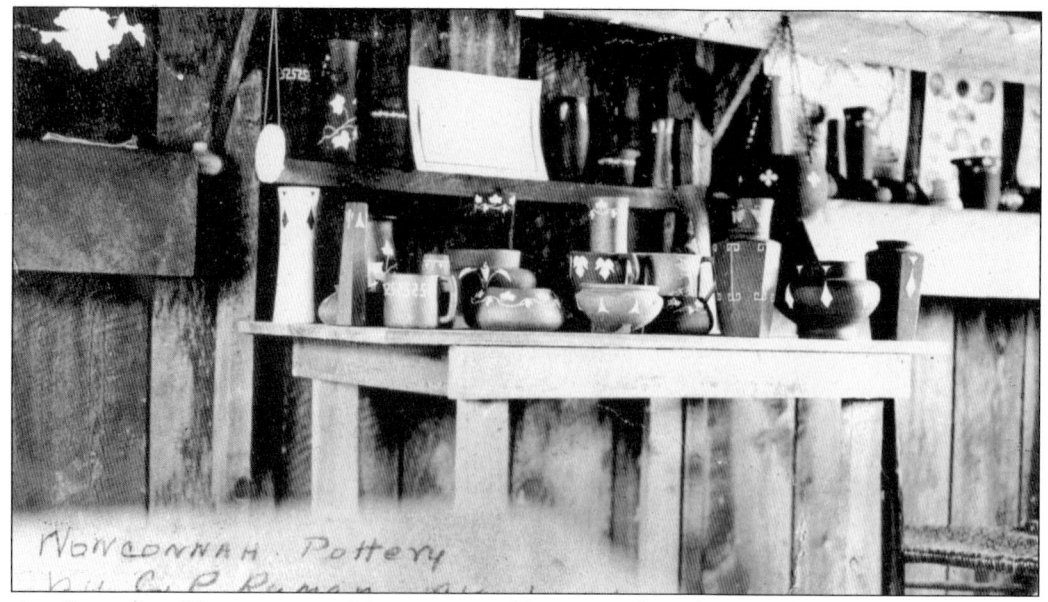

AN INTERIOR VIEW OF THE NONCONNAH POTTERY. Samples are displayed on a wooden tabletop and on wall shelves. (Gift of Mrs. James Morrison, Ryman's daughter.)

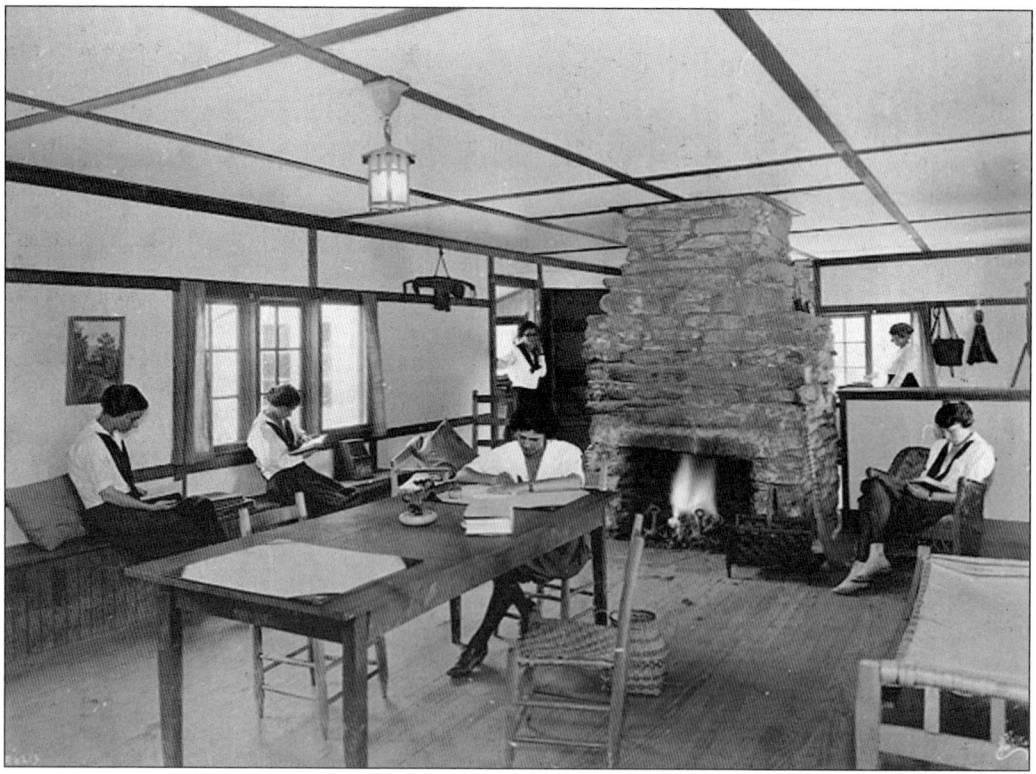

CHUNN'S COVE CAMP, C. 1919–1921. Four campers are seated inside the craft cabin; three are reading and one is writing—note the inkbottle on the table. The woman standing in the right background may be Mary Louise Allis. The cabin featured a stone fireplace, a hardwood floor, and cane-bottom chairs.

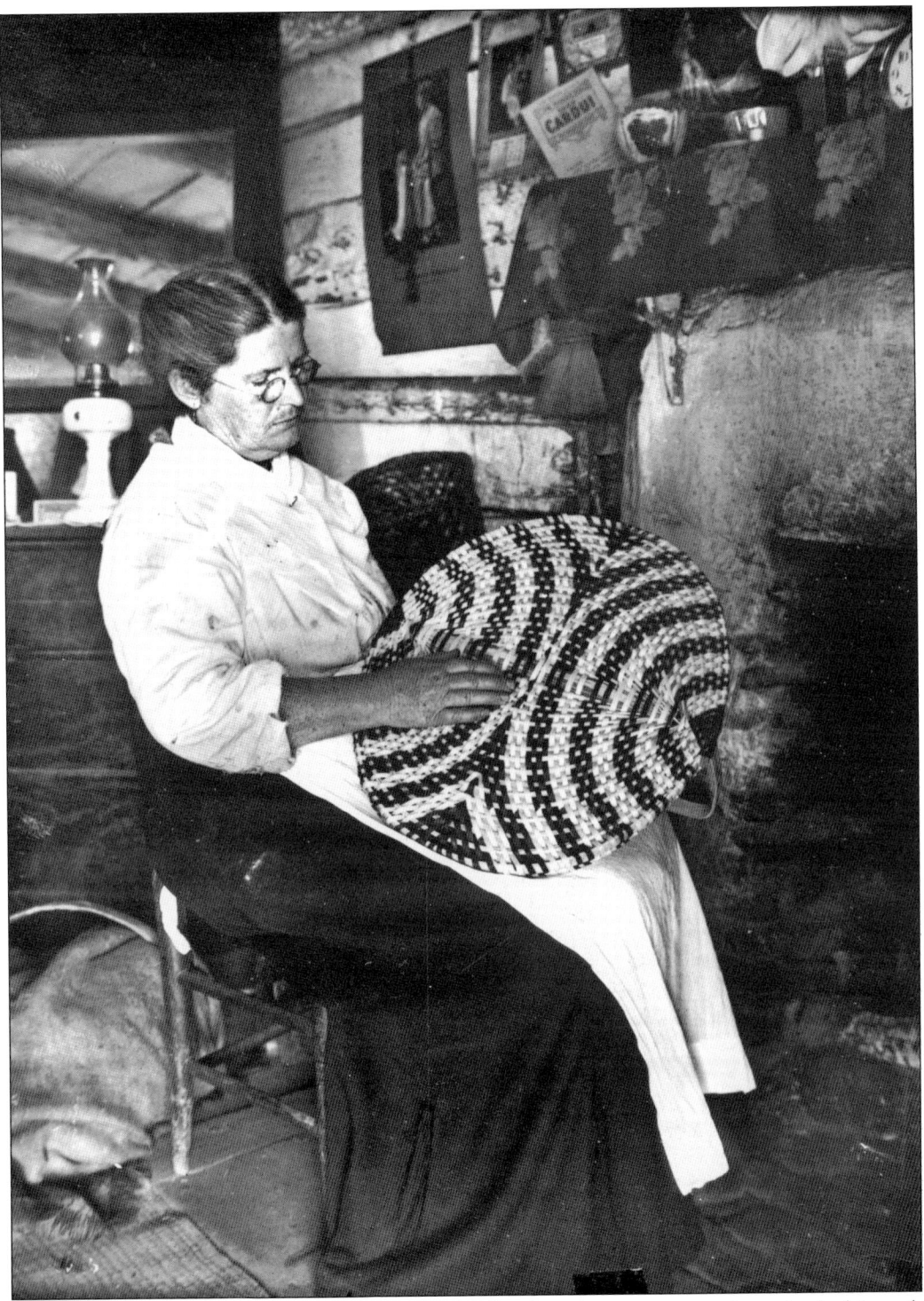

BASKET-WEAVING. Mrs. Littrell sits inside by the fireplace, weaving a tray from dyed white oak splints in the Skyland-Fletcher area of Buncombe County, c. 1915.

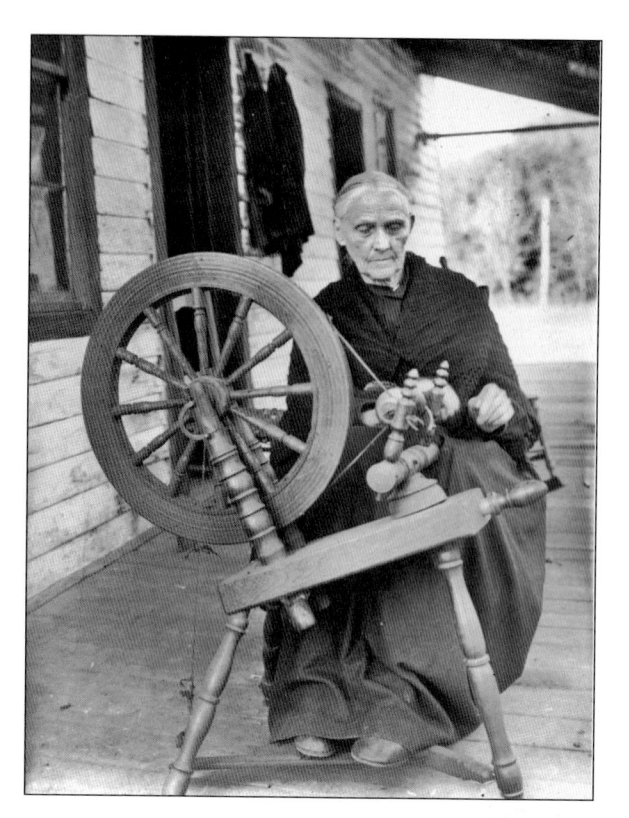

SPINNING WOOL. Mrs. Thomas O'Kelly sits on her porch spinning wool on a small wheel usually used for flax, *c.* 1920–1922.

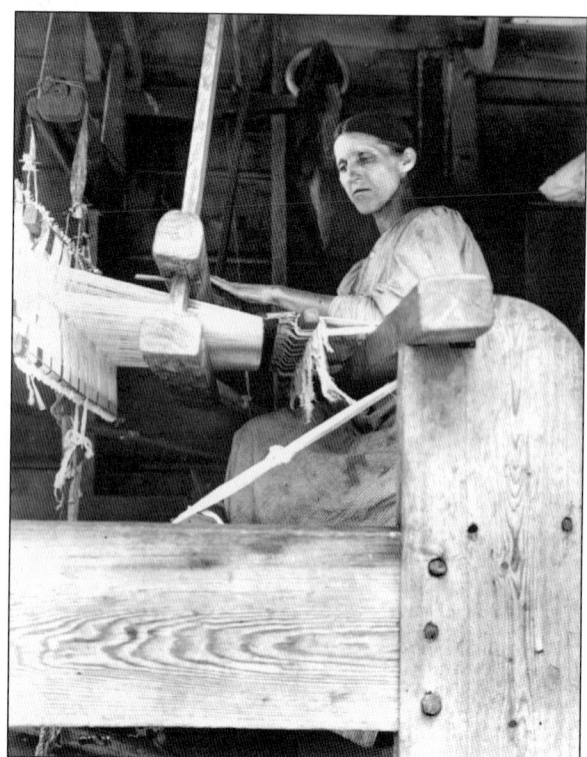

THE WEAVERS. Lucinda "Cindy" Netherton (Mrs. John) Warren, 70, works at her loom on the porch of her home in the upper Hominy section of Buncombe County *c.* 1915.

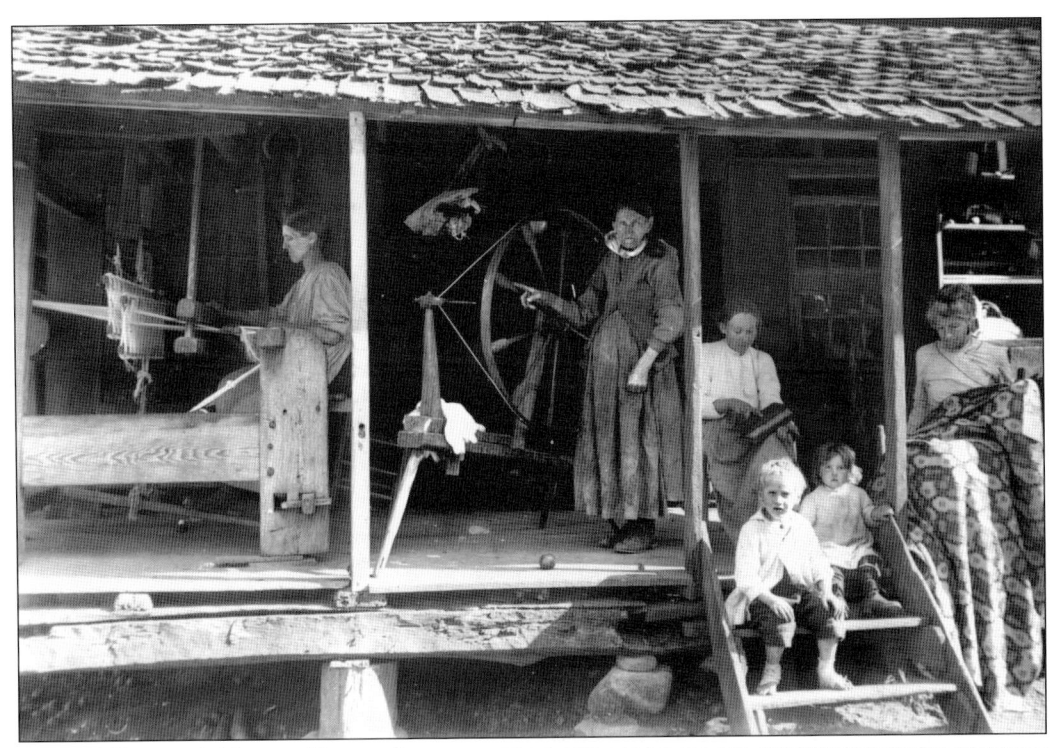

Cindy Warren's Place. Pictured on this *c.* 1915 porch in the upper Hominy section of Buncombe County are, from left to right, Lucinda "Cindy" Netherton (Mrs. John) Warren, weaving; Eliza Candler Netherton, 88 years old and mother of Cindy and Elizabeth, by the spinning wheel; Cora Warren, carding, her two children by her; and Elizabeth Netherton Brown Warren, holding a finished coverlet.

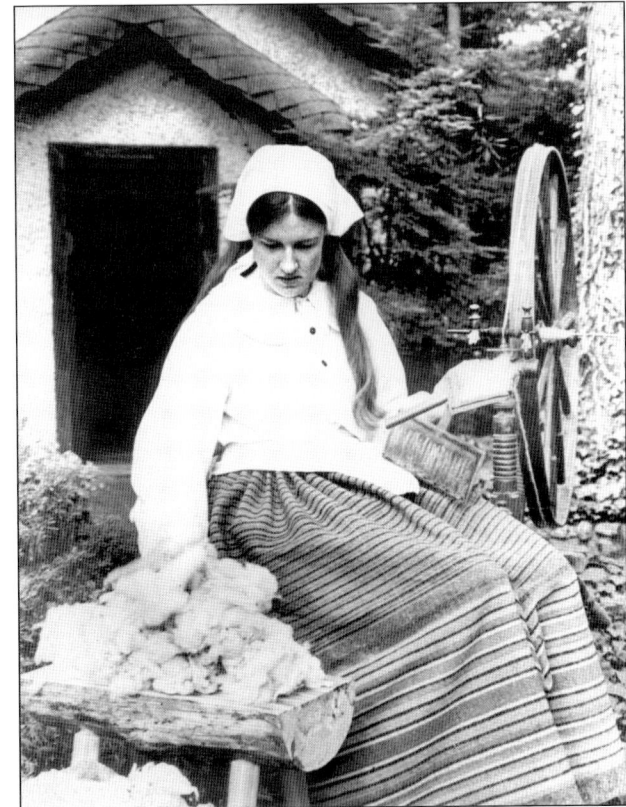

Biltmore Industries. This woman in colonial costume, carding wood, sits outside beside a spinning wheel, in front of the Biltmore Industries office.

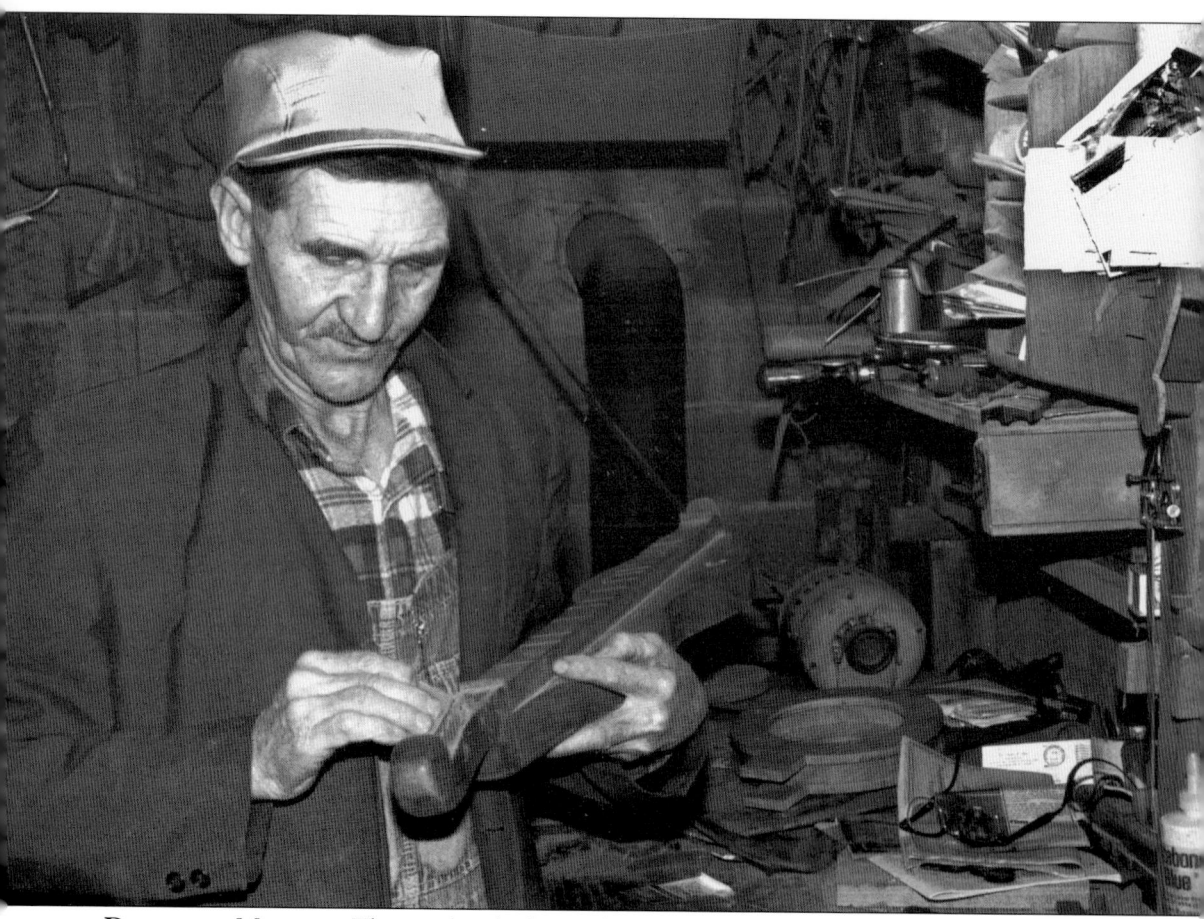

DULCIMER MAKING. This undated photo shows Stanley Hicks at his workbench making a dulcimer.

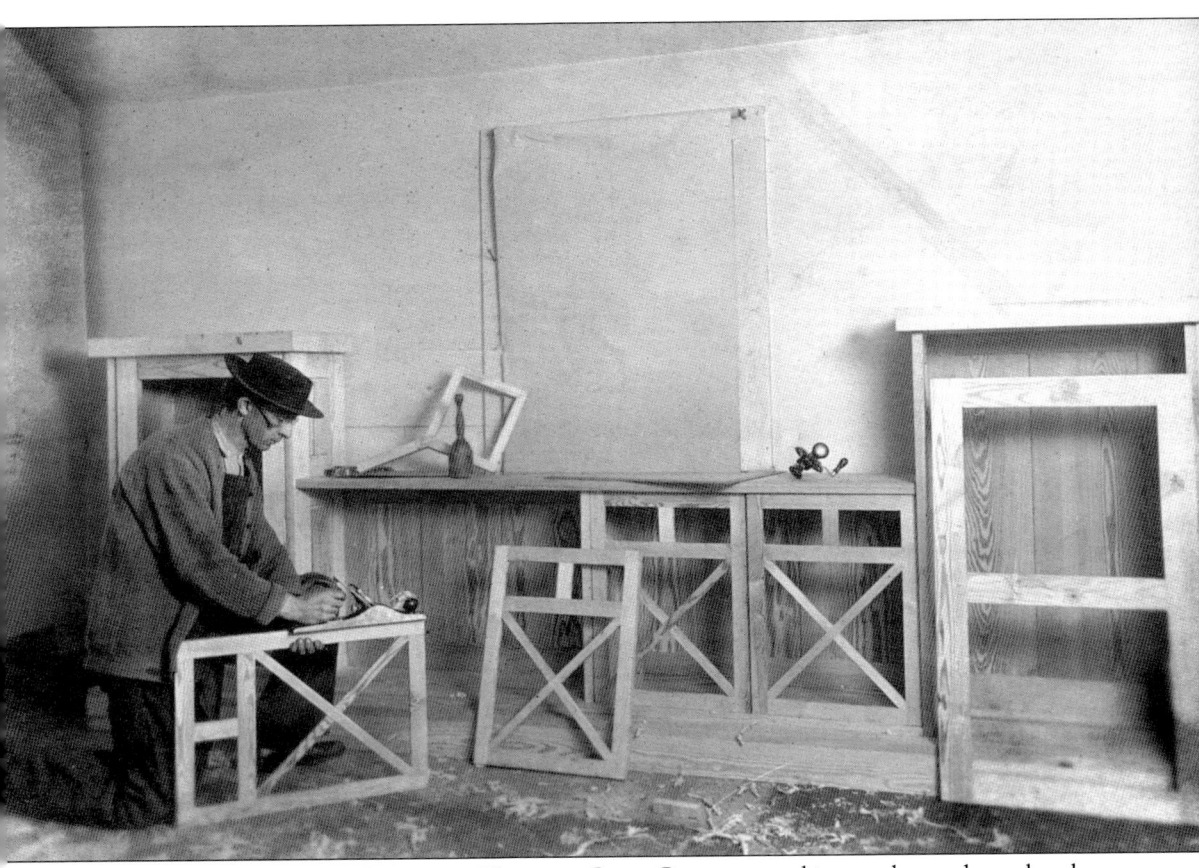

The Cabinet-makers at Biltmore Village. Oscar Creasman, cabinetmaker and woodworker for Biltmore Estate, is shown working with a plane on a cabinet door front. Other unfinished cabinet parts and tools are shown. The photograph was donated by Creasman's daughter, Jeanne Lance, who says this was taken in the Biltmore Village cabinet shop, where Mrs. Vanderbilt had Italian artisans teaching.

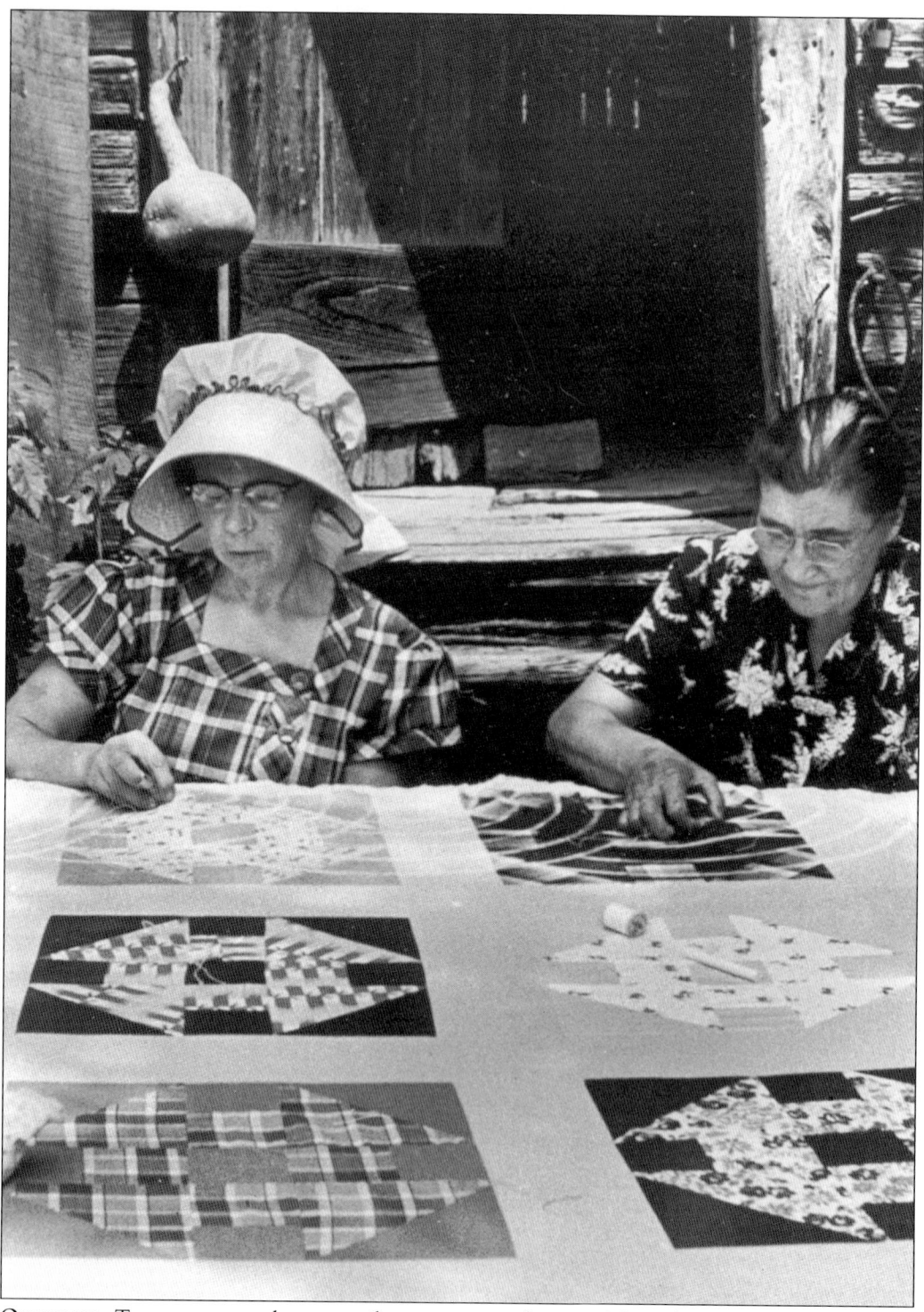

QUILTING. Two women work on a quilt; one wears a bonnet. Note the gourd hanging beside the door.

MICA PRODUCTION. This is a log single-pen cabin with a stick-and-mud chimney and a low-pitched wood-shingle roof. Sheets of mica are propped against the side of the building. A small group of people stands outside, including two female workers sitting at a table splitting the mica.

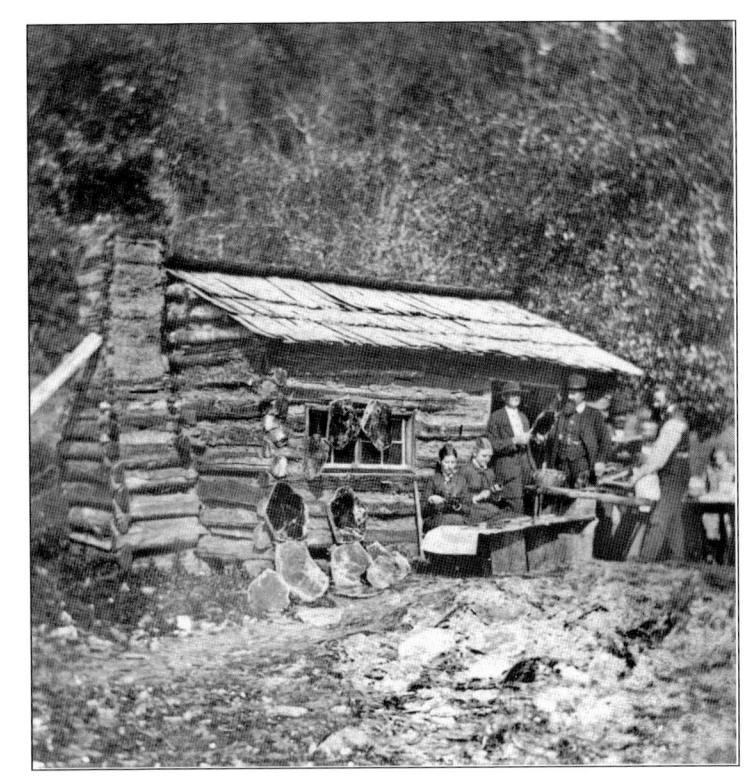

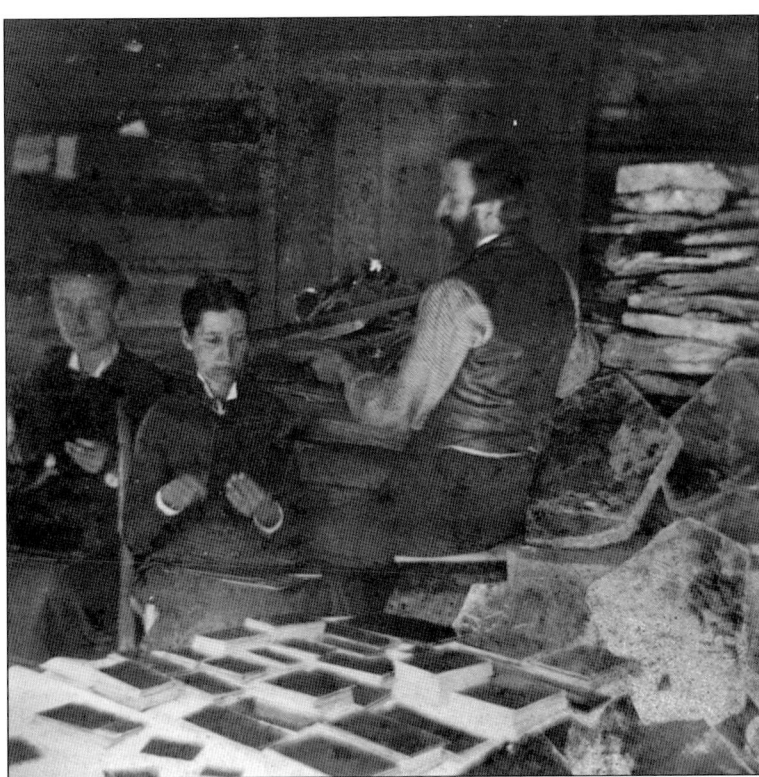

AN INTERIOR VIEW OF THE MICA HOUSE. This interior view of the outside wall shows finish planks over the chinking between the logs. Sheets of mica are stacked against the wall by the door. Three workers are visible, including two women sitting, splitting the mica, and a man standing, cutting the mica. A wide array of various rectangular pieces is laid out on the table before them.

111

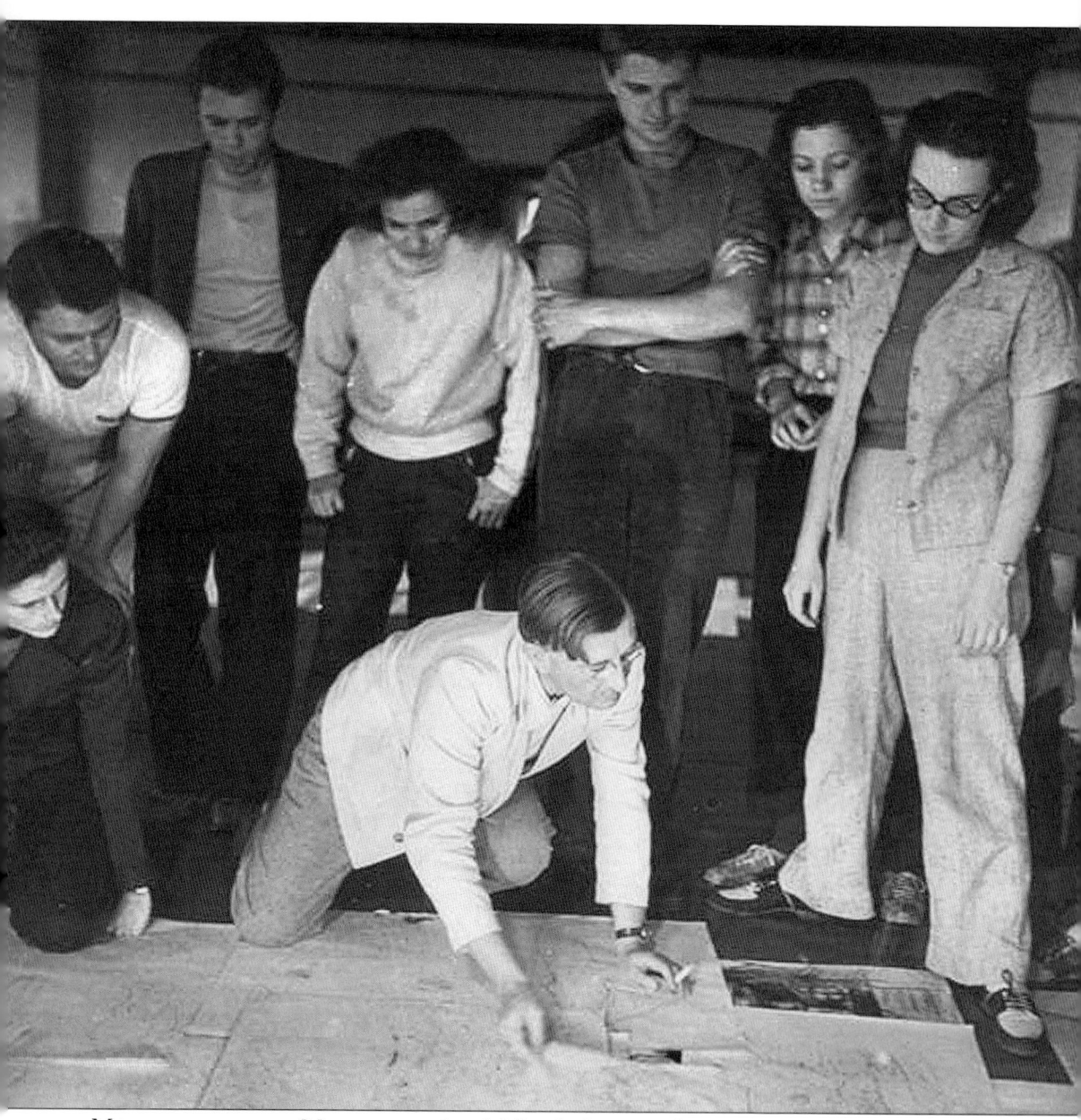

MODERNISM IN THE MOUNTAINS. Josef Albers's drawing class, c. 1939–1940, is, from left to right, Lisa Jalowetz, Bela Martin, Fred Stone, Betty Brett, Albers (kneeling), Robert de Niro, Martha McMillan, and Eunice Shifris. Black Mountain College was begun in 1933 by a group of teachers and students from Rollins College in Winter Park, Florida. Between 1933 and 1956 the college was a center for groundbreaking artists, composers, and writers of the period. Black Mountain College continues to exist as the mythical artistic birthplace of everyone from John Cage to Robert Creeley. Instructor-artists included Josef Albers, Kenneth Noland, Willem de Kooning, Franz Klein, dancer and choreographer Merce Cunningham, poets Charles Olson and John Wieners, composers Lou Harrison and Stefan Wolpe, and even the unclassifiable Buckminster Fuller. (North Carolina State Archives photo.)

Isaac Nakata. This Black Mountain College student participates in the work program. Students and instructors alike helped develop the campus at Lake Eden in Black Mountain, originally part of a lodge for the Biltmore Estate. The studies building they constructed in the Modernist style still stands. (North Carolina State Archives photo.)

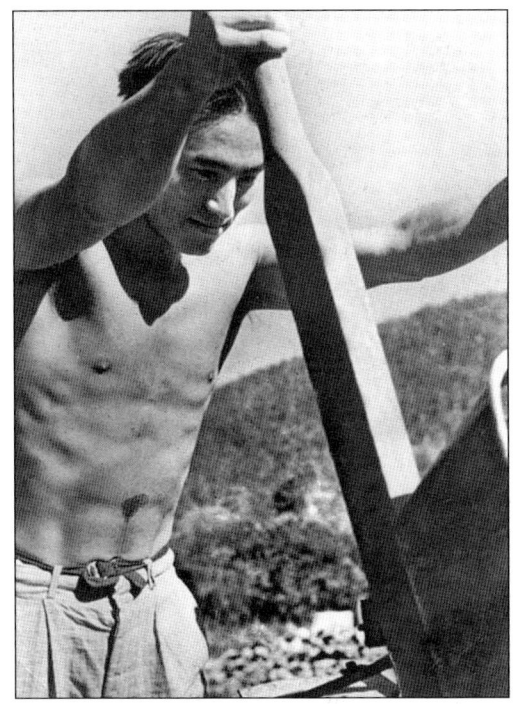

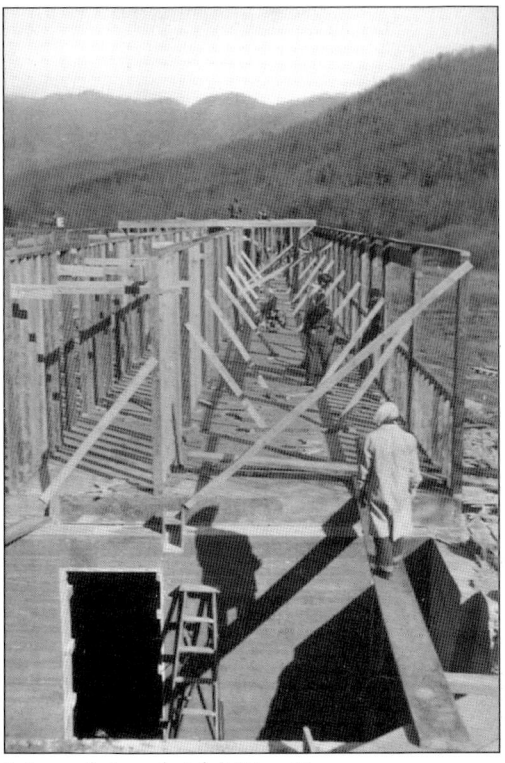

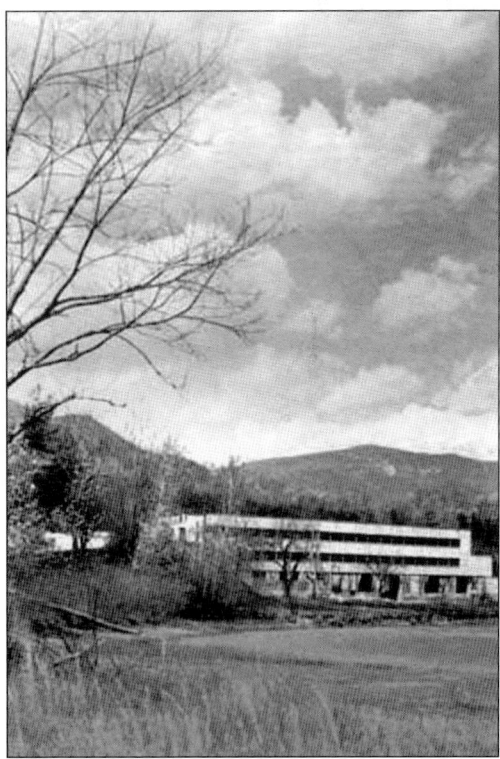

(above, left and right) **The Construction of the Studies Building, Lake Eden Campus.** The skeleton of the first floor studies and the hall begins to take shape in November 1940. It is shown to the right nearing completion in 1941. (North Carolina State Archives photos.)

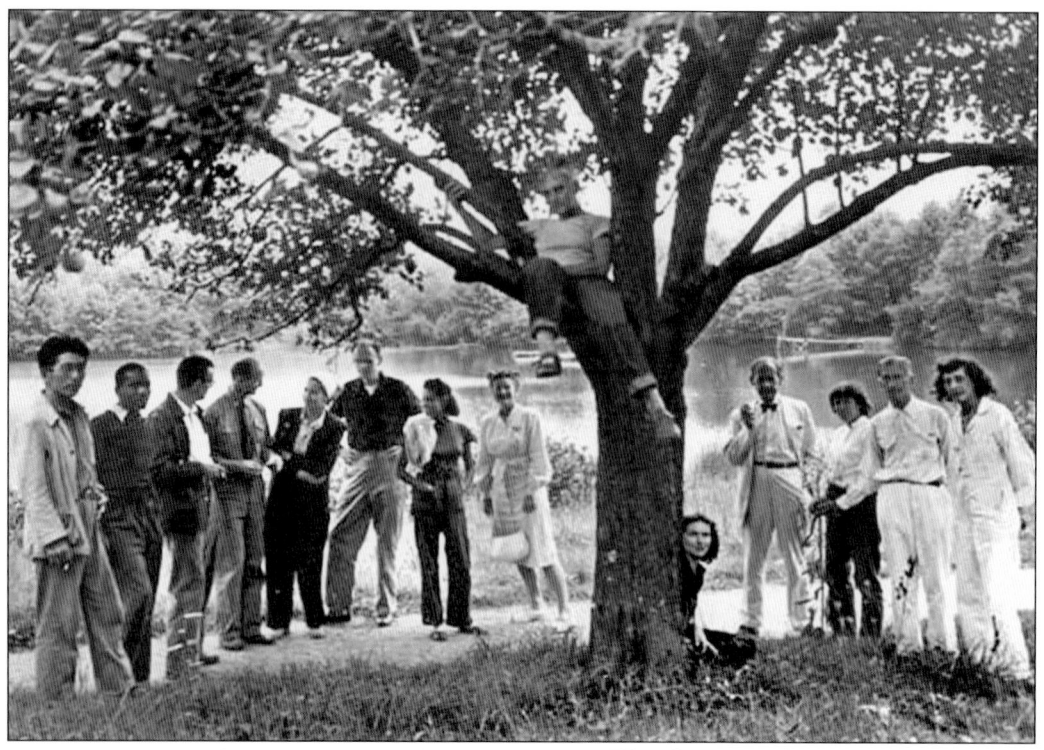

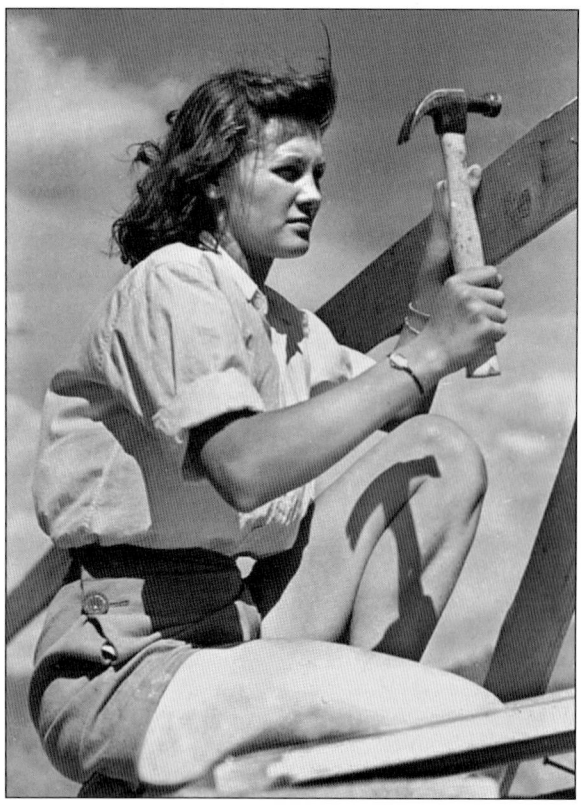

THE SUMMER ARTS INSTITUTE FACULTY IN 1944. The faculty is, from left to right, Leo Amino, Jacob Lawrence, Leo Lionni, Ted Dreier, Nora Lionni, Beaumont Newhall, Gwendolyn Lawrence, Ise Gropius, Jean Varda (in tree), Nancy Newhall (sitting), Walter Gropius, Mary "Molly" Gregory, Josef Albers, and Anni Albers. (North Carolina State Archives photo.)

CONNIE SPENCER. Connie Spencer was a Black Mountain College student from 1940 to 1942. Here, she is likely working on the construction of the Studies building. (North Carolina State Archives photo.)

Eight

AN ARCHITECTURAL TIME CAPSULE

The development of Asheville might not have been envisioned by your average "city father." The topography of Asheville is dotted with hills and ridges, contributing to what many have described as the town's distinctly European flavor, with its winding, hilly downtown streets. It would be much easier on some flat land with a simple grid pattern. Fortunately, Asheville today is much more of an architectural feast. The skilled craftsmen that architects and builders of the late 19th and early 20th centuries employed contributed greatly to these masterpieces. The skills they passed to locals cannot be overlooked.

One of the few surviving antebellum buildings in Asheville is the Ravenscroft School, a brick villa with Italianate and Greek Revival influence. The design likely came from A.J. Downing's popular 1842 plan book, Cottage Residences. A great number of downtown commercial buildings from the later 19th century have survived with or without modification. The most notable 19th-century building has to be the Drhumor Building at 48 Patton Avenue. The building is a four-story brick structure with limestone built in the Romanesque Revival style. A limestone frieze in high relief on the first floor of the exterior features lions, angels, men, women, mermaids, and shells. Other 19th-century buildings that have been well preserved include a group of commercial buildings on the southwest corner of Pack Square, including One Biltmore Avenue, an 1889 commercial building with Romanesque influence; the Young Men's Institute, designed by Richard Sharp Smith as a two-story brick and pebbledash Tudor building; the First Presbyterian Church, an 1884 Gothic Revival building at the corner of Church and Aston Streets; and the Vance Monument, an 1896 obelisk monument honoring Civil War governor and U.S. senator Zebulon B. Vance, who died in 1894.

Commercial buildings of the early 20th century that remain in downtown Asheville include an Art Deco masterpiece, Douglas D. Ellington's 1928 City Building at City County Plaza. The pink-orange brick building with a pink Georgia marble base blends Art Deco and Beaux Arts elements. It is crowned with an octagonal roof of red and green tile that is surrounded with a feathered, jagged roofline described by Ellington as "lightly reminiscent of the Indian epoch." This building was controversial in its time, resulting in a much more sedate sister building, the county courthouse that followed in 1929. Ellington had designed a pair of Art Deco buildings, but county commissioners fought the outlandish design, opting instead for Asheville's conservative eighth courthouse. County Commission went instead with the design of Washington, D.C. architects Milburn and Heister. The 1924 Jackson Building was Asheville's first skyscraper. Architect Ronald Greene wrapped the steel frame building with brick and terra cotta, providing Gothic influences complete with gargoyles near the summit. The building is located on the site of W.O. Wolfe's stonecutting shop of the 19th century. The 1926 Asheville Art Museum, which was originally the Pack Memorial Library, is a three-story Renaissance Revival building faced in white Georgia marble designed by the New York Library architect Tilton. It was named for George Pack and replaced a turreted library building that burned in 1923.

Churches of Asheville have great architectural significance. Foremost among these is the Basilica of St. Lawrence, designed by Rafael Guastavino and Richard Sharp Smith between 1905 and 1909 in the Spanish Baroque Revival. Gaustavino, who had completed adorning Biltmore Estate with his unique, self-supporting tile work, declared that Asheville needed a bigger Catholic church. The 85-foot sanctuary features a herringbone tile pattern within the domed church. Guastavino died before the church was completed. Douglas D. Ellington's work on the 1927 First Baptist Church is an instantly recognized Asheville landmark. Mixing early Christian church architecture with Beaux Arts and Art Deco detailing, Ellington designed the domed church with red-orange bricks and red and green roof tiles that bear similarity to his later work on the 1928 City Building.

A favorite building in Asheville is the Public Service Building on Patton Avenue. Built in 1929, just before the crash, by the Frank Coxe Estate for Carolina Power and Light, it was designed by Greenville, South Carolina architects Beacham and le Grand. The building exhibits Romanesque and Spanish elements in multicolored terra cotta. Just down the street, Ellington designed in 1929 another Art Deco gem in the S&W Cafeteria Building. His use of sparkling color on the exterior includes two-story, arched windows and geometric uses of terra cotta. Proof that life existed in Asheville after the Great Depression, Henry I. Gaines designed the Woolworth Building in 1939. This late Art Deco building features the popular cream and orange terracotta. The building today has been completely restored and is open to the public as a collective of independent artists and galleries.

For speculators and developers in this modern age, no building could be more on their radar screen than the Battery Park Hotel, designed in 1924 by New York architect William L. Stoddart. The 14-story brick hotel built by E.W. Grove was a 1920s transformation of Battery Park Hill and replaced the previous Queen Anne style Battery Park Hotel built in 1886. After standing vacant for some time, it was renovated as apartments for senior citizens. After Grove completed the Battery Park Hotel, his last great work was the Grove Arcade Building. Begun in 1926 and completed after his death in 1929, the building never got the skyscraper that Grove intended. Designed in the Tudor style, griffins guard the north entrance, while inside serpentine staircases and wooden storefronts reflect a distinctly medieval spirit. The building is one of Asheville's more recent rebirths, with a downtown grocery, shops, and galleries now open for business. While heavily subsidized by the city, the success of the Grove Arcade is an important element in Asheville's future.

THE DRHUMOR BUILDING. Located at 48 Patton Avenue and the southwest corner of Church Street, the building is shown here before the tower was removed and after the frieze was added. A Romanesque Revival four-story structure, trimmed with rock-faced limestone, it was built by Ephram Clayton and designed by Allen L. Melton for William J. Cocke Sr. and his relatives, Miss Mattie Johnston and Mrs. Marie Johnston. "Drhumor" comes from the Johnston's family's ancestral home in Ireland. Sculptor Fred Miles carved the high-relief limestone frieze on the first floor and the paired columns on pedestals with Byzantine foliate-carved capitals that support the frieze. Wachovia Bank bought the building in 1929, when a limestone frontispiece was added to the north side of the building, and the entrance was moved from the corner. The photo is from a glass plate negative found in 1988 at 235 Pearson Drive. (Courtesy of Mr. and Mrs. Ed Siler.)

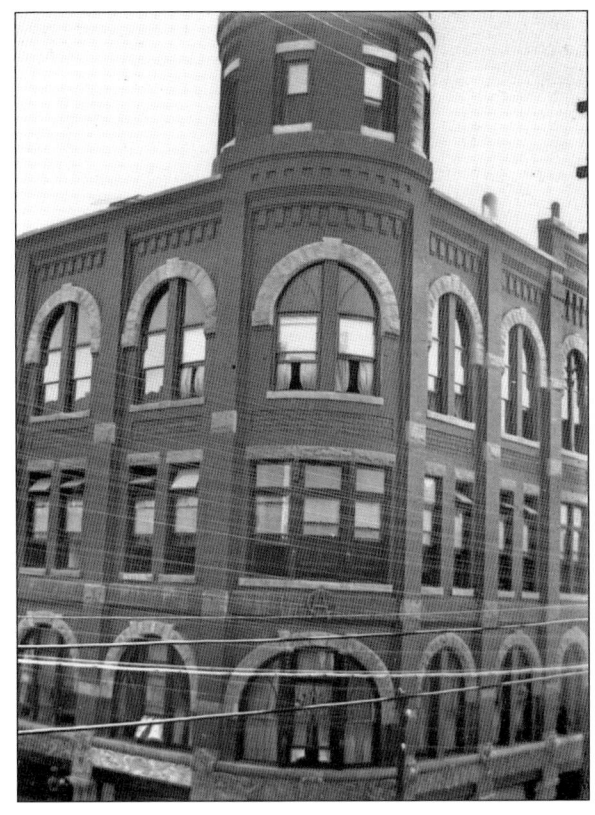

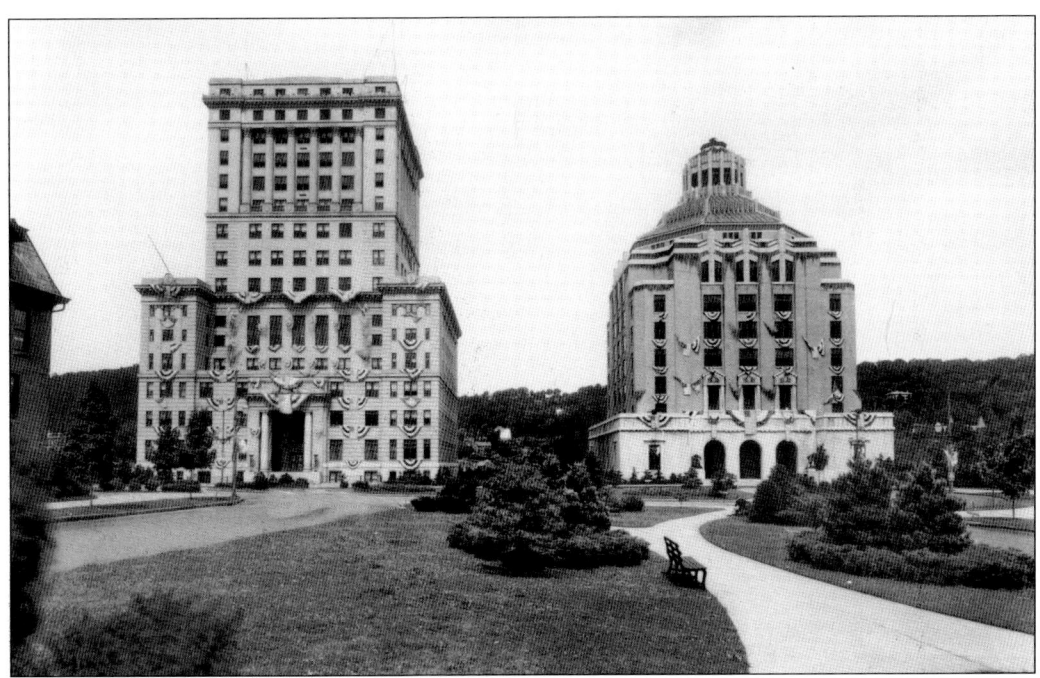

CITY COUNTY PLAZA. This view shows the 1926 Asheville City Hall and the 1928 Buncombe County Courthouse decorated with bunting.

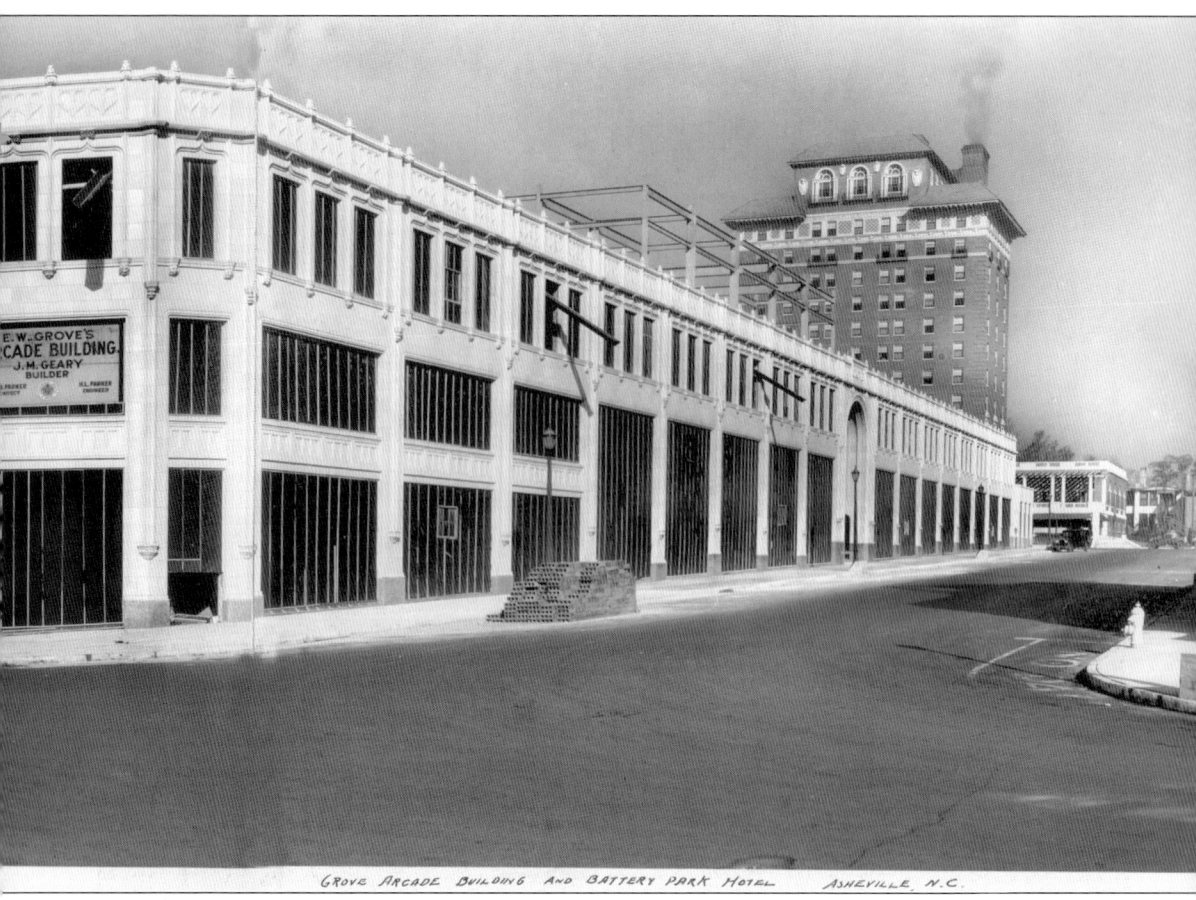

The Grove Arcade Building. The building is shown under construction from the southeast in 1927. Charles N. Parker is the architect. Visible to the right are #37 Battery Park Avenue, the Battery Park Hotel, and Page Avenue.

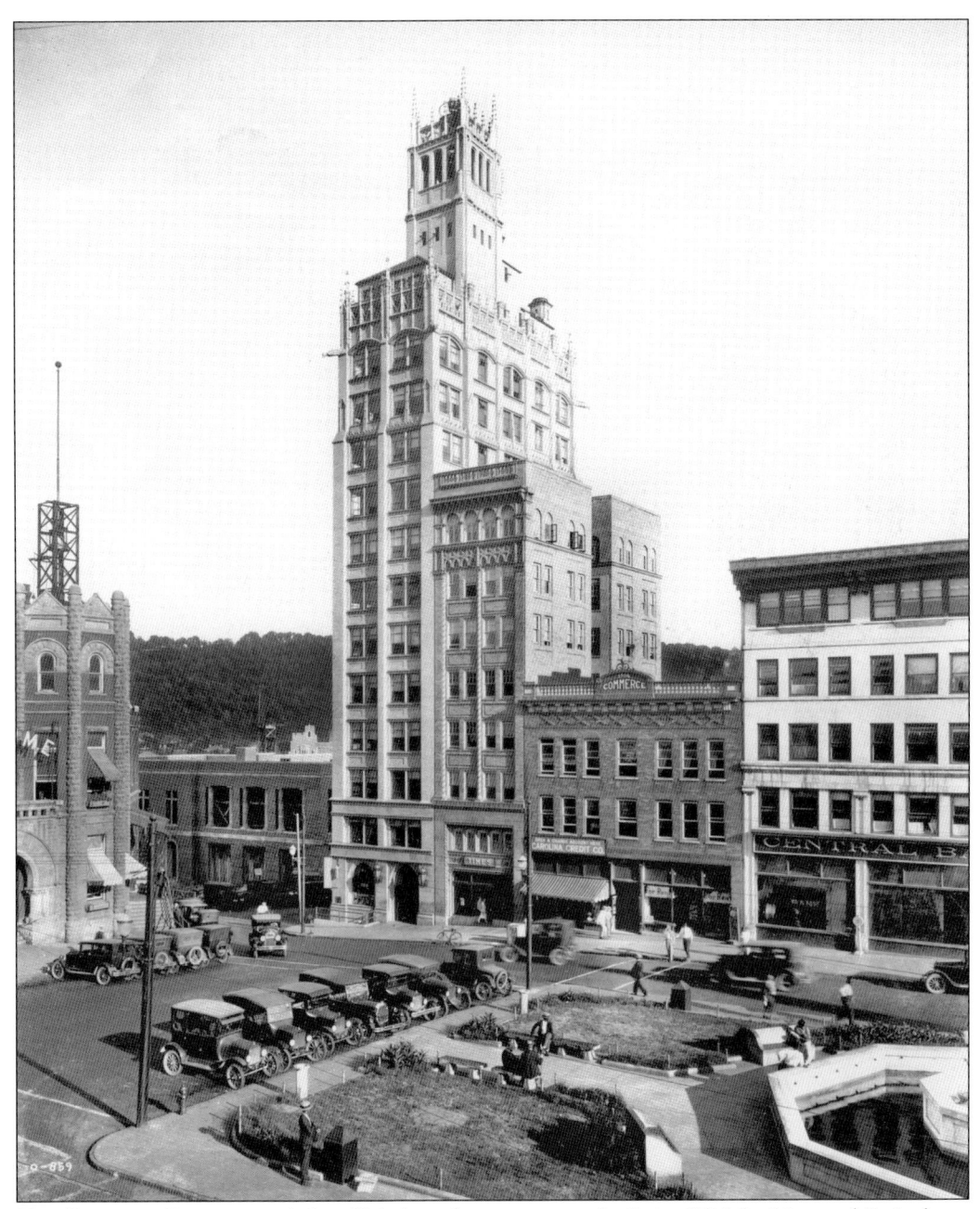

THE JACKSON BUILDING. Asheville's first skyscraper was built in 1924 for Linwood B. Jackson by Ronald Greene. The 1892 city hall is to the left. The Central Bank Building, Commerce Building, and Westall Building are also shown. The City Market Building is under construction, c. 1925–1926.

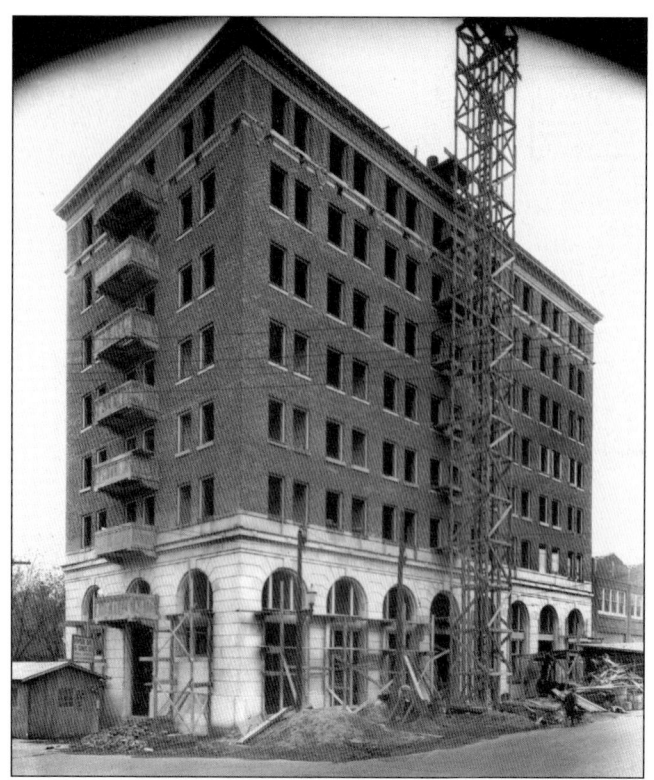

THE ASHEVILLE-BILTMORE HOTEL IN 1926. The hotel is shown under construction at 76 Market Street N. The hotel is in the Classical style and featured red brick with limestone trim; it has 100 guest rooms.

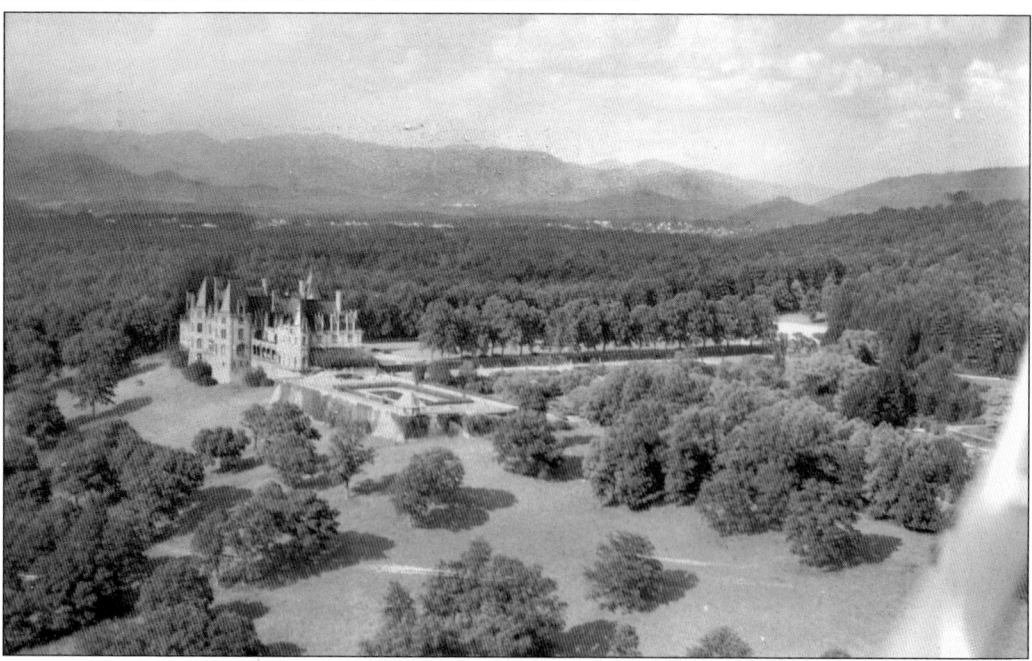

THERE'S THIS REALLY BIG HOUSE . . . No history of Asheville could be complete without mention of the Biltmore Estate. Many books have been dedicated to this, the largest private home in America. This unique Bingham aerial view is titled *Biltmore House from Southwest, July 1948*.

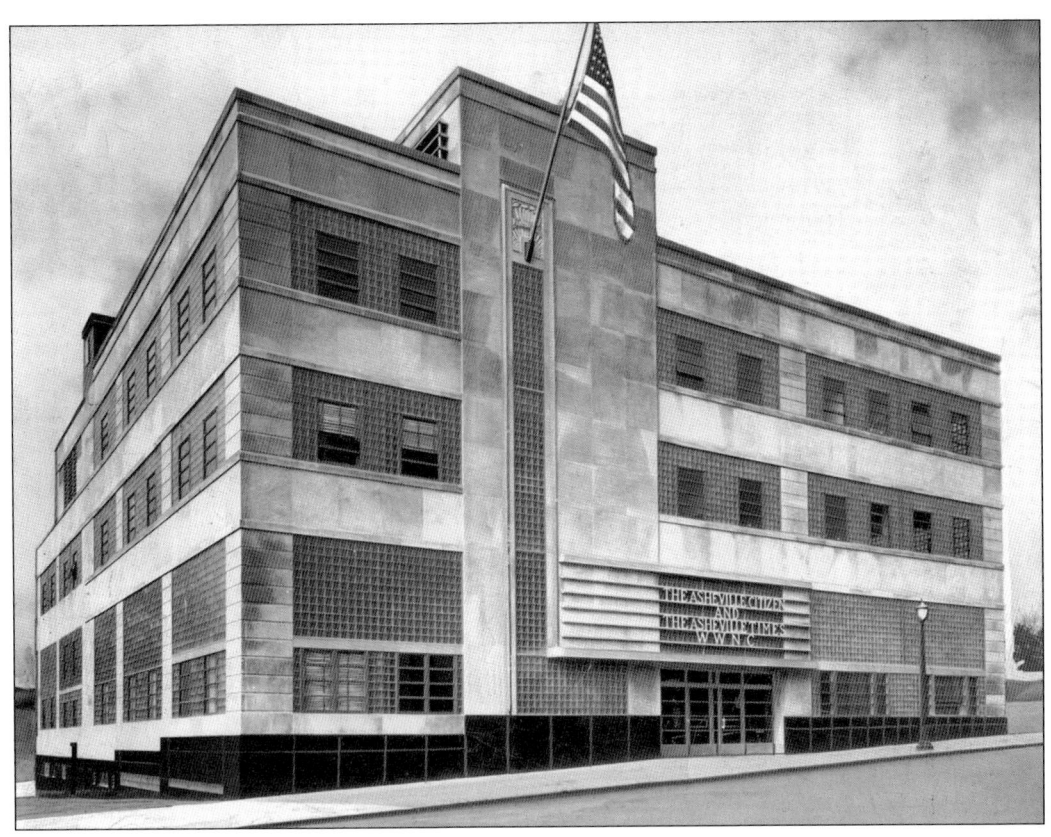

IN THE INTERNATIONAL STYLE. Architect Anthony Lord designed the 1939 Citizen-Times Building at 14 O. Henry Avenue with a limestone block facade and glass block window strips over a concrete structure. The front of building reads "The Asheville Citizen and The Asheville Times WWNC."

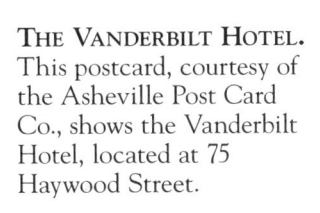

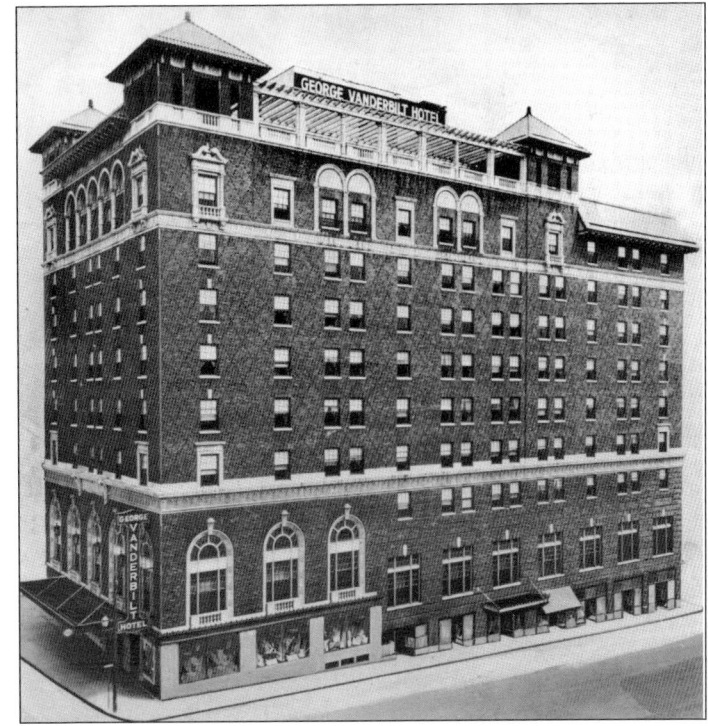

THE VANDERBILT HOTEL. This postcard, courtesy of the Asheville Post Card Co., shows the Vanderbilt Hotel, located at 75 Haywood Street.

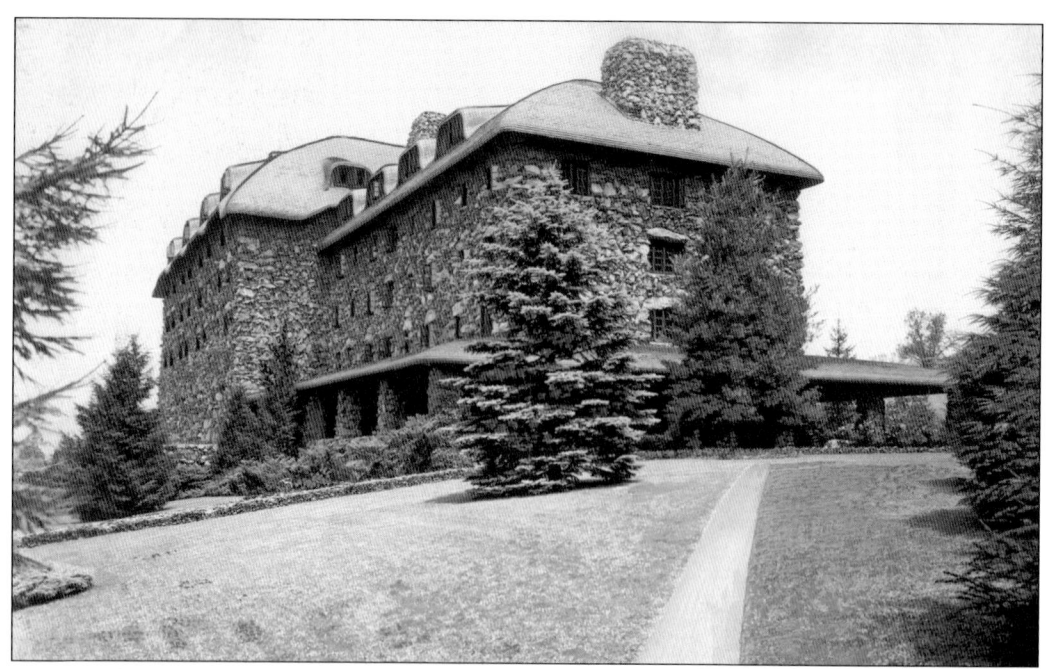

THE GROVE PARK INN. Fred Seely designed this massive stone hotel in the Arts and Crafts style, with many furnishings and lighting provided by the Roycrofters of New York. The building was inspired by the Grand Canyon Hotel in Yellowstone Park.

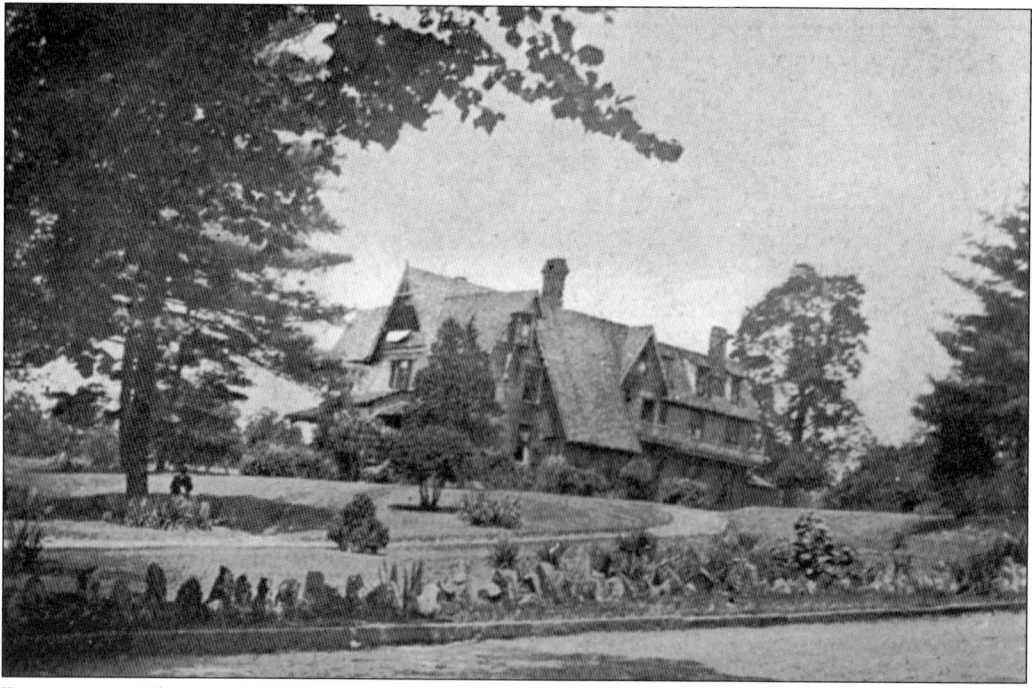

ROSELAWN. This *c.* 1910 view shows the spacious lawn of Roselawn, first listed in the 1906 city directories at 52 Merrimon Avenue. It was renamed as Commodius Gothic Mansion in 1912 after being remodeled and refurbished and given a well-shaded lawn with hammocks and swings.

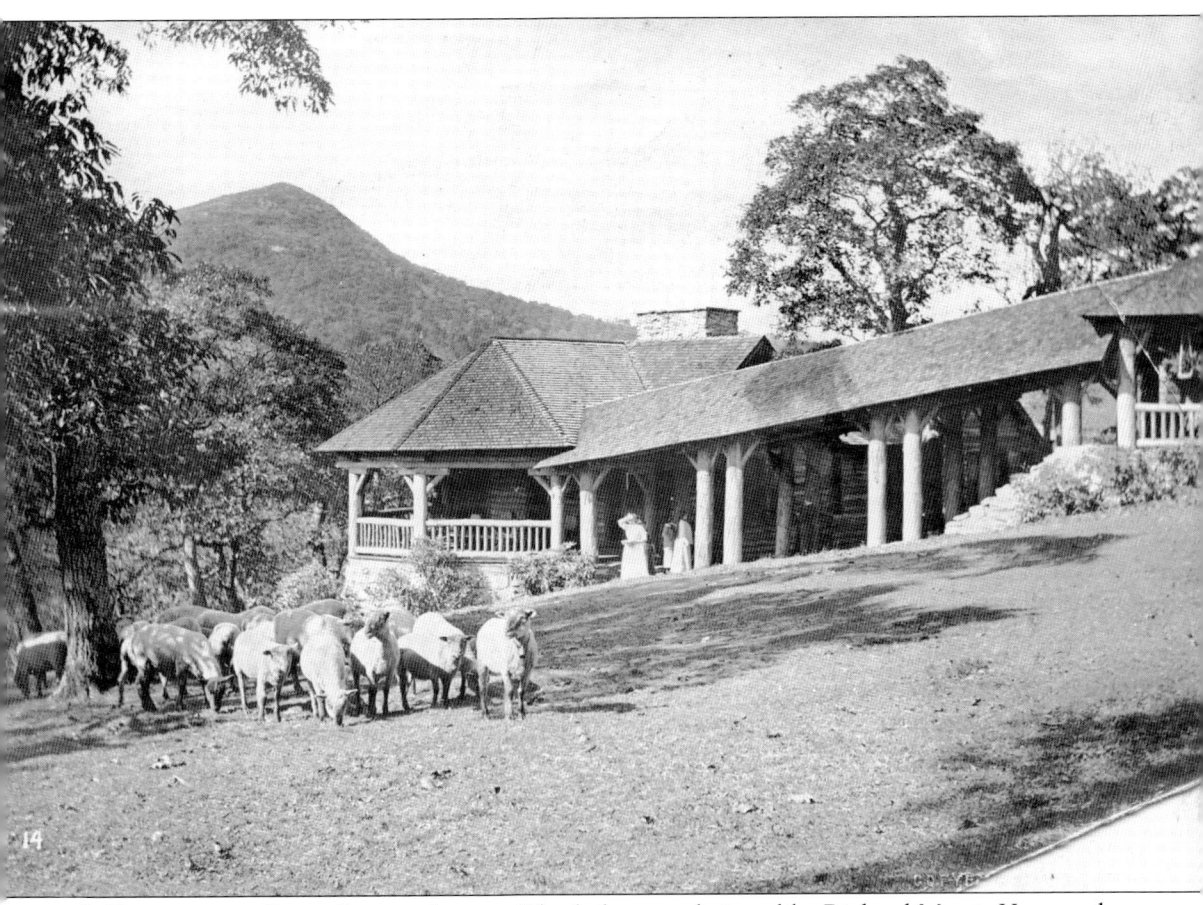

A VIEW OF THE BUCK SPRING LODGE. The lodge was designed by Richard Morris Hunt and built on Biltmore Estate Grounds near Mount Pisgah, now Pisgah National Forest. A few women are standing near the building, and a group of sheep are in the foreground in the shade of a tree.

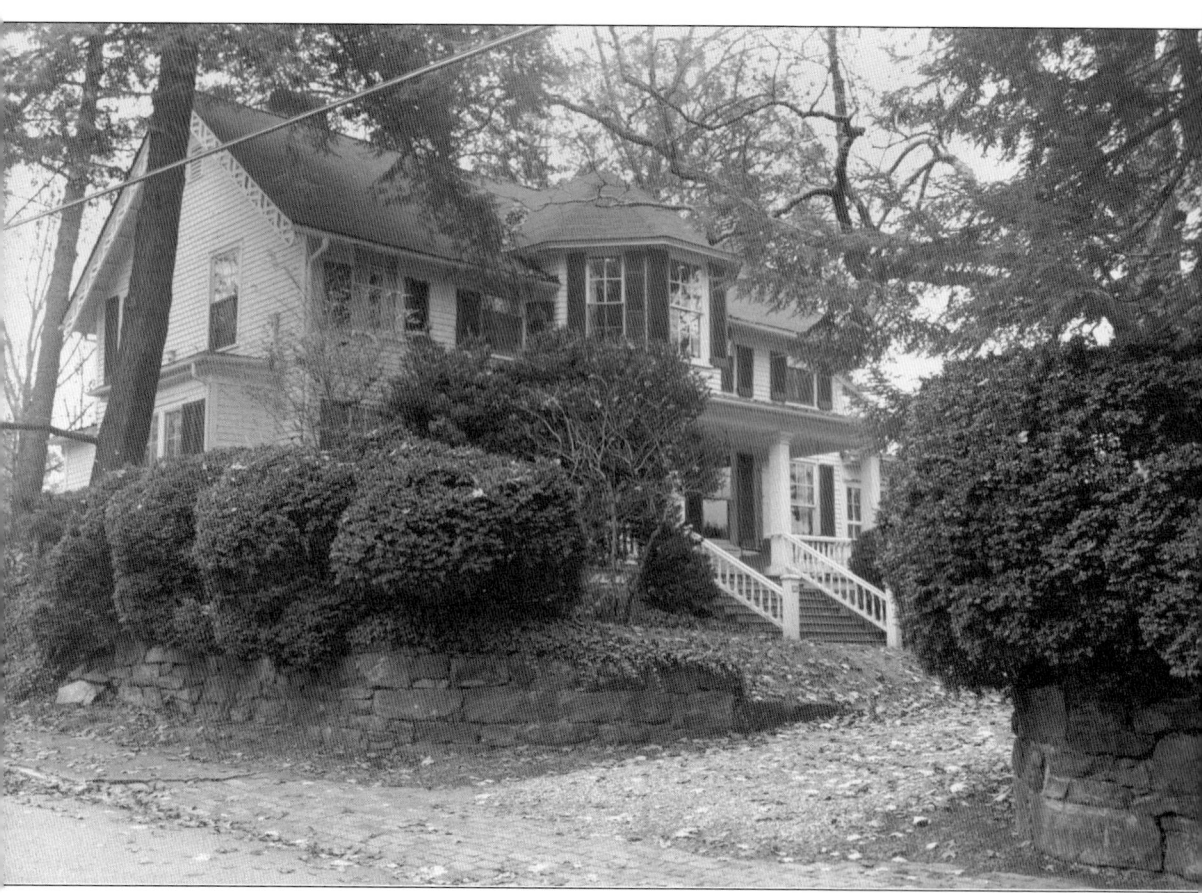

A LOCAL LANDMARK. The Parker home at 95 Charlotte Street was the site of Camp Patton during the Civil War. The house was built by former Asheville mayor Thomas Walton Patton in 1868 and made a local historical landmark in March 2000. The first meeting of North Carolina suffragettes was held at this house in 1894.

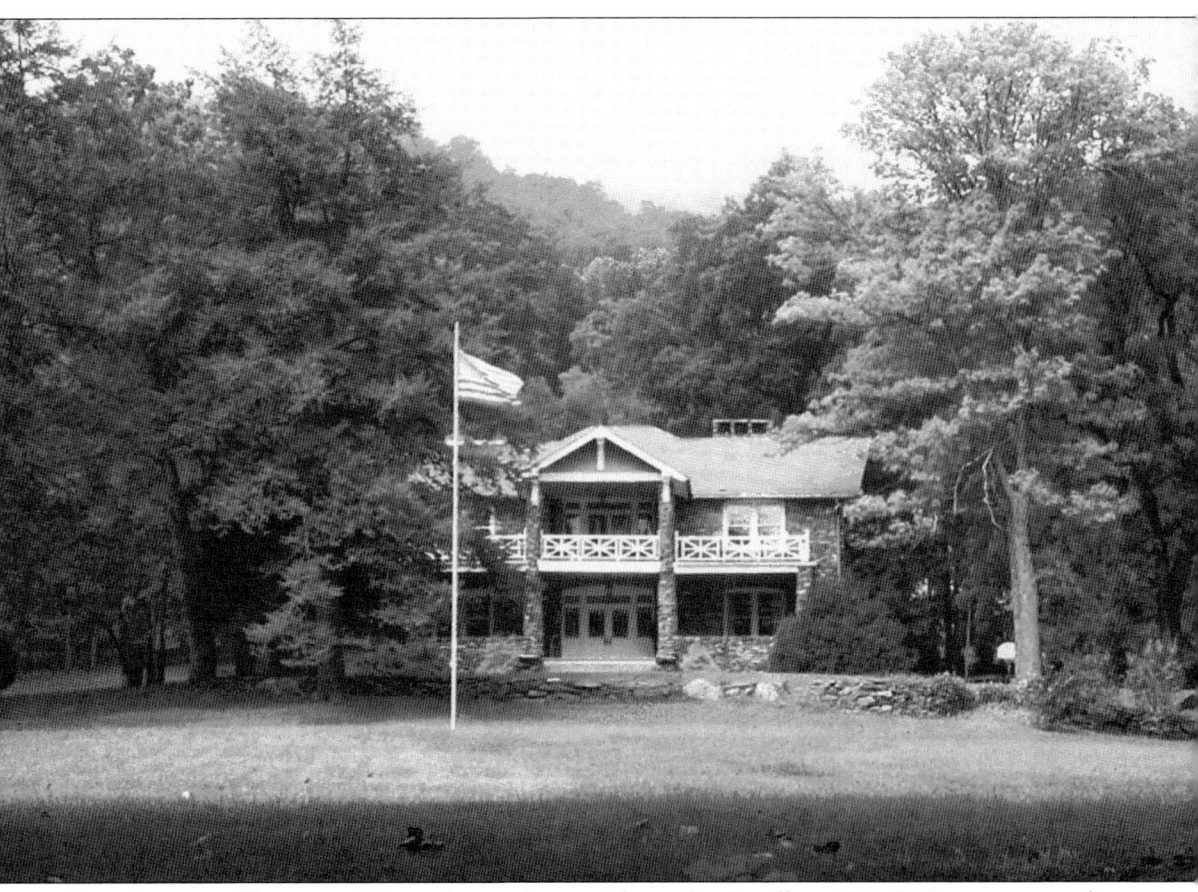

THE SONDLEY HOME IN HAW CREEK. Foster Alexander Sondley, 1857–1931, was a noted Asheville historian who published his history of Buncombe County in two volumes in 1930. He was elected historian of Buncombe County in 1927 by the Buncombe County Board of Education. In his preface, he pines that "for many years the author has hoped to see a history of Buncombe County. For many years that hope has been disappointed." And so he wrote his own, not necessarily to his own satisfaction.

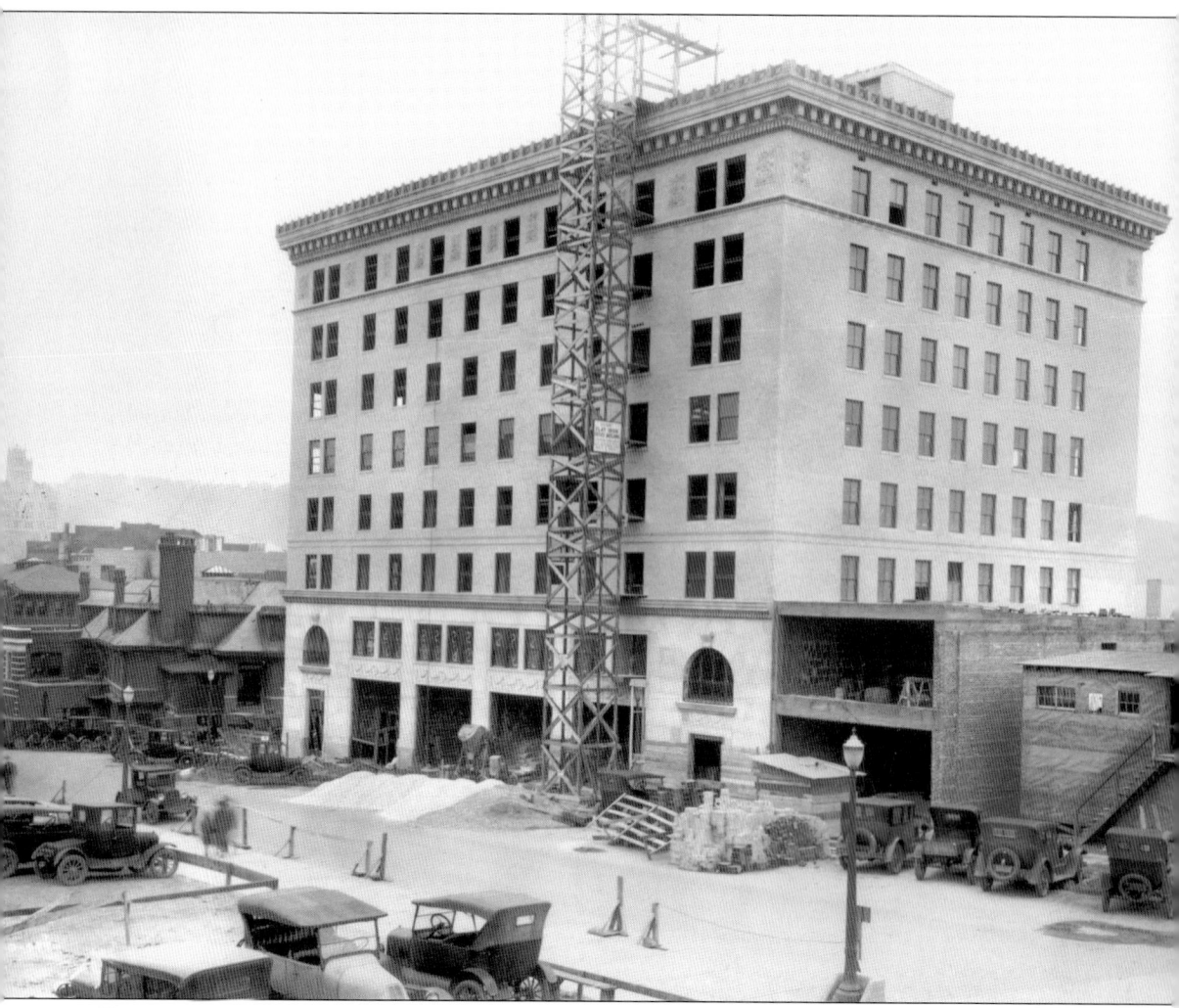

The Flatiron Building. The back of the Flatiron Building is shown under construction, c. 1925–1927. It was designed by Albert C. Wirth with six stories of tan brick on a two-story limestone base in the classic urban wedge design. It was built as part of the Grove development of the Battery Park area.

ACKNOWLEDGMENTS

This book is dedicated to my wife, Faith, and our five-year-old son, Jacob Knox Chandler McDaniel. Without them, nothing would be possible, and none of it would really matter. We fix houses together, we try to fix neighborhoods, and we both make and preserve a little history of our own.

This book is my first, but it is not mine. It belongs to Asheville. It is an attempt to collect and put in proper perspective a modest history in not too many pages with more than a few photographs—a quite ambitious undertaking by any measure. Perhaps differently than some other books about Asheville, the story does not begin as is usually told, with white settlers and their slaves crossing over into the Swannanoa Valley.

I want especially to acknowledge Ann Wright, Zoe Rhine, and Mollie Warlick at the North Carolina Collections Desk at the Pack Memorial Library. As you peruse the North Carolina Collection at Pack Library, you see their hands guiding you, their passion for preserving the history and heritage of Asheville in everything they do, from annotating and re-annotating images to getting in the car and photographing landmarks and treasures before they disappear.

I want to thank David Holcomb with the Preservation Society of Asheville and Buncombe County for guiding me early on with some of the lesser-known historical threads that make up the history of Asheville. I want to thank Stacy Merten with the Asheville Historic Resources Commission for providing very valuable information on quite short notice. I also want to thank Scott McKenzie, a WCU student whose recent paper "Slavery in Asheville" guided me toward some essential resources, including Inscoe.

I would be remiss if I did not acknowledge some of the very important Asheville photographers of the 19th and 20th centuries who are the true historians, including Rufus Morgan and W.T. Robertson for some of the earliest stereoscopic views of Asheville dating to the 1850s; Herbert W. Pelton, who photographically duplicated some of these stereoscopic views and then added famously to the photographic history of Asheville; George Masa (1881–1933), a Japanese immigrant who began his life in Asheville as a valet at the Grove Park Inn but quickly became a "Kodak finisher" for other photographers before taking over the Creasman family studio and becoming a legend of his own in his brief professional life; as well as John D. Caldwell, William A. Barnhill, and others, including those we were unable to include in the book like E.M. Ball Sr. and Jr.

Finally, I want to thank Betsy Chandler Drake for her support and her willingness to lend her home, the Drake Duck Blind B&B as the family refers to it, in Black Mountain. It has become our home away from home as I developed this book. Thanks Mom.

BIBLIOGRAPHY

Adamic, Louis. "Education on a Mountain: The Story of Black Mountain College." *Harper's Magazine*, April 1936.

Beck, Robin A. Jr. "From Joara to Chiaha: Spanish Exploration of the Appalachian Summit Area, 1540–1568." *Southeastern Archaeology*, Volume 16, No. 2. 1997.

Bishir, Catherine W., Michael T. Southern, and Jennifer F. Martin. *A Guide to the Historic Architecture of Western North Carolina.* Chapel Hill, North Carolina: The University of North Carolina Press, 1999.

Black, David R. and James Summer. *Historic Architectural Resources of Downtown Asheville, North Carolina.* Asheville, NC: City of Asheville, 1979.

Buncombe County. *1860 Census Population Slave Schedules.* Asheville Pack Memorial Library, Micro Copy Number M653, Roll 920.

Clayton, Lawrence A., Ph.D., Vernon James Knight Jr., Ph.D., and Edward Moore, Ph.D. *The de Soto Chronicles: the Expedition of Hernando de Soto to North America in 1539–1543, 2 Volumes,* Tuscaloosa: The University of Alabama Press, 1939.

Mooney, James. *Myths of the Cherokee: From Nineteenth Annual Report of the Bureau of American Ethnology 1897–98, Part I.* Washington, D.C.: Smithsonian Institution, Bureau of Ethnology (GPO), 1900.

Sondley, Dr. F.A. *A History of Buncombe North Carolina Volumes I & II.* Asheville, North Carolina: Advocate Printing Company, 1930.

Turner, William H., and Edward J. Cabbell. *Blacks in Appalachia.* Lexington, Kentucky: The University of Kentucky Press, 1985.